The Writing of War

Crosscurrents

GAINESVILLE

TALLAHASSEE

TAMPA

BOCA RATON

PENSACOLA

ORLANDO

MIAMI

University Press of Florida   JACKSONVILLE

William Cloonan

The Writing of

War

French and German Fiction and World War II

04 03 02 01 00 99 6 5 4 3 2 1

LIBRARY OF CONGRESS CATALOGING-IN-PUBLICATION DATA
Cloonan, William J.
The writing of war: French and German fiction
and World War II / William Cloonan.
p. cm. — (Crosscurrents)
Includes bibliographical references and index.
ISBN 0-8130-1685-1 (cloth: alk. paper)
1. French fiction—20th century—History and criticism.
2. German fiction—20th century—History and criticism.
3. World War, 1939–1945—Literature and the war.
4. Literature, Comparative—French and German.
5. Literature, Comparative—German and French. I. Title.
II. Series: Crosscurrents (Gainesville, Fla.)
PQ637.W35C66   1999
833'.91409358—dc21   98-48013

PORTIONS OF chapter 8 have previously been published in
an essay, "Le Roi des Alunes: Myth as Fiction, Fiction as
Myth," in vol. 3, pp. 32–36, of *Romance Languages Annual*
(1991). Copyright, Purdue Research Foundation, West
Lafayette, Indiana.

THE UNIVERSITY PRESS OF FLORIDA is the scholarly publishing agency for the State University System of Florida, comprised of Florida A&M University, Florida Atlantic University,
Florida International University, Florida State University, University of Central Florida, University of Florida, University
of North Florida, University of South Florida, and University
of West Florida.

University Press of Florida
15 Northwest 15th Street
Gainesville, FL 32611–2079
http://www.upf.com

For Harry Blair and Phil Karrh

Contents

Foreword

Human consciousness changed in 1910, according to Virginia Woolf, and with that comment she justified the abrupt alteration in narrative technique that emerged in the early part of the twentieth century. Her implication was that shared cultural assumptions of at least the British if not all Europeans had collapsed shortly after the turn of the century, and a new literature was responding. If confirmation were needed for her prescience, it came in August of 1914, at least for the participants in the Great War. Since the war was heavily censored, civilians would confront images of human evil, suffering, and degradation four years later. For Woolf and her allies in a literary revolution we now loosely call modernism, human consciousness turned back into itself and became the domain of the artist.

Little more than twenty years after the Great War, machinery was set in motion that would renew the assault. The impact of World War II on the human psyche is still being assessed, but it was clear by 1945 that whatever vestiges of those shared cultural assumptions survived the First World War were obliterated by images from a liberated Auschwitz, Dachau, and Buchenwald, by the obscenely aesthetic mushroom clouds over Hiroshima and Nagasaki. Language seemed to fail before such images. Not even the denotative precision of numbers could communicate the horrors. More than a war had ended in 1945. Philosophers like Theodor Adorno would proclaim, at least for a time, that the idea of art after Auschwitz was obscene. And yet something continued, if contorted. The composer Olivier Messiaen, a member of the French forces captured in the summer of 1940 and imprisoned in Gorlitz in Silesia, composed for the only musical instruments available in the camp: violin, cello, piano, and clarinet. *Quatour pour la fin du temps* premiered in January of 1941, and as Messiaen later recalled, "Never have I been heard with as much attention and understanding." Its apocalyptic imagery announced "The End of Time." As William Cloonan sensitively argues in his introductory remarks to *The Writing of War,* that ruptured or contorted consciousness in response to the Final Solution is perhaps best captured in the third of Samuel Beckett's sequence of postwar novels, *L'Innommable (The Unnam-*

able). For Beckett, those coherent entities that in literature we call story and character were exposed as frauds for much of the twentieth century, and his French writing, the *Quatre nouvelles*—the three postwar novels, *Molloy, Malone meurt,* and *L'Innomable,* and their residua, *Textes pour rien*—detail the disintegration. After *The Unnamable,* fiction had nowhere to go; and yet, paradoxically, it continued, if only to go nowhere. For Beckett all that was possible after the war were shards, fragments, residua, *Texts for Nothing,* for "The End of Time." These then were the limitations, the necessary incoherence and fragmentation within which the writer was obliged to work in the post-Auschwitz era in order to convey something of the lived experience of the world: "I'm here, that's all I know, and that it's still not me, it's of that the best has to be made" (*Text* III). The Irishman Beckett was writing through a postwar consciousness in a language that for him had escaped the assumptions—ideological and narratological—to which English was attached. After the war Europe was a new land, and a new language, a new system of representation, was needed to deal with the experience. For Beckett it was French.

In *The Writing of War: French and German Fiction and World War II,* William Cloonan examines a representative series of attempts by European writers to deal with the century's second major assault on human consciousness, with circumstances in which the only meanings remaining were invented ones. He examines the "postwar moral malaise" through major literary movements like Gruppe 47 in Germany and the *nouveau roman* in France and focuses on a set of "six novels that I believe offer original responses to World War II": Claude Simon's *La Route des Flandres* (*The Flanders Road*); Christa Wolf's *Kindheitsmuster* (*Patterns of Childhood*), especially within a broader context of women's writing; Celine's trilogy, *D'un chateau l'autre* (*From Castle to Castle*), *Nord* (*North*), and *Rigodon* (*Rigadoon*); Gunter Grass's *Blechstrommel* (*The Tin Drum*); Michel Tournier's *Le Roi des aulnes* (*The Ogre*); and finally Siegfried Lenz's *Deutschstunde* (*The German Lesson*).

Such insights as Cloonan offers, then, constitute an exemplary addition to the Crosscurrents series, which is designed to foreground comparative studies in European art and thought, particularly the intersections of literature and philosophy, aesthetics and culture. Without abandoning traditional comparative methodology, the series is also receptive to the latest currents in critical, comparative, and performative theory, especially that generated by the renewed intellectual energy in post-Marxist Europe. It will, as well, take full cognizance of the cultural and political realignments of what for the better part of the twentieth century have been two separated and isolated Europes. While Western Europe is now moving aggressively toward unification in the European Community, Eastern Europe—with the collapse of Communist hegemony and the breakup of the twentieth century's last major, overtly colonial empire, the Soviet Union—is subdividing into nationalistic and religious enclaves. The intellectual, cultural, and literary significance of such profound restructuring, how history will finally be rewritten, is difficult to anticipate. Having had a fertile period of modernism snuffed out in an ideological coup not long after the 1917 revolution, the nations of the former Soviet Union have, for instance, been denied (or spared) the age of Freud and Jung, most modernist experiments, and postmodern fragmentation. While Western Europe continues reaching beyond modernism, Eastern Europe may be struggling to reclaim it. Whether a new art can emerge in the absence—or from the absence—of such forces as shaped modernism is one of the intriguing questions of post–Cold War aesthetics, philosophy, and critical theory.

The Writing of War, then, forms precisely the sort of comparative social and literary study that the Crosscurrents series was designed to foster. The series henceforth will continue to critique the developing, often conflicting currents of European thought through the prism of literature, philosophy, and critical theory.

S. E. GONTARSKI,
series editor

Acknowledgments

I would like to thank a number of friends who have been extremely helpful in the preparation of this manuscript. For their time, patience, suggestions, and senses of humor, I am deeply grateful to Summer Allmann, Alexander Dunlop, Stan Gontarski, Jean-Philippe Postel, Gervais Reed, Harry Rosser, Robert Saba, Bettina Soestwohner, Gabriele Stellmacher, the late Jerry Stern, and Lori Walters.

Florida State University provided me with a summer COFRS grant that greatly facilitated the completion of this manuscript.

I would like to offer a special expression of thanks to my wife, Betty LaFace, whose presence and support were so instrumental in my actually finishing this project.

Unless otherwise indicated, all translations are my own.

Introduction: The Writing of War

I

If you could lick my heart, it would poison you.

Words of a Warsaw Ghetto survivor, in Langer, *Admitting the Holocaust*, 40

If people once thought that limits existed to human degradation, that certain moral standards, however contested, nevertheless could not be totally disregarded, World War II exposed this belief as an illusion. The debatable use of atomic weaponry against Japan, the cynical terror bombings of Dresden and Canterbury were shocking enough, but no event so pulverized traditional moral sensibility as the Final Solution. Quite aside from the historical reality of the concentration camps, delimited as they were in time and space, the Final Solution was destined to become the most prominent symbol for all the new and doubtless unwanted information about human cruelty that World War II would bequeath to its survivors.

The Final Solution permanently altered the moral, intellectual, and aesthetic climate in which French and German literary artists tried to write about World War II and its aftermath, and these authors' problems, failures, and successes are the subject of this book. Nathalie Sarraute, who aptly termed the postwar era the "Age of Suspicion," dated its birth from the moment she discovered the existence of the gas chambers, where "all feeling disappears, even scorn and hatred. All that remains is an immense and empty stupor, a total and definitive inability to understand" (*L'Ere du soupçon*, 65). The knowledge of the Final Solution challenged long-held assumptions about human decency and the possibility of progress in mutual understanding; it questioned the value of the Enlightenment heritage, and for some, it even created a caesura in history: "there was an Auschwitz, and there was an afterward . . . the two terms do not represent a chronology" (Langer, *Admitting the Holocaust,* 18). Theodor Adorno's celebrated (and later retracted) pronouncement that writing poetry after Auschwitz would be barbaric (*Noten zur Literaturen III,* 125) may well serve as the emotional counterpart to Sarraute's "immense and empty stupor," but both statements have in common the realization that in the aftermath of the Final Solution, the production of literary artifacts could not continue as in the past, as if nothing radically different had happened.

One might object, of course, that traumatic reactions from artists and intellectuals are a common enough occurrence after any major war. In his *A War Imagined: The First World War and English Culture,* Samuel Hynes points out the sorts of upheavals created by this earlier conflict: "Even as it was being fought the war was perceived as a force of radical change in society and in consciousness. It brought to an end the life and values of Victorian and Edwardian England; but it also did something more radical than that: it added a new scale of violence and destruction to what was possible—it changed reality" (xi). With specific regard to artists, Hynes writes that they "would see that if the past were indeed dead, then the future, the world after the war, would have to have a new beginning. The continuity of history had been broken" (4). In France, World War I transformed Henri Barbusse from a little-known, vaguely decadent novelist into the world-famous author of *Under Fire* (1916), a novel replete with "subversion, hatred of war, rejection of nationalism, and an appeal for social struggle against passivity" (Relinger, *Henri Barbusee,* 87). World War I gave an impetus to Dadaism and Expressionism in Germany; it launched Surrealism in France.[1] And, according to Hynes, it constituted the guiding spirit of modernism: "Modernism means many things, but it is most fundamentally the forms that the post-war artists found for their sense of modern history: history seen as discontinuous, the past remote and unavailable, or available only as ruins of itself, and the present a formless space emptied of values" (*War Imagined,* 433).

Nobody would deny the tremendous impact of World War I on the arts, or on human consciousness in general, but in a fundamental way the trauma it induced was different from the upheaval produced by World War II. The innovation of World War I involved traditional tactical developments being pushed to levels the world had never seen, coupled with the hardening human reaction to what this weaponry could achieve. The introduction of airplanes, tanks, and poison gas, the stench of the battlefields where the dead were left to rot, the apparent indifference with which commanders on both sides sent their troops into combat—these were but some of the "advances" that gave World War I its unique place in the history of warfare:

The immobility of trench fighting, the stunningly high casualties, which made the Duke of Wellington's famous estimate in the Napoleonic Wars— that no army could sustain more than 30 percent losses and survive—seem an antiquated irony, the new technologies of submarines, tanks, barbed wire, airplanes, machine guns, and bullets designed to wound with the maximum damage and pain, the lethal poison gas banned by mutual agreement at the meeting of nations at The Hague in 1907 and in use nonetheless—these factors defied all previous notions about what military destruction could mean. (Douglas, *Terrible Honesty*, 156)

World War II was certainly a development of this technology in the service of destruction; from this perspective it marked a difference in degree, but not in kind.

The heightened firepower of World War II does not distinguish it from earlier wars. It was the Nazi implementation of the Final Solution that moved World War II beyond the realm of traditional warfare; it gave a new dimension to the concept of war waged against civilian populations. Concentration camps served no military purpose and had no strategic value; they cannot even be said to have served as means of terrorizing citizens since the Nazis attempted to keep their existence largely secret. They were places where death was practiced for its own sake.

Given the understandably high emotional atmosphere that often accompanies discussions of the Final Solution and its consequences, I need, before turning to the novels I wish to analyze, to distinguish between the immediate and the more lasting ramifications of the Nazis' genocidal policies; the former were as gruesome as they were dramatic, while the latter remain more subtle but ultimately more frightening.

The discovery of places like Auschwitz shocked the postwar world. The liberation of the concentration camps, accompanied by the worldwide dissemination of their contents through photos, newsreels, radio broadcasts, and newspaper articles, added a new dimension to the meaning of the word *inhumanity*. The Final Solution quickly became the standard against which other crimes committed during World War II were judged. For instance, in the midst of the Japanese war crime trials, the president of the Tokyo tribunal, Sir William Webb, noted that "the crimes of the Germans accused were far more heinous, varied and extensive than those of the Japanese accused" (Buruma, *The Wages of Guilt: Memories of War in Germany and Japan*, 168). Also, the uniqueness of the indictments handed down at Nuremburg against the surviving perpetrators of the Final Solution for their "crimes against humanity" illustrates that the Nazi activities were sufficiently beyond the bounds of wartime hatreds and excesses as to merit a new terminology, a new category of guilt.

This wholesale condemnation of the Nazis and the implicit exculpation of the Allies' wartime strategies were not, however, without their critics. William Golding probably speaks for many of his contemporaries who refused to believe that the evil unleashed in World War II was a uniquely German phenomenon; at the same time, he sounds a prescient note concerning the difficulties the war would create for the subsequent writing of literature:

The experiences of Hamburg and Belsen, Hiroshima and Dachau cannot be imagined. We have gone to war and beggared description all over again. These experiences are like black holes in space. Nothing can get out to let us know what was inside. It was like what it was like and on the other hand it was like nothing else whatsoever. We stand before a gap in history. We have discovered a limit to literature. (Hewison, *Under Siege*, 172)

In a similar vein, Ian Buruma, writing about the Japanese reaction to the dropping of the atomic bomb, points out that in modern Japan "Hiroshima is a symbol of absolute evil, often compared to Auschwitz" (*Wages*, 92). Yet later on in this same study, Buruma makes the sort of distinction typical of those who wish to differentiate between the dropping of the atomic bomb, as well as other alleged Allied atrocities, and the Final Solution: "the case of Hiroshima is at least open to debate, the A-bomb *might* have saved lives; it *might* have shortened the war" (105, emphasis in text). Richard Rubenstein offers a variation on this argument, one that stresses the gratuitousness of the Nazi mass murders: "The American assault ceased as soon as the Japanese surrendered. During

World War II, German mass violence against enemy civilians was inten-sified *after* the victims surrendered" (*The Cunning of History,* emphasis in text, 7).

Distinguishing between acts of war, however debatable or downright senseless, and the unprovoked destruction of people because of their ra-cial or ethnic origins is a common motif among commentators who feel compelled to mark the special quality of the Final Solution in the context of World War II. Alain Lercher recently published a history of the Nazi slaughter of the inhabitants of Oradour, a French village without any strategic importance. An S.S. division, Das Reich, decided to annihilate the town in response to harassment from the French Resistance. Lercher's well-researched account of this incident is particularly moving since he lost relatives in the massacre. Nevertheless, at the end of his study Lercher offers a telling reflection concerning the place of Oradour on the list of wartime horrors:

I understood a little while ago that Oradour was not comparable to geno-cide, because the massacre at Oradour, as horrible as it was, can be associ-ated with the dynamics of the war, like the bombings of Cologne and Dresden, which equal it in horror. While the genocide of a people without a homeland, who threatened nobody, from whom one had nothing to take, cannot be associated with anything one could endow with a histori-cal sense, unless it was the particular destiny of the Jewish people. (67–68)

Lercher's singling out the Jews is at once understandable and typical. Of all those the Nazis chose for destruction—gypsies, political dissenters, Slavs, homosexuals—the Jewish people were by far the largest group. Jews have traditionally been the scapegoats for Christianity's various insecuri-ties, and anti-Semitism has long been an integral part of the fabric of Western society. Perhaps for these reasons some scholarly accounts of Nazi genocide give the impression that the Jews were the only victims. Dominick La Capra, in his *Representing the Holocaust,* cites with approval Eberhard Jäckel's frequently quoted explanation for the uniqueness of the Final Solution:

The Nazi extermination of the Jews was unique because never before had a state, under the responsible authority of its leader, decided and an-nounced that a specific group of human beings, including the old, the women, the children and the infants, would be killed to the very last one, and implemented this decision with every means at its disposal. (49)

Without for a moment denying the fundamental truth of Jäckel's statement that the Nazis engaged in gratuitous brutality against essentially harmless and defenseless human beings, it remains nonetheless true that placing an exclusive emphasis on the destruction of the Jews, or for that matter any other specific group, at a particular historical moment, risks obscuring the second, more far-reaching implication of the Final Solution.

The enduring ramification of the Final Solution may ultimately have less to do with the identities of the victims as Jews, homosexuals, gypsies, or political dissenters than is often supposed. The Final Solution demonstrated human beings' willingness and ability to facilitate the emplacement of a carefully developed bureaucratic structure capable of wide-ranging murderous acts, while at the same time freeing its various functionaries from any sense of personal responsibility for the activities they directed. As terrible as were the Nazis' professed aims—the annihilation of specific groups—the mindset of "persons who are permitted to commit murder without remorse by a language stripped of conscience" (Wolf, *Patterns of Childhood*, 237) is at least as daunting. Thus the Nazi genocidal policy was much more than the ugliest phenomenon of World War II; it was and remains a potent blueprint for the future, in which any group or groups can be chosen for extermination, and those who carry out the task will do so without remorse or doubts:

The passing of time has made it increasingly evident that a hitherto unbreachable moral and political barrier in the history of Western civilization was successfully overcome by the Nazis . . . and that henceforth the systematic, bureaucratically administered extermination of millions of citizens or subject peoples will forever be one of the capacities and temptations of government. (Rubenstein, *Cunning*, 2)

The existence of Auschwitz, Buchenwald, and other prisons made apparent both the human capacity for massive, wanton destruction and the ease with which traditional ethical constraints could be shunted aside by relatively large numbers of people in the interest of serving the State. Extrapolating from the German experience, one comes to realize that genocide can be the potential policy of any government. When Marguerite Duras declares in *The War: A Memoir* that in order to endure the idea of a concentration camp, "we must share the crime" (50), it is easy to dismiss her statement as a reaction more emotional than rational. The Nazis ran those places and killed those people; we did not. Yet what lies behind the shock and outrage motivating Duras's words is the possibility that while we are not those Nazis, we are perfectly able to act like them. These nefarious acts could have been, or could be in the future, "committed by anyone" (Duras, *War,* 50). Christa Wolf succinctly sums up this fear: "We, the people of today, don't put anything past anybody. We think that anything is possible. This may be the most important difference between our era and the preceding one" (*Patterns,* 242).

Without mitigating the Nazis' responsibility for the events that transpired in the concentration camps during World War II, an awareness of the Final Solution's broader ramifications helps explain the puzzling reaction of some German intellectuals to the often-reiterated insistence by the Allies on their nation's guilt. When a German writer like Hans Egon Holthusen insists upon Germany's continuing responsibility and need to remember its crimes, his remarks are generally greeted with approval within the international intellectual community: "the past, as we know, has not faded or become indifferent . . . but rather stronger, more terrifying, more unbearable, and one would like to add, more incomprehensible" (in Bosmajian, *Metaphors of Evil,* 17). However, one is initially taken aback by the comments of the poet and political activist Hans Magnus Ensensberger: "the reality of Auschwitz shall be exorcised as if it were the past, specifically the national past, and not a common present or future" (in Bosmajian, *Metaphors,* 12). Or, for that matter, Heinrich Böll's insistence that the ill-treatment he received in a prisoner of war camp increased his desire to express himself not simply as a writer, but as a specifically German writer who was proud of his national identity: "When for months at a time you are treated as a fucking German Nazi, and kicked in the behind, then you think, not just kiss my ass, but also that in spite of everything I am a German, and I will write" (*Eine deutsche Erinnerung,* 102)

Neither Ensenberger nor Böll can be accused of harboring any latent Nazi sympathies, and their words and actions have never denied the historical reality of the Final Solution. Their anger, I would suggest, stems from the self-righteous condemnation of Germany by her conquerors and occupiers. These writers resent the holier-than-thou attitudes they encountered from victors whose wartime activities, however much they remain within the loosely defined category of "military strategy," contributed also to our awareness of the lengths to which human beings would go in order to intimidate and kill their fellow creatures. The atomic bombings of Japan, the terror attacks unleashed on civilians by both sides during the war, certainly are more open to debate than is the Final Solution, but they too contributed to the creation of a postwar climate characterized by extreme suspicion of any individual's or group's claims to moral authority.

The Final Solution as a historical phenomenon that can be described and dated is horrific enough; nevertheless, to limit our understanding of that experience to the events themselves constitutes a serious misreading of just how greatly the Final Solution has challenged or even destroyed moral values once considered sacrosanct in Western culture. Hannah Arendt points to the enormity of the issues raised when she argues that Nazi Germany's methods of domination and destruction "must cause social scientists and historical scholars to reconsider their hitherto unquestioned fundamental preconceptions regarding the course of the world and human behavior" (cited by Korman in "The Holocaust in American Historical Writing," 48). And Lawrence Langer goes as far as to make the Final Solution the catalyst for the twentieth century's growing disenchantement with the values that have contributed to Western society's belief in social and moral improvement:

Textbook theories about self-actualization, the intrinsic goodness of the human spirit, moral growth, social progress, and the valuable lessons of history collapse into pretentious evasions of the grim legacies that twentieth century reality has left us: the Holocaust above all, but only as the chief example of companion forms of mass dying through war, revolution, famine, repression and genocide. (*Admitting*, 12)

Among the many casualties of the Final Solution was the time-honored notion that there existed inherent limitations to the cruelty of which people were capable, and that to transgress these boundaries was to forgo one's humanity. Just how tenacious has been that belief is illustrated in Michel Borwicz's *Ecrits des condamnés à mort*. The author cites camp inmates whose language illustrates their inability, in the face of their own imminent deaths, to ascribe what was being done to them to their fellows. These victims speak of their Nazi torturers "as bloodthirsty creatures from another planet disguised as men" (137). Such language represents a desperate and doubtless unconscious effort to hold onto the belief that there remained sane parameters to human behavior, limits that individuals, regardless of their aims or anger, could not exceed without reverting to an animal state. The truth was the opposite, and Edmond Jabès, writing in almost direct response to the prisoners' imagery, pointed out years later the error in thinking that the Nazis were "brutes descended from another planet" (*Du Désert au livre,* 93). The German novelist Martin Walser was even more specific and unyielding when he described the oppressors and their victims: "Auschwitz was not Hell, rather a German concentration camp. And the 'prisoners' were neither the damned nor the half-damned of the Christian cosmos, rather innocent Jews, Communists, and so forth. And the torturers were not fantastic devils, but men like you and me. Germans, or those who wanted to become such" ("Unser Auschwitz," 11).

Walser's comment is exemplary not simply for its content but because of its matter-of-fact tone, free of rhetorical excess. He states the truth of the situation and eschews any effort to find greater, potentially redemptive significance in what had occurred. Walser's language is atypical; most commentators find it difficult to write about the Final Solution, or matters related to it, without finding some reassuring moral meaning, or using it as a club against individuals or groups. Two controversies provide examples of this difficulty: one is of considerable semantic importance, the other indicative of the polemical power the Final Solution continues to generate. I am referring to the use of the word *holocaust,* and the argument surrounding the wartime journalism of Paul de Man.

The very word *holocaust* is controversial since it is essentially a religious term. In their *Approaches to Auschwitz: The Holocaust and Its Legacy,* Richard Rubenstein and John Roth describe the origins of the expression: "In the Septuagint, a Greek translation of the Jewish Scripture dating from the third century B.C.E. (before the common era), *holokausten* is used for the Hebrew *olah,* which literally means 'what is brought up'. In context the term refers to a sacrifice, often specifically to 'an offering made by fire unto the Lord'" (6–7). "Sacrifice" connotes a willing or willed loss for a greater purpose, and as such has been applied by both scholars and theologians most often, but not exclusively, to Jewish victims of the concentration camps (Rubenstein and Roth, *Approaches,* 4). The problem with the term is that it implies that these people's deaths have some vaguely understood redemptive or didactic quality. The use of "Holocaust" suggests that the victims' destruction serves a higher purpose, that the living will discover some moral reinforcement from their deaths. Nothing, however, indicates that this ideal is true, or that something reassuring about the human animal can be garnered from this particular slaughter of the innocent: "To speak of a 'Holocaust' is a self-serving misrepresentation, as is any reference to an archaic scapegoating mechanism. There was not the least 'sacrificial' aspect in this *operation,* in which what was calculated coldly and with maximum efficiency and economy . . . was pure and simple *elimination*" (Lacoue-Labarthe, *Heidegger,* emphasis in text, 37). Even among some scholars who continue to use the term, "Holocaust" is deprived of any redemptive implication: "the Holocaust is an event without a future—that is, nothing better for mankind grew out of it" (Langer, *Admitting,* 38). My own choice of the phrase "Final Solution" reflects my agreement with Lacoue-Labarthe and Langer on this question.

The controversy surrounding Paul de Man's wartime activities demonstrates the Final Solution's persistent ability to foster reactions that owe more to emotion than to logic. The facts are simple enough. As a young man in occupied Belgium, de Man wrote a series of newspaper articles, several of which have a clear anti-Semitic slant. Just how, if at all, this affected his subsequent work as a literary theorist is at best highly speculative. Nevertheless, Jacques Derrida's efforts in the pages of *Critical Inquiry* to exonerate his deceased friend from charges of anti-Semitism ("Like the Sound of the Sea Deep within a Shell: Paul de Man's War") created a storm in academic circles. Shoshanna Felman's impassioned plea on behalf of de Man provides a good example of the excessive rhetoric still characteristic of so many discussions related to the Final Solution:

It is no longer possible to distinguish between heroes and knaves, regeneration and destruction, deliverance and entanglement, speeches and acts, history and faith, idealistic faith and (self)-deception, justice and totalitarianism, utmost barbarism and utmost civilized refinement, freedom of will and radical enslavement to historical manipulations and ideological coercions. ("Paul de Man's Silence," 719–20)

If Felman's strategy in championing de Man was to blur all distinctions, Derrida chose instead to be haughty and dismissive toward those who attacked his former colleague. In the end his defense of de Man became a defense of deconstruction. Apparently Derrida foresaw this literary issue, since whatever might have been latent in some of the criticisms of Paul de Man's alleged anti-Semitism during World War II became transparently clear in a subsequent publication by David Hirsch, who mangaged to extend the ramifications of the Final Solution directly into the realm of literary theory: "In fact, are we not in all honesty to say that the real-world endpoint of Heideggarian (and now Derridean and de Manian) deconstruction of the logocentric tradition is precisely Auschwitz?" (*Deconstruction*, 87).

All the arguments and controversies mentioned here attest to the ways the Final Solution has affected, and continues to affect, postwar cultural life. The implementation of the Nazi genocidal policies was the catalyst that provoked among artists and intellectuals, as well as among many ordinary citizens of different nationalities, a profound distrust in the possibility of human decency. In fact, Western intellectuals came to question the Enlightenment tradition that has so marked their own thinking over the last three centuries. The disgust created by the discovery of places like Auschwitz added a further dimension of horror to wartime activities such as the dropping of the atomic bomb, the terror bombings of cities like Dresden, and the wanton destruction of villages like Oradour. These latter phenomena, although secondary in importance to the concentration camps, in turn contributed to the creation of the postwar moral malaise, a malaise that would make the writing of fiction about World War II particularly difficult.

The elements of the malaise that would directly affect the creation of literature in the postwar context are brilliantly illustrated in a novel published a mere eight years after the end of World War II. The visceral numbness that characterized Sarraute's "Age of Suspicion" found a powerful fictional embodiment in Samuel Beckett's *The Unnamable* (1953), the final installment of a trilogy that included *Molloy* (1951) and *Malone Dies* (1952). *The Unnamable* can be read as a series of questions that allude to complex issues without ever providing anything resembling coherent answers. This novel offers no resolutions to conflicts; where a reader might expect clarification, there is only contradiction.

It is inappropriate to speak of a narrator in *The Unnamable;* instead, a constantly self-contradicting narrative voice oscillates between several real and/or imagined identities. At times the voice associates itself with Mahood, a word that seems to contain allusions to manhood, but aside from the homonymic similarity, nothing justifies such a conclusion, nor is anything gained by attempting to make this connection. Mahood, we learn, is also Basil, but Basil is as much a cipher as Mahood, except that the voice implies that Mahood lacks a foot (42). Is the absence of a foot a physical embodiment of some sort of moral crippling? Perhaps, but also perhaps not. Once again nothing permits such a conclusion, as the text flatly denies such facile symbolic relationships. The narrative also refers to someone named Worm, but Worm seems less a person than a possibility, a tentative and stillborn effort to establish a human identity.

The disembodied narrative voice that flits from one name to another suggests what remains of individual identity after the war. Certainties of any kind are suspect, and for anything the voice can utter about human beings, the opposite is equally plausible. Given this situation, to the extent that the novel progresses at all, it is through questions: "Where now? Who now? When now?" (3); and through negative assertions: "Pupil Mahood, repeat after me, Man is a higher animal. I couldn't" (69).

The force of *The Unnamable,* as well as its appropriateness as a starting point for a discussion of the postwar novel, is in its negation: without being able to affirm what truths, if any, remain, it clears away the debris of false certainties, of consoling assumptions. Christian Prigent's comment about the entire trilogy is particularly germane to *The Unnamable:* "[Since] it resists the constitutions of figures and meaning, mechanically erodes and dissipates settings, and frustrates the expectation of positive endings, this literature, simultaneously frugal, denuded, and rhetorically complex, seizes in a new way on the real" ("A Descent," 11). In this instance the "real" is the postwar world.

Among the intellectual/moral casualties of World War II were the optimism about the decency of mankind and the confidence in the possibility of human progress—ideas frequently, albeit somewhat loosely, associated with the Enlightenment. The French expression for "Enlightenment" is *le siècle des lumières* (the century of lights). Light is a source of disturbance to the narrative voice in *The Unnamable,* yet typically the voice is uncertain about "complaining about the disorder of the lights, this being due simply to my insistence on regarding them always as the same lights and viewed always from the same point . . . disorder of lights perhaps an illusion, all change to be feared, incomprehensible uneasiness" (9). Yet for this voice that at one point imagines itself as "the blessed pus of reason" (92), the lights continue to be a problem. For one thing, they hiss as they go out (95), thus providing more noise than clarity. Despite their annoying features, however, the lights remain perhaps the only means of showing what progress has been made (95). In any case, as the voice remarks, "this question of lights deserves to be treated in a section apart, it is so intriguing" (95).

To the extent that light imagery constitutes an allusion to the declining, if not moribund, Enlightenment influence, it is an allusion of the slightest sort, as if to suggest that this decline may be true, but even if it is, the discussion of the matter can be deferred until "time is not so short, and the mind more composed" (115). The alleged decline of the Enlightenment's influence is discussed in chapter 2.

The Unnamable also questions the function of language. The problem is not that information is lacking but whether language in its present state can cope with what has occurred. The voice wonders if it might best proceed by "aporia pure and simple . . . or by affirmations and negations invalidated as uttered, or sooner or later" (3). It then quickly confesses that "I say aporia without knowing what it means" (4). The voice poses the possibility that to comment clearly on the present circumstances would require verbal structures (future and conditional participles) that do not exist (16), thereby implying that traditional grammatical forms are inadequate to the current situation. Reexamination of the function of language in the postwar era constitutes part of chapter 3.

Given the semantic and linguistic condition the voice describes, what role, if any, does literature play as a means of understanding postwar experience? To the degree that the voice offers any response to this question, it is largely negative. Toward the end of *The Unnamable,* there is an effort to tell a story involving a boy, a girl, a mother-in-law, and love found and lost. This attempt is quickly abandoned; the story goes nowhere and says nothing (167–68). If this fumbling narrative has any purpose, it is to suggest that literature, in its traditional formats, no longer has much validity and might best be consigned to history's junk heap. What appears to endure is typically contradictory: the impossiblity of speaking, the impossibility of remaining silent, and solitude. In a novel where every statement elicits its opposite, it is worth noting that the need to speak is nonetheless asserted at the beginning (4) as well as at the end (173), even though the voice seems to imply throughout that it learns nothing from its own remarks. Although it comes as no surprise that *The Unnamable* terminates in confusion—"where I am, I don't know, I'll never know, in the silence you don't know, you must go on, I can't go on, I'll go on" (179)—a slightly earlier statement matters more for the writing of postwar fiction: "quick now and try again, with the words that remain, try what, I do not know" (178). Parts of chapter 2 deal with early attempts and failures at finding the right words.

In his discussion of *The Unnamable,* Wolfgang Iser argues that the novel's contradictions create potentially useful paradoxes: "Only by accepting incomprehensibility is it possible to see through the fictions that pretend to know the unknowable. . . . But in addition to this, it is the incomprehensibility of reality, and indeed of the ego itself, that gives rise to fiction" ("When Is the End" 57). For Iser, Beckett's endless questioning, his debunking of facile explanations and reassuring fictions, is ultimately "a great comfort for literature and a great nuisance for ideology" (57).

With regard to the present study, the abiding merit of *The Unnamable* lies in its effort to describe, as best words can, the postwar climate in its confusion and opaqueness as well as the difficulty this state of affairs presented for the writing of fiction.

Other novelists, working in the immediate aftermath of World War II, would prove less rigorous in their approach, more comforting in their intentions, and finally less aware of how greatly the war had altered the direction literature was going to take. Hence Beckett's style, his pained, precise prose would have no imitators of consequence, and other authors would eschew his bleak mindscapes. Nevertheless, the vision of a world without meaning, except for invented ones, along with the constant need to subvert the literary text, would come to characterize the best writing about World War II.

For reasons of clarity and chronology, this study is presented in two phases. The first consists of two chapters that mingle literary history and textual analysis in an attempt to explain how World War II radically affected the writing of novels in Germany and France. The second contains six chapters examining successful efforts to create fiction about the war.

Twentieth-century French and German literature is an area of professional interest to me, which to some extent explains my limiting this study to novels in these languages. However, it is also true that in the initial stages of World War II, France and Germany were the principal continental belligerents, whose lands comprised the main battlegrounds on the Western front. This situation provided citizens of these nations with a wartime experience quite different from and arguably more intense than that which the Americans or even the British encountered, in that their countries were never invaded.

The question of battlegrounds aside, of all the elements that contributed to focusing on French and German fiction, the most important is the relationship of both these countries to the Enlightenment tradition. Paris was at the very least the propaganda center of the Enlightenment, the focal point from which so many of the ideas associated with *philosophes* of all nations were disseminated. Yet this two-hundred-year-old tradition seemed to fail when tested by the onslaught of Nazism. As Michèle Cone remarks concerning the Occupation period: "During those four years, France, a country that had acquired the reputation of being a haven—or *terre d'accueil*—for the talented and persecuted, reaches a peak of xenophobia, anti-Semitism, and sectarianism that caused drastic changes in the art world" (*Artists under Vichy,* xvii). It need not be belabored that these "drastic changes" extended to nonartists as well.

Germany contributed one of the most idealistic statements about the possibility of humanity's advancement with Kant's *What Is Enlightenment?* (1784); Lessing's *Nathan the Wise* (1779) is one of the first dramas to take as its theme religious tolerance, while Moses Mendelssohn was in the vanguard of the struggle for Jewish emancipation. France and Germany, where artists and intellectuals had done so much to create a climate favorable to human progress, were to be the sites of a conflict that would severely jeopardize the very tradition those forebears had struggled to establish. It seems to me that a study claiming that the implications of World War II challenged many of the humanistic assumptions of modern Europe must necessarily deal with the literatures of the nations that contributed so greatly to the establishment of these beliefs.

Chapter 2 opens with a discussion of the threat to the Enlightenment heritage engendered by World War II, and I then focus on four early examples of serious writing about the war. The texts I have chosen are Thomas Mann's *Doctor Faustus* (1948), Albert Camus' *The Plague* (1948), Ernst Jünger's *War Diaries* (1941–43), and Jean-Paul Sartre's *Death in the Soul* (1949). In my treatment of these authors I endeavor to show how, for a variety of cultural and aesthetic reasons associated primarily with their reliance on Enlightenment values and their use of Romantic prototypes, their struggles to deal adequately with World War II are largely unsuccessful.

In chapter 3, I describe the origins and aims of the Gruppe 47 (Group 47), which strove to reorient German literature after the war. Efforts to rethink the writing of literature in postwar France took the form of the *nouveau roman* (new novel), and in the second section of the chapter I indicate how this movement, more amorphous than the Group 47 and less viscerally connected to the war, nevertheless constituted a reaction to that conflict.

The six chapters that follow center on six novels that I believe offer original responses to World War II, responses that articulate, in a variety of fashions, how that war was different from preceding ones and would have lasting ramifications for the writing of literature. Obviously, the choice of six texts out of so many possibilities requires some explanation.

Anyone endeavoring to justify a limited selection of novels about a war that has spawned so much literature will find some solace in Susan Suleiman's forthright presentation of her reasons for the choices she made in *Authoritarian Fictions: The Ideological Novel as a Literary Genre:* "a combination of personal preference, professional intuition and pure chance, which, despite all efforts at objective justifications, presides over any activity that has literature as its object" (17). Yet, when a subject is as controversial as a world war that has inspired a plethora of literary activity of widely different value, one's personal preference, however understandable, is not sufficient.

My original desire was to concentrate on novels that managed to be serious in their intent and even complex in their form but nevertheless had a strong popular appeal and were read by relatively large audiences. In the concluding chapter I develop my reasons for believing that contemporary literature can still have an important social function and that its readership need not and should not be limited to the academic community. The avoidance of closure was also a quality I was looking for in the books to be discussed because I believe the finest fiction about the war raises more questions than it answers and, by doing so, indicates that many social and literary issues stemming from the war remain unresolved today.

Despite my initial intention to limit this study to works that achieved a good degree of success with the general public, repeated readings of Claude Simon's *The Flanders Road* (*La Route des Flandres*, 1960), an admittedly difficult work associated with the nouveau roman, convinced me that this novel was integral to my study. This work illustrates brilliantly that however great was the desire to break with the Enlightenment heritage and earlier literary techniques, the power of the past continues to impinge upon the present. *The Flanders Road* is the subject of chapter 4.

When I began to investigate fiction written by French and German women about World War II, I made the rather surprising discovery that there appeared to be no major novels written by women. Anna Seghers' *The Seventh Cross* (1942) certainly achieved popular success, but it was written during the war and thus obviously does not deal with the implications of the conflict. Nevertheless, as I pursued the question of women writers and World War II, I realized that if there were not many texts by women that one could readily describe as novels, women did a great deal of writing about the war, especially after May 1968. These works at times appeared as memoirs, but what proved far more interesting than the simple memoir was the consciously orchestrated combination of memoir techniques with elements of fiction. This hybrid form provides a fascinating expression of an effort to articulate a means of writing about the war that is specific to women. Christa Wolf's *Patterns of Childhood* (*Kindheitsmuster*, 1976) offers an excellent example of World War II viewed from a woman's perspective. In Chapter 5 I discuss the general question of women writing about World War II, with special attention given to *Patterns of Childhood*.

My most controversial choice was doubtless Céline's war trilogy, *From Castle to Castle* (*D'un château l'autre*, 1957), *North* (*Nord*, 1960), and *Rigadoon* (*Rigodon*, 1969), discussed as one novel. The controversy has to do with Céline's role as a collaborator and his well-deserved reputation as an anti-Semite. Without denying either of these truths, it remains impossible to escape the power emanating from these novels. It is also self-evident that Céline's instinctive grasp of the human animal's capacity for stupidity and hatred dates from his early novels, but the war gave his pessimistic vision an impetus that finds its fullest and darkest expression in the trilogy. Céline's war trilogy is the subject of chapter 6.

Günter Grass is an uneven novelist whose obsession with World War II has marred some of his writing, but *The Tin Drum* (*Blechstrommel,* 1959), the subject of chapter 7, remains a model of controlled rage and of the use of laughter as a political tool.

I know the writings of Michel Tournier from an earlier project, and probably more than anything else it was the discovery of *The Ogre* (*Le Roi des aulnes,* 1970) that inspired the present study. The focus of chapter 8, this is a novel examining the personal and political dangers inherent in the conviction that an individual or a nation possesses some great destiny that must be fulfilled.

Siegfried Lenz's *The German Lesson* (*Deutschstunde,* 1968) is arguably the best German novel about World War II; it provides a brilliant example of the power of understatement. Hitler is scarcely mentioned, and violence rarely exceeds the destruction of a cow by an errant bomb. More than any other novel I discuss, *The German Lesson* addresses the issue of unanswered questions related to World War II. For this reason it was my choice for the penultimate chapter.

In the concluding chapter I argue for literature's value as an instrument for the examination of social issues. I discuss the growing tendency to imagine that serious literature is the exclusive property of the academic community, whose members alone are sufficiently educated to understand and explicate texts that are too sophisticated in their techniques and allusions for the average reader. In this chapter I hope to reestablish that literature continues to possess the vitality to involve literate people of all backgrounds in the effort to confront issues that, despite their origins in a now somewhat distant past, continue to affect the present.

The Present Made the Past

Germans sometimes refer to 1945 as *Jahre Null* (year zero), and the expression is well chosen. The political and physical shambles of Europe at the end of World War II made imperative the need for a new beginning, yet the enormity of the devastation led Europeans and Americans alike to imagine the required changes primarily in concrete forms. What the situation required was a new, democratic form of government for Germany, retribution against the designers and implementers of the Nazi genocidal policies, and immediate food and shelter for the survivors. However, for some, the war's devastation was more than physical; it called into question traditional ways of thinking about the individual's relation to self and others and to society at large. World War II provoked a reassessment of the Enlightenment heritage; it gave impetus to a debate that has continued to the present day.[1]

When Theodor Adorno and Max Horkheimer published their *Dialectic of the Enlightenment* in 1944, they took pains to insist that "the retreat from enlightenment into mythology is not to be sought so much in the nationalist, pagan and other mythologies . . . but in Enlightenment itself when paralyzed by the fear of truth" (xiii–xiv). This "fear of truth" that Adorno and Horkheimer detected at the heart of the Enlightenment would take a very curious form. For them the Enlightenment was flawed, perhaps from its very inception, by what appeared to be one of its finest qualities: the desire for intellectual clarity. As Adorno and Hork-heimer put it: "False clarity is only another name for myth; and myth has always been obscure and enlightening at one and the same time: always using the devices of familiarity and straightforward dismissal to avoid the labor of conceptualization" (xiv). For these two philosophers, writing as the war came to an end, the error of the Enlightenment was to limit the analyses of the individual and society only to what could be articulated in a logical, systematic fashion; they believed that little importance was ac-corded to the power of irrationality or to ideas not deemed "universally" true. In one of history's uglier ironies, the very impulses and ideas that Enlightenment thinkers chose to ignore asserted themselves with dread-ful effectiveness in World War II.

The problem in approaching the arguments for and against the En-lightenment and its alleged failure is the broadness of the concept itself; it is a term having meanings that vary among scholars, and its use is wide-spread and not confined to the academic community. As Peter Gay puts it: "I can think of no area of historical study in which the gap between the scholar and the general public is as wide, and as fateful, as it is with the Enlightenment" (*The Party of Humanity*, 262). One reason for this dispar-ity of opinions, which certainly exists as much among scholars as between scholars and the general public, is that we are all, as Michel Foucault insists, "beings who are historically determined . . . by the Enlighten-ment" ("What Is Enlightenment?" 43).

Although Foucault is frequently numbered among those who belittle the Enlightenment heritage (J. G. Merquior speaks of his "systematic disparagement of the Enlightenment," *Foucault*, 145), his point here is well taken.[2] Like it or not, define it as one may, the Enlightenment is an integral part of our Western heritage and as such has contributed to the intellectual formation of literate people. For the purpose of this study, what is required is not a detailed study of the Enlightenment with all its complexity and contradictions but rather an assessment of how the En-lightenment, regardless of whether it be well or poorly understood, has affected nonspecialists in that field, namely authors whose writings about World War II betray to some degree the influence of the eighteenth century's most important and amorphous contribution to Western cul-tural history.

In what follows I provide a brief survey of certain Enlightenment assumptions that have achieved wide currency among artists and intellectuals, then argue that the inability of several well-known authors to take a distance from these values contributed to the failure of their books to deal with the unique aspects of World War II. This failure was in turn compounded by these authors' dependence upon techniques and upon concepts of heroism rooted in Romanticism. The result was not to engage with the present but to reinvent the past.

Peter Gay maintains that the commonly held conviction that the *Aufklärer* possessed a near-blind confidence in human progress "has the status of an established truth, and yet it is a myth" (*Party,* 271). Myth it may be, but this "myth of the Enlightenment" has proven extremely influential. Jean-François Lyotard sums up this nonspecialist perception and suggests its implications for the future: "The thought and actions of the nineteenth and twentieth centuries are governed by the Idea of the Emancipation of humanity. This Idea develops at the end of the eighteenth century in Enlightenment philosophy and the French Revolution. Progress in technical sciences, the arts and political liberty will free all humanity from ignorance, poverty, lack of culture, despotism, and will not only make men happy, but, especially thanks to the State, enlightened citizens and masters of their destiny" (*Le Postmoderne expliqué aux enfants,* 129).

Let us consider some aspects of Enlightenment thinking that contributed to the situation Lyotard describes. According to Ernst Cassirer in his *The Philosophy of the Enlightenment,* Diderot believed in the "immutable moral nature of man and in a firm principle of justice arising from this nature" (246). He adhered to the notion of natural laws: "Let nature rule, let her obey only herself without fetters or conventional hindrances, and by this she will also realize the true and only good, the happiness of man and the welfare of the community" (247). The existence of *Rameau's Nephew,* that brooding, deeply ironic work written at various moments throughout Diderot's career, and never published during his lifetime, makes one wonder whether the editor of the *Encyclopedia* sustained this optimism until the end of his busy and harried existence, but Cassirer's paraphrasing of Diderot underscores what is frequently perceived as a widespread trend in Enlightenment thought: the perfectibility of the human species through recourse to its natural instincts.

The eighteenth century is considered the century of light in part because the *philosophes* believed that the application of reasonable concepts
to human problems would illuminate the underlying causes of concern
and thus provide means for resolution. Cassirer writes: "If there is one
formula by which the period of the Enlightenment can be characterized
and which can be attributed to the period with absolute certainty, it
would seem to be that it is an era of pure intellectualism, that it uncondi-
tionally upholds the primacy of thought and pure theory" (165). An essential component of the proclivity for theorizing is the confidence in the
power and universality of human reason: "The eighteenth century is imbued with a belief in the unity and immutability of reason. Reason is the
same for all thinking subjects, all nations, all cultures" (6).

Although the Enlightenment frequently invokes the "individual," what
is usually meant is something more akin to the "citizen," the "social being." Even an iconoclast like Rousseau—who toward the end of his life
broke with the main current of eighteenth-century thought by rejecting
society for nature, the city for the country—essentially acknowledged
that the individual was a social animal. While it is true that in his *Discourse on the Origin of Inequality* (1754) he imagines human beings alone
and isolated from one another, yet happy in their personal freedom, for
him this idyllic situation is a hypothetical state, one that probably even
for him never really existed and which in any case can never be recreated.
Despite his dislike and distrust of social constraints and his fantasy about
the putative unfettered individual, Rousseau, for the greater portion of
his career, accepted society as a necessary reality, something that could be
changed and improved but certainly something that would never disappear. As *The Social Contract* illustrates, Rousseau believed that human
nature was essentially good and that human corruption and enslavement
were the result of an unjust social system. For him, a better society would
allow its members to express their inherent decency and mutual respect.

The Enlightenment obviously had its share of dissenters, the most
prominent doubtless being David Hume. Nevertheless, within the context of the present discussion, it seems fair to maintain that, *mutatis
mutandis,* the Enlightenment heritage is a resolutely optimistic one. Humanity is by nature reasonable, social, and prone to goodness. The march
of history entails the possibility of a continuous improvement in the arts,
philosophy, and sciences, the ultimate and realizable goal of which is the

fulfillment of the human personality within a positive social setting.

However contested the current status of the Enlightenment, negative reactions to it began long before the twentieth century. In his *The Romantic Ideology: A Critical Investigation,* Jerome McGann describes a nineteenth-century attitude toward life and art that contrasts markedly with the Enlightenment sensibility: "The idea that poetry, or even consciousness, can set one free of the ruins of history is the grand illusion of the Romantic poet. This idea continues as one of the important shibboleths of our culture, especially—and naturally—at its highest levels" (91). If the Enlightenment *philosophe* sought to *discover* truth, the Romantic believed the artist could *invent* it. One of the greatest creations (delusions?) of Romanticism is precisely this notion that art and culture could somehow serve as refuges from the shambles of history. In this respect the Romantic is condescending toward the pettifogging workings of reason, since the goal is a higher level of consciousness where the Beautiful is willed into Truth, and where destruction and pain justify themselves by becoming the source of artistic creation. Hans Eichner provides a clear summary of this complicated and radical change in Western thinking: "the Romantics never wholly rejected reason, but they dethroned it, assigning it only the more menial services; to attain those truths that really matter they relied on the irrational faculties of the mind—unmediated insight, 'enthusiasm, intellectual intuition,' and the imagination, concepts that the Romantics did not always differentiate. The claims made by the Romantics on behalf of the imagination, in particular, are as ubiquitous as they are, to the modern ear, excessive" ("Rise of Modern Science," 17).

Given this intense subjectivity and the attendant claims for what the individual imagination can accomplish, it is not surprising that the heroic figure in Romanticism is most often the poet himself. The Romantic poet, whether the allegedly politically active Lord Byron, the deranged Hölderlin, or Vigny's suffering Chatterton, is a mythic figure whose traits, despite some personal variations, can be readily adumbrated. The Romantic poet (hero) is at once extremely gifted and sensitive, qualities that isolate him from his fellows. He is a person engaged in a doomed struggle against the forces of evil, which usually take the form of bourgeois society. What matters is not the success of his efforts but the struggle itself; his self-esteem depends upon his unceasing opposition to an infinitely powerful opponent. The issues the Romantic hero confronts are always titanic, and his failure to surmount them is no disgrace. His activity is its own justification, and his art compensates for any lack of practical success. If the intellectual tradition that dominated much of the present century has been strongly marked by the Enlightenment heritage, the heroic figure of the modern novel displays many vestiges of the Romantic hero.

In fact, there is no logical reason to assume that art *necessarily* has any moral or social value, and this banal and self-evident truth becomes especially significant when art's subject is something as barbaric as World War II. Nevertheless, the best art can bear witness to events. It can point to inconsistencies and deceptions; it can insist that the explanations proposed do not really provide answers; it can disconcert, indispose, and insist that the questions remain. To the extent that a work of art can achieve these ends, it may be said to possess a social value.

It is precisely these sorts of goals that much of the writing immediately after World War II failed to attain, because so many of the authors who attempted to respond to the war were imbued with faith in rational discussion and in heroic struggle. These beliefs led to a corollary confidence in human decency and in the ability of art to wrest beauty out of ugliness. Such attitudes are part of the legacy of Enlightenment and Romantic thinking.

The books I discuss in this chapter all fall prey to the Enlightenment and Romantic influences I have briefly sketched. Thomas Mann's *Doctor Faustus* (1948), Albert Camus' *The Plague* (1948), Ernst Jünger's war diaries—*Gardens and Roads* (1939–40), *First Parisian Journal* (1941–43), *Second Parisian Journal* (1941–43)—and Jean-Paul Sartre's *Death in the Soul* (1949) are thoughtful and at times compelling works, but each falters in its treatment of the war because of an adherence to techniques and attitudes that tend to turn the present into the past.

Doctor Faustus

Adrian Leverkühn is clearly at the center of the novel; he is the focus of the story and the character whose genius, accomplishments, and miseries parallel those of the German nation. While Leverkühn is certainly the novel's towering figure, the infinitely more modest Serenus Zeitblom, Ph.D., proves more important for my discussion. Critics tend to stress the parodic elements when considering Zeitblom. Donna Reed argues in

The Novel and the Nazi Past that "Mann's parody of his *Bildungsburger* Zeitblom often transforms him into a *Bildungsphilister* (17). At times Zeitblom seems to encourage such judgments by his repeated confessions of inadequacy and ineptness, a tendency evident from the first page: "Indeed, my mind misgives me that I shall only be awakening the reader's doubts whether he is in the right hands, whether, I mean, my whole existence does not disqualify me for a task dictated by the heart rather than by any true competence for the work" (1). Because such confessions abound in *Doctor Faustus,* it is easy to forget just who Zeitblom is and what he has achieved in his sixty years. Zeitblom is a well-educated and accomplished man; he knows classical and modern languages, has studied mathematics and the sciences, is conversant with contemporary theological speculations, plays the *violon d'amore* well enough to participate in recitals with first-rate musicians, and is sufficiently gifted in the arts to have composed the libretto for Leverkühn's version of *Love's Labors Lost.* In short, Serenus Zeitblom has a more extensive *Bildung* and greater artistic talent than most of us who comment upon his role in the novel.

Zeitblom's impressive education and achievements constitute his great weakness. He is the product of a distinguished European tradition; all he has done, thought, or learned makes it impossible for him to understand either his friend Leverkühn or the thousand-year Reich, which is literally crumbling around him. In the introduction to his early novel *Life Is Elsewhere* (1973), Milan Kundera quotes Heidegger as saying that "the essence of man has the form of a question" (vii), and it is certainly true that the nature of the question asked determines the parameters of the answer given. Zeitblom's questions are geared toward explaining the present in terms of the past; his superb academic background makes it nearly impossible for him to perceive what is unique and unanticipated in a contemporary situation. Mario Praz notes in *The Romantic Agony* that "it is romantic to consider concrete expression as a decadence, a contamination" (33). Zeitblom reflects this implicit disdain for the self-evident, especially when it is brutal and ugly, through his penchant for formulating issues in grandiose terms: "What sphere of human endeavor, even the most unalloyed, the most dignified and benevolent, would be entirely inaccessible to the powers of the underworld?" (9).

The reference to satanic powers might easily appear atavistic, a ploy by which Mann can suggest Zeitblom's old-fashioned ways of thinking, but whatever the author's desire to distance himself from his narrator, the schoolteacher's interest in raising great questions and then offering even greater answers is Mann's interest as well. As Judith Ryan observes in *The Uncompleted Past: Postwar German Novels and the Third Reich,* in the immediate postwar period the tendency of German writers was to "view the historical development of Nazism as an inevitable process. . . . *Doctor Faustus* presents a sophisticated version of this view" (12). The notion of inevitability is an extremely dangerous concept when applied to history. It either totally frees the individual from the burden of choice and responsibility or considerably lessens these burdens. Also, since the inevitable by definition resists alteration or opposition, it allows people to avoid concrete questions and clear analyses of specific historical circumstances. Precisely this approach to events and human beings' involvement in them permeates *Doctor Faustus* and allows its author to avoid issues anchored in Germany's *Realpolitik* for vaster and vaguer ones. By means of his narrator, Mann is forever posing questions on a scale that precludes serious answers. If his aim were to do so in order to illustrate the inadequacy of such an approach, his novel might have been more instructive, but this is clearly not the author's intention.

Thomas Mann, whatever his gifts for irony, structured *Doctor Faustus* in such a way as to imply that Hitlerism, and the involvement of the German people with their leader, could somehow be illuminated in cosmic terms.[3] This tendency, widespread in postwar literature and apparently common in some historical writing, merits the rejoinder of a historian of the Final Solution: "The historian who assigns causal responsibility to those 'vast impersonal forces' rather than to the movers and shakers who made events happen has abdicated his professional obligation, for if he cannot locate the human factor in explaining historical events, he cannot then decipher the import of those events" (Dawidowicz, *Holocaust and Historians,* 146).

A more interesting aspect of the structure of *Doctor Faustus* involves the use of allegory, the constant, implicit analogy between Leverkühn and the Germany enamored of Hitler. Judith Ryan provides a clear synopsis: "We are to understand that it is the nature of Leverkühn's (and Germany's) genius which gives rise to the involvement with evil, that genius and evil are in a sense two faces of one coin" (*Uncompleted Past,* 47). Mann's allegory of World War II, despite its cosmic overtones, is very much anchored in a real time period; it draws a relatively straightforward correlation between aspects of Leverkühn's and Hitler's genius and purports to offer serious insights into a specific historical event. Furthermore, the rigidity of the allegorical structure easily leads to political and moral absurdities. Ronald Gray underscores this tendency when he notes that the parallelism between Leverkühn, who creates masterpieces because of his bondage to evil, and Germany's adherence to Nazism implies that "both pacts might end in a miraculous new uprising, that both were the truly theological path to salvation" (*German Tradition*, 222). From Gray's perspective, the novel becomes a misguided, simplistic attempt to conjure some kind of spiritual rebirth out of a reality of wanton destruction.

The allegorical pattern in *Doctor Faustus* further strains credibility and common sense in trying to equate the artist's egocentricity and exploitation of his entourage with Hitler's policies and abuses of the German people. Leverkühn, like Hitler, is ego driven, obsessed with his own genius, and convinced that the dictates of his own destiny free him from the constraints of commonly held moral convictions. If the majority of the German people succumbed to their Führer's self-image and tended to treat him as a deity, Zeitblom's view of his friend is disquietingly similar. Toward the end of the novel, he describes Leverkühn's agonized face as "something spiritualized and suffering, even Christlike" (483).[4] It is tempting to consider such a remark as another example of Zeitblom's limitations, but in a novel where allegory labors to poeticize the artist's torments, and implicitly Germany's as well, it would be difficult to imagine that in this instance the schoolteacher's words were to be read ironically. It seems truer to the novel's tenor to take this comparison seriously and conclude that, in Mann's view, Germany's misdeeds and sufferings, like the artist's pain, have some redemptive value.

The real irony of *Doctor Faustus* as an example of writing about World War II is that it occasionally does provide glimpses of a possible break with the past and new ways of thinking in a postwar context. Not surprisingly, these moments are associated with Leverkühn. Except for the musician's description of his pact with the devil, his mad speech at the novel's end, and some brief remarks interspersed throughout the story, little is known of Leverkühn's thinking about the world in which he lives. What does emerge, however, shows him to be a man largely free of the values and inhibitions of his contemporaries. Despite the personal suffering his activities exact, Leverkühn's intermittent comments reveal a willingness to break with artistic and intellectual traditions and to reformulate problems from a distinctly modern perspective. In a discussion with Zeitblom, whose university education and personal temperament have encouraged traditional ways of thinking, the artist responds to his friend's rather hackneyed contention that the alternative to culture is barbarism by suggesting that "barbarism is the opposite of culture only within the order of thought which it gives us. Outside of it the opposite may be quite different or no opposite at all" (59). Leverkühn's words imply that the unthinkable can and may have to be thought, that long-standing dichotomies may be the result of language rather than inherent in reality, and that the experience of the present risks being obfuscated by the inclination to analyze it in terms of the intellectual and moral categories of the past.

To cite another of the all too rare examples of openness to the present, there is the scene in which Leverkühn chides his friend for his "tendency . . . to inquire after the objective, the so-called truth, to question as worthwhile the subjective, pure experience: that is petty bourgeois" (242). The artist is calling Zeitblom's attention to his inability to see the class origins of his assumptions and their influence on his thoughts. More generally, Leverkühn is inviting a reevaluation of the methods employed in structuring, delimiting, and hierarchizing experience; he is allowing for the possibility that the irrational has been consistently undervalued in Western thinking. Unfortunately, ideas like these remain undeveloped and scattered throughout a novel in which the allegorical format does exactly what the principal character criticizes: the allegory provides a false sense of continuity and coherence between particular events and allows for the possibility that there may be some transcendent significance to what is occurring.

The writing of *Doctor Faustus* caused Thomas Mann considerable physical and psychological suffering, and his devotion to the work was enormous: "I am attached to this book as I am to no other. Whoever does not like it, I do not like anymore. Whoever shows himself sensitive to the extreme emotional tension under which it was created, to him belongs all my gratitude" (Reed, *The Novel*, 1). It is saddening to read these words and nonetheless realize one must place oneself in the camp of the opposition. Perhaps Mann was indeed "the last bourgeois artist," a man well schooled in the values and traditions of the nineteenth century, and for that very reason he was so adrift in the world of postwar Europe. From the perspective of over fifty years after the novel was published, *Doctor Faustus* seems consistently to confuse vagueness with complexity and hence to shed little light on the causes and ramifications of World War II. It ultimately gives credence to Michel Hamburger's strongly worded judgment: "If Thomas Mann had not been a writer of fiction—however 'philosophical,' however ambitiously intent upon dealing with the principal issues of the age—no one would have the slightest interest in his ideas" (*From Prophecy to Exorcism,* 84).

The Plague

Conor Cruse O'Brien describes *The Plague* as "less a novel than a sermon in the form of a fable" (*Albert Camus,* 64). Developing this thought, he adds: "*The Plague* is not a novel. It is an allegorical sermon" (65). Camus made the precise nature of the allegory clear when, in a letter to Roland Barthes, he stated that his book has "as its obvious content the struggle of the European Resistance against Nazism" (O'Brien, *Camus,* 63). Camus' allegory is more pointed and less portentous than Mann's effort, but it too suffers from large-scale simplification. The rats, which represent the Nazis, come from nowhere and eventually disappear for no discernible reason. The resistance fighters, the doctors, the simple citizens like Grand and Rambert, the intellectuals like Tarrou, and the priest Paneloux, unite harmoniously, albeit after some hesitation, in an altruistic combat against the common enemy. In no way does this correspond to the internecine struggles between the competing Gaullist and Communist resistance factions and the Vichy government. This rift was so large, so destabilizing for France that its effects linger into the present. According to Henry Rousso, "the civil war . . . played an essential role . . . in the difficulties the people of France have in reconciling themselves to their history" (*Vichy Syndrome,* 9). Nor do the activities of the pathetic Cottard clarify anything essential about the collaboration.

The central weakness in Camus' allegory, and also of allegory in general when applied to World War II, is its dehistoricalization of specific events. Stephen Ullman is quite right when he remarks that "the allegorical significance of the plague is . . . wider: transcending the limits of a particular crisis in history, it becomes the symbol of evil in general, and raises the whole problem of the human predicament and of man's predicament and of man's attitude in the face of an absurd universe" (*Image,* 256). While Ullman might find much to praise in this universalization of evil and absurdity, from another perspective his comment indicates how *The Plague* transforms concrete occurrences in Europe between 1939 and 1945 into a vast, existential drama and, in so doing, reintegrates the war, along with anything that might have been different about it, into the mainstream of Western anxiety. World War II thus becomes yet another example of the types of problems that have existed in the past and will doubtless persist in the present.

Camus' existential hero is the Romantic hero reborn. Dr. Rieux is the strong, taciturn figure who towers over others, speaks the uncompromising language of Saint-Just (12), and is relentless in his efforts to destroy the evil threatening him and those he has sworn to protect. Like his Romantic counterparts, Rieux excites the admiration of men, while he deals with the absence and loss of women with exemplary stoicism. Danger and death move him to philosophical speculation and harden his determination to continue the fight despite the odds against him. Rieux may be the finest example of Camus' "absurd hero," but the unimpeachable rightness of everything he does, especially when measured against the mindless enemy (rats = Nazis), appears too facile and encourages a positive response to George Steiner's question about whether "the banality of Camus' plays, and all but the first of his novels, does not connote the persistent vagueness, the statuesque but airy motion of his thought?" (*Language and Silence,* 10).

There are, nevertheless, other elements in *The Plague* that display a toughness of vision not characteristic of the novel as a whole but pointing toward later, more successful treatments of the war. If Rieux is the positive embodiment of the Romantic hero, Tarrou is the parody of the same personage. His self-proclaimed desire to be a "saint" (237) and his tendency to revel in dramatic and dangerous situations place him clearly in the tradition of Romantic literature.

Tarrou's death, essentially provoked by his lack of desire to live in a modern, plagueless world, contrasts markedly with the attitude of another, more interesting character. Joseph Grand—the ridiculous, admirable little clerk, who under pressure chooses life over art and prefers persistence in necessary, inglorious tasks to grandiose gestures—does what is perhaps the most courageous thing a human being can do amid awful circumstances: he survives. As Rieux correctly observes, Grand is the true hero of the story. This modest, unassuming man, lacking in heroic physique, limited in intelligence and artistic talent, yet determined to live his life even if that means fighting when no other options are available, is the most striking exemplar of modern heroism in the novel.

Rieux also has moments when his character exceeds the boundaries of the novel's allegorical structure and Romantic ambience. In opposition to Tarrou he insists that heroism and sanctity hold no appeal for him. What he desires is to learn to be a man (238). Unfortunately, just what constitutes manhood is never really developed. In any case, such instances of breaking away from Romantic patterns and posturings are rare in *The Plague*. Despite repeated gestures toward stoicism, Rieux's values are grounded in a visceral optimism, only occasionally tempered by some protestation of life's meaninglessness. As the novel ends he sums up his experience of the plague as having taught *us* that "there are more things to admire in human beings than to despise" (287). Rieux's conclusion, which is probably Camus' as well, provides a quick and dismissive response to one of the ugliest questions the war raises: is there indeed any reason to continue to believe in the fundamental decency of one's fellows or oneself?

Camus' and Mann's choice of an allegorical method eviscerated their respective treatments of World War II. As previously mentioned, Steiner described Camus' thought as "airy," and the allegorical approach can only increase the propensity for vast generalizations and strained analogies. This type of writing succeeds so poorly because it attempts so much. The late Edmond Jabès, who had devoted so much of his talent to finding a means of writing about World War II, made a pun in *El, ou le dernier livre* (El, or the last book) that encapsulates the weakness inherent in such a broad approach to the war: "Le mot *aérien* est menacé, dans son propre sein, par le mot *rien*" (89). The literal translation is: "The word *aerial* is threatened, in its own breast, by the word *nothing*." The pun being in French on *aérien* (aerial) and *rien* (nothing).

War Diaries

In his war diaries, Ernst Jünger uses the past as a barrier and protection against the present. As a result these diaries fail to clarify, or really even confront, what is happening either on the battlefield or in the political arena. They serve instead to create a fictional universe that seals the author (and reader) off from what is actually transpiring. Failing that, they blunt the impact of events. In his *Second Journal* (*First Parisian Journal 1941–1943*) he mentions that he seems to move about in a world for which he is not suitably prepared (251). The three war diaries largely confirm this judgment.

Jünger's diaries take him from the heady days of the *Blitzkrieg* and the triumphant marches through Belgium and France to the Paris of the Occupation; later he visits the Russian front, and finally, in anticipation of the Allied victory, the author returns to his home in Kirchhorst to await the inevitable. Throughout the narration Jünger's prose serves to distance him from what is happening around him. During the initial German victories he notes the beauty of the landscape while lamenting its devastation. Only occasionally does a harsher reality intrude with sufficient force to provoke a momentary reflection on what he has witnessed in his lifetime. In his first journal Jünger recognizes the implications of his wartime experience: "I looked at . . . the barbed wire, which, along with explosives and exploding shells, are the symbols of our time" (*Gardens and Roads* 117).

Jünger's awareness of Germany's cultural tradition and his pride in his own distinguished record in World War I, in which from his perspective soldiers on both sides comported themselves honorably, seem to blind him to what is at stake in the present conflict. Neither a Nazi nor an anti-Semite, Jünger disliked Hitler intensely and throughout the diaries referred to him condescendingly as "Kniebolo." Yet these honorable attitudes did not prove sufficient to prevent his active participation in the German war effort, even though he was technically too old to fight. There is doubtless no simple explanation for the seeming disparity between Jünger's beliefs and activities, and one can only hazard a guess that Jünger was so imbued with a sense of Germany's great aesthetic and intellectual heritage, along with the perceived wrongs done to this nation by the Treaty of Versailles (1917), that the evil he was sufficiently well placed to witness remained somehow unacknowledgeable.

Certainly Jünger's literary taste helped to turn his eyes from the present. He praises one of the last works of Oswald Spengler, *The Early Period of World History* (1936), because "the mystery of his discourse is that it has strength, and can confront great catastrophes" (*Gardens,* 58). Yet the strength of Spengler's discourse, his means of confronting "great catastrophes," takes a peculiar form: "There is in his prose a certain impetus toward barriers that must be jumped" (*Gardens,* 58). What Jünger appears to admire is a use of language that can move beyond problems, jump over them rather than face them. As authors often do, he praises a quality in a colleague's work that his own writing possesses. Spengler, like Jünger, can find the literary means to avoid annoying particularities that interfere with his propensity to accede, as quickly as possible, to some cosmic level. What charms Jünger about Spengler's writing is how the latter, like himself, by a combination of *idées fixes* and an inspired choice of words, can make precise details diminish in importance.

In another distraction from the wartime events, Jünger also praises the works of Edgar Allen Poe. He cites with approval the Goncourt brothers' assessment that Poe's "The Descent into the Maelstrom" qualifies the American author as "the first writer of the twentieth century" (*Gardens,* 71). Jünger shares the Goncourts' respect for Poe's ability to describe the ways in which human beings are reduced to the status of robots. Later, in his third diary (*Second Parisian Journal 1943–1945*), written as Germany's collapse accelerated, he lauds Poe for offering in "The Maelstrom" one of the "greatest prophetic visions of our catastrophe, and especially the best image of it" (93–94). Like many writers of his generation who attempted to react to World War II, Jünger gravitated toward apocalyptic language and imagery, which, while they can convey an overwhelming apprehension of finality and loss, nonetheless say little that is concrete about causes and effects.

Jünger's fascination with Poe, aside from the ahistorical context of the American's narrative, stems largely from the image of the human being reduced to a robot. Just as Spengler's broad view of history as expressed in *The Decline of the West* (1922) considered the demise of Western civilization to be inevitable, and hence the individual's role in preventing it insignificant, the idea of the robot likewise circumvents the question of human responsibility. In his diaries Jünger would seem to imply that although the Germans were at fault for permitting Hitler to turn them into automatons, once this happened there was nothing to do except allow the historical drama to move toward its catastrophic dénouement.

The simplicity of Jünger's historical vision emerges most forcefully in his penchant to conflate the past and the present. In the first diary there is a scene in which, from the vantage of a cathedral tower, he surveys a horizon where the natural beauty of the countryside and the implements of modern warfare vie for his attention. He is so moved by the juxtaposition that he exclaims: "I felt the continuity between the past and our present era. I especially felt that the past should not escape me and I made a vow nevermore to forget what I owe to my ancestors" (*Gardens*, 185). Correlating the past with the present serves in this instance to remove the immediacy of the here and now by obscuring the significant differences between what is natural and what is manufactured, what is peaceful and what is warlike. Also, the equation of the two loosely defined time periods creates an aura of continuity and eternal recurrence: "one senses here the formidable power of future centuries still in the bud" (*Gardens*, 185). In short, he escapes thinking about the present either by conflating it with the past or by musing about the future.

Jünger constantly uses language to obscure significant differences. He praises the participants in the war without addressing the goals they represent. For Jünger World War I created a sense of community among those who survived (*Gardens*, 236), and, initially at least, he tries to see a continuation of this putative camaraderie extending from the First to the Second World War. His efforts to achieve this end involve his using an inflated rhetoric that hinges on a comforting, albeit limp, imagery: "The images of the two wars are going, perhaps after all, to melt into a single one in the eyes of memory" (*First Parisian Journal*, 37). The infinitive "to melt" softens distinctions between the two conflicts, while the further distancing created by the mixed metaphor "the eyes of memory" manages to evoke a general impression rather than a clear idea.

A comparable deviation occurs when Jünger describes his reaction to the Nazis imposing the yellow star on Jews in Occupied Paris: "Such a spectacle cannot but provoke a reaction—thus I immediately felt embarrassed to be in uniform" (*First Journal*, 142). These words succeed at directing attention from the center to the periphery of the issue, from a lethal insult to a group of threatened human beings toward a gentleman's reaction of displeasure, and by so doing turn a degrading act into a question of bad taste. Such an attitude makes comprehensible Hamburger's assertion that "Jünger is truly representative of those cultured Germans

who disassociated themselves from Nazism out of an aesthetic or aristo-
cratic fastidiousness" (*Prophecy,* 124).

As the war accelerates, the diaries reflect the author's ever-increasing
distancing of himself from events. He notes that he is strangely unmoved
by the invasion of Russia (*First Parisian Journal,* 44). Later in the same
diary, he complains that theologians are lacking to answer important
questions concerning why men become robots (141) but does not mention why theologians are best suited to this task. Eventually he admits that
liberty, as it was understood in the nineteenth century, would be impossible to reestablish (*First Parisian Journal,* 256), but he never considers
either why it should be or what possible alternatives might exist.

Ernst Jünger is in many ways the real-life equivalent of Serenus Zeitblom. As with Mann's character, Jünger's strengths are his limitations. His
background, learning, and literary sensitivity mark him as a man of the
nineteenth century whose ethical and political values reflect elements of
the Enlightenment heritage. He has an essentially positive view of human
nature, expressing more faith than distrust in the possibility of a just society and a strong sense of himself as a responsible citizen whose status
imposes obligations as well as privileges. Hence, when Hamburger concludes his discussion of Jünger by saying that his "literary gifts have failed
to coalesce with the realities of the postwar age" (*Prophecy,* 127), this judgment may not be as damning as it initially appears. Because of the special
nature of World War II, the wanton and massive destruction of civilian
populations, intellectual and political history would take such a radical
turn that many artists, especially those whose aesthetic formation pre-
dates the war, are simply unable to keep apace.

Just as there are moments in *Doctor Faustus* when the reader seems to
sense the burgeoning emergence of a new consciousness in the world,
Jünger's texts also contain hints that history is neither necessarily progres-
sive nor subject to some form of eternal recurrence. A sentence in his last
diary displays the tension between his penchant for explaining the present
in terms of the past and a disturbing premonition that something new
and ugly has come upon the scene: "One might say that all the old errors
will be repeated, and that the world, instead of being warned by the existence of Kniebolo [Hitler], inclines to take him as a model" (*Second Parisian Journal,* 337).

Death in the Soul

Jean-Paul Sartre ought to have been an ideal person to write an effective, original novel about World War II. Always interested in contemporary aesthetic and intellectual movements, galvanized by the war into involvement with the political controversies of his day, an excellent writer who was already the author of an innovative novel, *Nausea* (1938), Sartre had all the tools to produce one of the first important works of fiction about the war. His attempt to do so took the form of a trilogy, *The Roads of Liberty*, which he originally intended to be a tetralogy. The three completed novels are *The Age of Reason* (1945), *The Reprieve* (1947), and *Death in the Soul* (1949).

Although the trilogy tells several stories at once, the focus of attention is most often Mathieu, a young intellectual who fancies himself free of the moral, political, and philosophical inhibitions of the bourgeoisie. His girlfriend's unexpected pregnancy shatters Mathieu's complacency and compels him to realize how enmeshed he is in middle-class values. He begins to appreciate the extent to which he profits from the privileges accorded him as a member of that social class. Meanwhile, as Mathieu struggles to untangle his personal problems, Europe is moving rapidly toward war, a situation that largely escapes this bourgeois intellectual's notice. The grave danger is, however, apparent to his Communist friends, whose trust in Stalin Mathieu cannot accept. In what follows, I intend to concentrate on *Death in the Soul* (translated as *Troubled Sleep*, but I prefer the literal rendering) in order to show how Sartre's effort to deal with World War II failed, in a large measure because of his dependence upon situations and posturings that reflect a Romantic sensibility.

Death in the Soul details the demoralizing defeat of France. Toward the novel's end, Brunet, a French Communist and prisoner of war, is attempting to establish a Communist cell in the prison camp. Eventually he is overwhelmed by the seeming futility of his efforts. Wandering in a drizzling rain, "he does not think of anything, he feels hollow and empty . . . death in the soul" (393). "Death in the soul" is despair, the total absence of hope felt by the French in the face of the speed and thoroughness of the German victory. This attitude of helplessness and defeat before an infinitely more powerful enemy is the backdrop for the novel. While such an emotional state may accurately reflect a widespread sentiment at the historical moment of France's collapse, it precludes any serious analysis of what took place, of how this state of affairs actually came about. In *Death in the Soul,* thought usually takes the form of positing grandiose statements in a physical setting, such as in the example already mentioned, where the environment (the rain) mirrors the mood of the speaker. The use of nature to reflect the emotions of a human being is, of course, the pathetic fallacy, a technique much loved by Romantic artists.

In this novel Sartre owes much to Romanticism. Aside from the frequent use of the pathetic fallacy and the propensity for grand generalizations about the human condition, there is the presence of Mathieu, the bourgeois intellectual transformed into the Romantic hero. Mathieu abandons thought for heroic and desperate action; he casts aside common sense and, with an explanation worthy of a Byronic character, joins a suicidal effort to halt the German advance: "I decided that death was the secret sense of my life, that I lived to die; I am dying to bear witness to the impossibility of living" (253). Shortly thereafter, Mathieu's words risk becoming reality when, as the last living French soldier, perched gun in hand on top of a tower the Germans have surrounded, "he fired: he was pure, he was all-powerful. He was free" (281). The hesitant, introspective bourgeois of *The Age of Reason* exits in *Death in the Soul* as the Romantic hero. (Actually Sartre does not let him die; Mathieu reappears in the fragment of the fourth novel.)

It is tempting but mistaken to imagine that Sartre is using Mathieu to illustrate the emptiness of a certain type of intellectual; the pattern of replacing effort to understand by either disillusionment or frenzied action is not confined to Mathieu. For example, Brunet, the Communist organizer, succumbs to a mindless despair as the train carrying the other prisoners and himself to Germany thunders across France: "ideas spurted out, indistinct, fell on the rails behind him, before he could recognize them" (435).

For the most part, Sartre's novel has little to say concerning what form the postwar consciousness might take. There is, however, one section in *Death in the Soul* that offers a brief but intriguing commentary on the possible relation between contemporary art and *engagement.* Toward the beginning of the novel, the political activist Gomez is a refugee in New York. At the Museum of Modern Art he comments cynically on American art lovers' enthusiasm for Mondrian. From his viewpoint, Americans appreciate Mondrian's spare canvases because these works do not "ask questions" (33). When his American acquaintance retorts that they most certainly do, Gomez at first seems to acquiesce, but then after a moment of reflection, he says that while Mondrian's paintings may indeed pose questions, they never are "the serious ones" (34). He then goes on to say that in the past he never had much confidence in revolutionary art, but now he has no belief in it at all (35). It never occurs to Gomez that the contemporary artist may indeed be posing "serious questions," albeit no longer in a traditional form. These different queries may just reflect contemporary experience more accurately than do his own questions. From this perspective Gomez may be objecting to art's new ways of framing reality and formulating the questions pertaining to it. A revolutionary in politics, he is very much a conservative in art. Gomez's disenchantment with contemporary art parallels Sartre's attitude during the postwar period. The Spaniard's pessimistic estimation of the capacity of art to affect social change was very much that of the Sartre who was soon to abandon the project of *The Roads of Freedom* and to turn away from the writing of fiction.

Whatever Gomez's limitations as an art critic, he remains an impressive figure in the novel. Unlike Mathieu and Brunet, he still believes that immediate, specific questions can and should be asked. Living in New York he is certainly in a safer place than his two friends, but he has been active enough in European politics to have been forced to become a political refugee. Putting aside for a moment the relevance of Gomez's remarks to Mondrian's work, or to the broader issue concerning the ways in which postwar artists or intellectuals may choose to frame their works, his perception that an artist's *oeuvre* may be popular with an intellectual elite because it presents no serious challenges may also be applied to *Death in the Soul* or Sartre's trilogy in general: these novels cultivate a trendy despair that discourages serious reevaluation of important questions, however difficult they may be to pose.

In *Human Being: The World of Jean-Paul Sartre,* Joseph McMahon cites Simone de Beauvoir's rather unconvincing explanation for Sartre's inability to complete the tetralogy: "With almost everyone dead, no one remained to raise the questions posed by the postwar period" (142). McMahon offers an unflattering but perhaps quite accurate gloss on de Beauvoir's comment: "That is the most succinct explanation of why the novel (the fourth) remains unfinished. It was not completed because history had gone its own way and had seemingly undone, even before they had a chance to be applied, whatever solutions the final volume might have outlined" (142). The postwar world did not turn out as Sartre had imagined; he had cast his trilogy in a fashion that was so committed, aesthetically and intellectually, to the past that it had no light to shed either on the uniqueness of the war itself or on the lingering impact of the conflict on society.

McMahon's assessment can easily be applied to the four writers whose works I have briefly discussed in this chapter. In an essay entitled "Conversations with Brecht," Walter Benjamin quotes the playwright as saying that the contemporary artist must learn to build "not on the good old days, but on the bad new ones" (*Illuminations,* 219). This is precisely what Mann, Camus, Jünger, and Sartre were unable to do. Rather than attempting to explore the new, they chose to transform it into the old. If World War II gave birth to a new consciousness, artists were initially uncertain how to baptize the baby. In the next chapter I discuss efforts in Germany and France to contend with this troubling and unwanted child.

Presenting the Present

3

I do not know whether you have come across the word Bullshit—it is an army word and signifies what I think I must get rid of—the mass of irrelevancies, of "attitudes," "approaches," propaganda, ivory towers, etc. that stand between us and our problems and what we are to do about them. To write on themes that have been concerning me lately in lyric or abstract forms would be immense bullshitting.

Hewison, *Under Siege,* 123

These words of the British poet Keith Douglas, who died in action during World War II, constitute a vulgar, albeit pertinent, statement of the changing attitudes toward the writing of literature that World War II engendered. What Douglas envisioned, of course, was not a rejection of the elegant in favor of the gross. Rather, he wanted a language freed of cultural complacencies, a style of writing that would permit an author to look as unsparingly as possible at the reality of a situation, that would touch upon what was different and unique in the present experience. This desire for a new approach to the making of literature was also an obsessive concern for many postwar German and French writers, and their efforts to achieve this end is the subject of the present chapter.

The beginnings of the Group 47, whose name was invented by Hans Georg Brenner and refers to the year of the group's first meeting, were as chaotic as anything else in Germany immediately after the war. Two writers, Alfred Andersch (1914–80) and Hans Werner Richter (1908–) were both prisoners of war transported to the United States, where they founded a revue called *Der Ruf* [The shout]. They continued producing this journal when they returned to occupied Germany, but in April of 1947, the American military government banned the publication on account of its "nihilism" (Demetz, *After the Fires,* 8). Largely at the initiative of Richter, young

German writers, most of whom were veterans, began meeting once and eventually twice a year in various parts of Germany. At these meetings they would discuss the current crisis of German letters as well as the best ways to articulate the experiences of past and present. One faction proposed a return to *poésie pure* and was against any form of political involvement. Their opponents, most of whom had previously published in *Der Ruf*, insisted upon a realistic, politically aware approach in which form would be sacrificed for content. Writing about a meeting at Bannwaldsee in 1947, Hans A. Neunzig described the proponents of the latter tendency: "they were honorable, they detested formalistic games and attempted to allot to Man, in the midst of a world of shattered values and lost illusions, a reliable position" (*Lesebuch der Gruppe 47*, 15). This, the more radical position, eventually won out and generally speaking became characteristic of the Group 47. As early as Bannwaldsee, "it was clear to people that this new time must be lived, experienced and written about differently" (Maria Eibach, "Die Epoche," in Lettau, *Die Gruppe 47*, 22; hereafter cited as Lettau).

The effort to write differently entailed breaking away from a prestigious tradition in German literature, the abandonment of artists like Goethe and Thomas Mann as literary models. Hans Georg Brenner captures the aggressive mood of the disillusioned young writers and particularly their contempt for the reigning literary luminaries: "They were not about to allow themselves to be instructed by their elders, who once again after the second collapse [i.e., World War II] wanted to discuss 'The Task of the Poet in His Time,' in order to retreat into their pleasantly polished inner lives; the tasks of the present burned their nails too hotly, and what was most disturbing was the realization that the tool kit of these would-be teachers, while brightly polished, was obtuse and useless. They decided to work together to procure a new tool kit" ("1952 Niendorf," in Lettau, 74).

Principal among these new tools was a simple, straightforward, unemotional style that many of the Group 47 associated with Ernest Hemingway. A journalist present at the 1949 autumn gathering in Ammersee captures just how suspicious were the early adherents of the Group 47 toward formalistic experimentation: "'Development is opposed to complexity' was in the ensuing discussion rarely contradicted" ("Herbstagung der Gruppe 47 am Ammersee," in Lettau, 50). This distrust of new literary trends, although occasionally opposed, persisted throughout the lifespan of the Group 47. As late as 1965 Marcel Reich-Ranicki could report that at the 1964 meeting in Sigtuna, "the trendy texttinkers . . . didn't have the slightest chance" ("Nichts als deutsche Literatur," in Lettau, 214).

Ilse Aichinger provided an example of how intensely felt was the desire to rethink the ways of writing the native language when she claimed that she wanted to relearn German "as a foreigner learns a foreign language, cautiously, warily, like someone turns on a light in a dark house, and then goes on his way" (Urs Widmer, "So kahl war der Kahlschlag nicht," in Lettau, 333). This new literary style, which came to characterize much of the writing associated with the Group 47, was christened by Wolfgang Weyrauch "Kahlschlag" (clearing away) prose.

One of the unique features of the Group 47 was the absence of any statutes or manifestos. Nor was there any formal membership list. Every year Richter would send handwritten postcards inviting various writers to attend the meeting and read from their work in progress. The invitation to read was something of a mixed blessing. The chosen author would have the privilege of sitting on a chair ("the electric chair," as it rapidly came to be known) facing the assembly of colleagues and reading from his or her work. When the reading ended, the author had to listen to any criticism offered without having the right to respond. The sessions were frequently boisterous enough to justify Mann's well-known characterization of the Group 47 as a "Rasselbande" (a bunch of troublemakers). These experiences doubtless created as many enmities as friendships, yet all of this was part of the remaking of German literature.

Inevitably the Group 47 became an institution, and while never as stuffy as the *Académie Française*, it did possess the ability to make or break careers. As time went on, the meetings began to attract publishers in search of new talent and received ample exposure in the press and on radio and television. By the 1960s the most famous of Germany's angry young men and women had become very much establishment figures. The inevitable reaction occurred at Princeton in 1966 when Peter Handke—speaking for the newly emerging generation of German writers, which obviously included himself—castigated the work of his immediate elders, the now middle-aged or elderly adherents to the Group 47, as writers of merely "description literature. Everything lacked creativity and was better suited for children's picture books. . . . the language was bleak, clipped, silly and idiotic. The criticism was silly and idiotic too" (Ernst Jochen, "Rowohlt wird unsicher," in Lettau, 404).

Whatever the weaknesses of the Group 47, it did have the great virtue of establishing that the war had created a new intellectual, artistic, and moral climate. To an extent the polemical, even dogmatic tone of those opposed to the group stemmed from the refusal of some prominent German intellectuals to accept this reality. In an essay that appeared in *Die Zeit,* Friedrich Sieburg took issue with the positions of the Group 47 and argued that there was really no difference between a child dying of an illness and another being destroyed by a bomb. Alfred Andersch's reply is as heated as it is accurate: "'Whether someone lost a child to meningitis in Switzerland or to a bomb in Dresden, it is the same suffering' speaks well for Sieburg's human understanding, but not for his ability to make intellectual distinctions. For throughout time children die from meningitis, but the monument particular to our time is that children en masse were killed by bombs. Thus it happens that the perhaps unsuccessful attempt of a writer to express in words this sign of the times and to mourn it passionately means more to us in itself than the depiction, however artistically rendered, of meningitis in Switzerland" ("Die Spaliers der Banalität," in Lettau, 343). Andersch ends his essay with the by now *de rigueur* attack on Germany's traditional cultural mavens: "Let the bad old gentlemen play peacefully with the 'European spirit'—they will never get to it—for where the European spirit really is, they will not find it!" (347).

The Group 47 was a vital force in German letters for about twenty years. Despite its weaknesses and reverse snobbism, it changed the writing of German literature. The works associated with the group were often of a high literary quality, but they were not intended exclusively for the literati. These writers produced novels, stories, poems, and plays aimed at the average literate German; in this respect they were decidedly antimodernist. The Group 47 wrote popular literature in the finest sense of the term; the readership is not condescended to but treated as an audience capable of dealing with complex issues, provided they are clearly developed.

At first the adherents to the Group 47 were as adrift as any other German writers with regard to the most effective methods for treating World War II. At the initial meeting in Bannwaldsee (1947), Heinz Friedrich read some scenes from a play in which he "demonstrated the problem of the present through the concept of Golgotha" (Eibach in Lettau, 22). One would be hard pressed to find a more traditional analogy, and if this standard were to be the norm, Mann's *Doctor Faustus* undoubtedly offered a richer elaboration. This approach, however, was not the one favored by the group, and in an excellent essay entitled "Günter Grass: der Faschismus als Kleinbürgetum und was daraus wurde" (Günter Grass: Fascism as lower middle class–ness and what came from it), Helmut Koopmann demarcates the differences between established German novelists' ways of dealing with the origins of the war and those of the younger writers such as Grass. Koopmann argues that authors such as Thomas Mann, Leon Feuchtwanger, and Stefan Zweig tended to explain the Hitler phenomenon in terms of distant historical and even religious or metaphysical antecedents. This approach failed to alert the German people to what was happening or had happened: "Neither references to historical parallels nor psychological significance, nor economic analyses, which were masked in the form of a novel, brought about any changes; these writers started no revolts" (in Wagener, *Siegfried Lenz,* 163).

Of course it must be said that it was a much more dangerous task to alert Germany to the dangers of the *Hitlerzeit* when the Nazis were in power than to condemn their brutality after the war. However, it can also be argued that self-consciously literary treatments of the issue, such as those practiced by Mann and Zweig, constituted a politically questionable way of making a point. Placing a realpolitik situation in such an established cultural context would serve to suggest that the events described were part of some timeless, perpetually recurring pattern, the latest manifestation of which was in the Germany of the 1920s and 1930s.

According to Koopmann, Grass's tactic, one that was typical of the Group 47, was to look for more modest and immediate causes for Germany's seduction by Hitler. He concentrated on the thwarted ambitions of the lower middle class, and in *The Tin Drum* as in other works, Grass's writing is suffused with an irony much different from Mann's. If Zeitblom's perceptivity in *Doctor Faustus* is open to question, just about everything in Grass's narrators encourages doubts about their integrity. Grass's method is to raise concrete questions about the interpretations of specific events, thereby placing readers in a position where their personal perceptions, memories, and evaluations had to be measured against the narrative voice. At their finest, the works about World War II associated with the Group 47 comprise a secular, everyman's version of Jabès's *Livre des questions* (Book of questions).

A modest example of the best of this type of writing is Heinrich Böll's *The Man with the Knives*. The story is quite simple. The narrator, a wounded veteran who was a lieutenant during the war, is talking to his former sergeant, who makes a living as a knife-thrower in a vaudeville show. The bombed-out city where the story takes place could be anywhere in Germany. The sergeant, Jupp, entertains his audience with knife tricks, but he needs a more gripping routine to satisfy his thrill-hungry clientele. The two former soldiers scarcely talk about the war; they concentrate their discussions on how to survive the present. Gradually, but predictably, the lieutenant realizes he will become part of his former subordinate's act; he will be the knife-thrower's target. While the narrator is standing on the stage he perceives the audience as "that glimmering, slavering, hydra-headed monster" (17). He explains his reaction to the crowd as "I simply switched off" (17). Meanwhile, as Jupp prepares to throw the knives, "he appeared to be casting a spell over the audience with this sorcerer's pose" (18). In a matter of seconds the show is over and the ex-lieutenant "realized that Jupp was my boss, and I smiled" (19).

In the English translation this story takes up only nine pages, yet it raises a variety of questions. The two men never discuss war guilt, but questions about the war are clearly implied. Should the reader interpret the narrator's acceptance of his role, both as a target for potential suffering and the butt of the audience's scorn, as some expression of culpability for his or even Germany's role in the war? Or should one imagine that the lieutenant is just happy to find a line of work he can do despite his infirmity? Is the audience merely looking for some moments of escapism in the midst of the postwar misery, or is there something in their bloodlust mentality that suggests reasons for the Nazi success in Germany? The former sergeant initially did tricks in which he risked his own life, but then he discovered that the crowd responded better to his putting others in danger. Is this sergeant-sorcerer an upgraded version of the Austrian-born corporal wounded in World War I who had so recently cast a spell upon the Germans? Is the lieutenant-sergeant reversal, the inferior controlling the superior, an implicit comment on what happened to the German psyche when Hitler came to power? These questions, all left for the reader to resolve, may appear pretentious in the asking, but they emerge from a narrative that is certainly not pretentious.

In one of the earliest meetings of the Group 47 a German correspondent reported the rather ironic comment of a foreign participant: "It sometimes seems to me, as young German experimental writers run after a train, that this train departed elsewhere twenty years ago" (Rohnert, in Lettau, 62). However condescending this comment, there was something very new afoot in theorizing about literature shortly after the end of the war, and to find out what it was, young German writers would have been well-advised to take a train to Paris.

The New Novel

Group 47's roots in the experiences of World War II are obvious; more debatable perhaps is the relationship between the *nouveau roman* (the new novel) and the war. This question is particularly important because frequently the new novel is perceived as apolitical and asocial. This viewpoint entails a gross oversimplification. For one thing, the impetus toward the rethinking of literature that led to the new novel is strongly marked by the war. One of the new novelists wrote: "There occurred forty years ago in France a catastrophe that was as much social and cultural as military. Germany's defeat of France ruined all the ideas that eighteen year olds had concerning the goals of society. Concerning narrative (*récit*), the defeat and the occupation ended a relationship that had existed between narrative and French society. One could no longer write in terms of narrative" (Claude Ollier, cited in Aas-Rouxparis, "Interview," 155).

The new novelists' rejection of the political commitment of a Sartre or a Camus parallels their disenchantment with these writers' literary strategies. Essentially theirs is a rejection of a particular artistic mode of expressing political involvement, an expression that is too bound up with a literary tradition unsuited for contemporary needs. As Claude Ollier put it: "We cleared the decks of the earlier systems (Gide, Mauriac) as well as the new (Sartre, Camus) in order to try and renew things at their base: to start with a minimum of narration, noun, verb, complement, and attempt to create new forms" (Aas-Rouxparis, "Interview," 155).

The generation of new novelists were after all a group who "had lived through Europe shocked by Nazism, who saw each day the French Republic and even socialism sucked into, and subsequently denying the Indochinese and then the Tunisian affair. This generation witnessed the final break of the bonds which attached it to France's glorious humanistic past" (Jacques Leenhardt, "Nouveau roman et société," in *Nouveau Roman*, 1:165, hereafter cited as *NR*).

Germany's defeat and moral humiliation left the country's writers little recourse but to confront its past. However, as Henry Rousso has shown in *The Vichy Syndrome,* the confusing combination of France's defeat, collaboration, and eventual victory has made it quite difficult for the French to assess the impact of the war years on their present situation. One might argue that the new novel was not entirely the result of World War II, but when one considers the radical changes in the writing of literature proposed by these novelists, it is apparent that the aftershocks of World War II as well as the ensuing conflicts in Indochina and North Africa affected theorizing about the writing of literature. Certainly the new novel attests to the need for change, to the belief that the postwar era would be radically different from what had come before, and that this difference requires a new form of literary expression. The strident antihumanism of the new novelists, coupled with their frequent polemics in favor of a radical rethinking of literature, reflects their belief in the necessity for change and the need for writing that abandons tradition in an effort to reexamine the bases for the creation of literary texts.

It should not be forgotten in any discussion of the new novel that the works of this disparate band of artists and critics were before all else *experimental,* and thus any evaluation of their success and failure must allow for the innovative nature of what was being attempted. From my perspective, the theoretical pronouncements are generally more interesting than the creative works, with the major exception of Claude Simon's *The Flanders Road.* The curious irony surrounding the theoretical pronouncements of the new novelists is that in their efforts to sever intellectual and artistic bonds with the past, their publications displayed the polemical skills that made them natural heirs of the Enlightenment philosophes.

Principal among the new novel's polemicists is Alain Robbe-Grillet. He entitles his autobiographical trilogy *Romanesques,* because it mingles fact and fiction. The three texts are *Le Miroir qui revient* (1985), *Angélique ou l'enchantement* (1988), and *Les Derniers jours de Corinthe* (1994). In these three volumes he details his upbringing in a politically conservative household, his experiences as a forced laborer in Germany during the war, and his subsequent career as a novelist and literary theorist. Despite his right-wing background and the seemingly apolitical nature of most of his fiction, Robbe-Grillet shared his generation's amazement and revulsion at the discovery of the concentration camps: "My personal relations with authority were deeply altered starting from the Liberation, and especially after the entrance of Allied troops in Germany, followed each day by monstrous revelations concerning the existence (*la matérialité*) of the camps, and all the dark horror which was the hidden face of national socialism" (*Le Miroir,* 122). Perhaps in implicit response to those who debunk the importance or even the reality of the gas chambers, he added: "Gas chambers or not, I do not see for my part any difference, from the moment that men, women and children were dying there by millions, innocent of every crime except to be Jews, gypsies or homosexuals" (*Le Miroir,* 122). In the trilogy's final installment he returns to the war's effect on his decision to write: "Old Europe crushed under the bombs, her historic past departed in flames . . . doubtless as well the bloody and repeated failure (from the war in the Vendée up to the extermination camps) of the beautiful Enlightenment humanism . . . this general collapse which I became aware of at the end of the 1940s was able to constitute the essential driving element in my decision" (*Les Derniers jours,* 142–43). Finally, when Robbe-Grillet describes his purpose for writing, he employs the sorts of postwar allusions one might easily ascribe to a member of the Group 47: "to construct despite fear and without blindness something solid on this debris, in the midst of the haze, the scorn, the dull noise reverberated by the wall panels which never stopped sinking" (*Les Derniers jours,* 143).

Robbe-Grillet's 1963 *Pour un nouveau roman* (*For a New Novel*) remains, after all these years, the most cogent expression of the concerns that animated the writers of his generation: "The term *New Novel* is not intended to designate a school, nor a definite and constituted group of writers who work in the same way; it is only a convenient tag encompassing all those who have decided to invent the novel, that is, to invent man" (*Pour,* 9).

A new expression for a new, and far from clear, sense of experience is what animates the new novel. Among the reasons the present cannot be written about with the techniques of the past is that whereas "the Old Novel was amply founded on the solidarity of the character . . . the New constitutes itself by . . . questioning this sort of literary character" (Jean Ricardou, "Le Nouveau Roman existe-t-il?," in *NR*, 1:13). The traditional novel (in France, Balzac's work usually serves as the prototype), however modest its purview, created a cosmos, an ordered universe peopled with fully drawn characters whose crucial thoughts and feelings were available to the reader. The very success of the great novels of the nineteenth century, the totality of their achievement, is what makes them unsuitable conveyors of contemporary experience. They simply explained too much. Olga Bernal makes this point when she notes that "if the nineteenth century novel was a novel of knowledge, the modern novel is essentially a novel of non-knowledge" ("La Fiction mot à mot: Claude Simon," in *NR*, 2:84).

Concomitant with the repudiation of the fully developed character and the omniscient narrator is the new novelists' deep suspicion of what has passed for psychological analysis in the novel. Robbe-Grillet identifies a tradition that he considers to date from Madame de La Fayette: "The sacrosanct psychological analysis constituted, already during this period [the seventeenth century], the basis of all prose: it presided over the conception of the book, the painting of the characters, the unfolding of the intrigue. A 'good' novel, since then, remained the study of a passion—or of a conflict of passions, or of an absence of passion—within a clearly demarcated milieu. Most of our novelists of the traditional sort—that is, those who properly receive the approval of the consumers—could copy long passages from *La Princesse de Clèves* or from *Père Goriot* without awakening the suspicions of the vast public which devours their production" (*Pour*, 15–16).

The pivotal words here are "consumer," "suspicions," and "production." For Robbe-Grillet the success of the popular novel stems from its ability to offer a prepackaged product that reassures rather than challenges the reader by presenting yet one more example of what is already known. This type of writing offers perhaps thrilling incidents, but no real surprises, while it in no way demands a reexamination of the act of reading by the literary consumer. In his own work, such as *The Voyeur* (*Le Voyeur*, 1955), and *In the Labyrinth* (*Dans le Labyrinthe*, 1959), to take two examples, Robbe-Grillet attempts to defy this tradition by rigorously avoiding any sort of established psychological exploration. In a similar vein Robbe-Grillet's elaborate and at times maddeningly detailed descriptions of objects at the expense of character development become a statement concerning what can and what cannot be known. A thing can be described—its height, weight, colors, etc., can be expressed in words—but the vagaries of the human psyche are other matters. Robbe-Grillet's novels, like much of the writing that figures under the rubric of the new novel, are essentially epistemological studies aimed at delimiting the current parameters of human knowledge. For Robbe-Grillet to avoid psychological analysis is not to say that it is either unimportant or potentially impossible to achieve. It is merely to state through negative example that the existing tools available are not sufficient to the task. Bruce Morrissette summarizes nicely Robbe-Grillet's attitude toward the use of psychology in fiction: "his so-called rejection of psychology . . . is in fact only a rejection of *psychological analysis*" (emphasis in text, 127). Rather than denying the potential for psychological investigation, Robbe-Grillet sets himself against the overarching accounts of human behavior (Freudian, Jungian, etc.) that provide the convenient explanations the reader is all too accustomed to encountering.

Not every new novelist was as adamantly opposed to psychologically based characterization as Robbe-Grillet, yet those willing to explore the issue did so gingerly. Those who undertook the task of rethinking the methods of approaching and depicting the complexity of the human mind tended to stress the tentativeness, ambiguity, and uncertainty of what can be known. The new novel was a form of research, and with regard to the domain of the psyche, no one has been more active in redefining the relationship between psychology and contemporary literature than Nathalie Sarraute.

Sarraute's 1956 collection of essays, *L'Ere du soupçon* (*The Age of Suspicion*), was to a great extent written in reaction to World War II. In an essay entitled, "De Dostoïevski à Kafka," she stresses that psychology has been the "source of so much disappointment and pain" (18), and in another essay, "Conversation et sous-conversation," she adds that "the word 'psychology' is one of those that no author today can hear pronounced about her without lowering her eyes and blushing. Something a little ridiculous, obsolete, cerebral, limited, not to say pretentiously stupid, is attached to it" (99). Nevertheless, despite her severe reservations concerning the uses of psychology in literature, Sarraute does maintain in the title essay, "L'Ere du soupçon," that it is on the psychological element "that all the effort of the novelist's research concentrates, and on it the reader's effort of attention is supposed to focus" (87–88). The specific form that Sarraute's research took is not at issue here, but her words do underscore the ambivalence about the use of psychology among the new novelists. Robbe-Grillet represents the extreme position of total rejection of psychological theorizing. Sarraute is more cautious, and with regard to this issue, more typical of the new novelists. Psychology for her is as suspect in the novel as it is inevitable. Inquiries of this nature, however, must be approached in such a way as to avoid dogmatism and the illusion of total coherence or explanation. More often than not, the psychological dimension of a piece of fiction will be most effective when it reveals its own weaknesses and lacunae.

A major assumption of Robbe-Grillet, one he shares with many new novelists, is that "the world is neither significant nor absurd. It quite simply *is*" (*Pour,* 18). The postwar human being is no metaphysician; the myth of life's deep meaning is another potential victim of World War II. Whatever significance life may have is "partial, temporary, even contradictory and always disputed" (*Pour,* 20). The contemporary novelist's obligation is to describe this state of affairs, where coherence is uncertain and the stability that exists confines itself most often to physical phenomena. One critic characterizes the willingness to undertake this task as the mark of the new novel's realism: "a new way of describing objects. . . . The anecdote, without disappearing, ceased to look for the coherence of an illusory verisimilitude. . . . The insistent and inexplicable presence of things, the isolated and feverish consciousness, the events disordered and uncertain, that is where the true realists rediscover the authentic" (Denis Saint-Jacques, "Le Lecteur du nouveau roman," in *NR,* 1:136–37).

Given the existence of a world without any metaphysical underpinnings, without any inherent significance, what then is accomplished by writing a novel, especially the sort of novel so seemingly limited in psychological scope, lacking in plot, and at times complex to the point of obscurity? The new novel performs the valuable service of contesting traditional ways of writing about the self and questioning the limits of knowledge. The *engagement* of the new novel is more theoretical than social, but the force of the former does not preclude the possibility of the latter. Claude Simon's *La Route des Flandres* (*The Flanders Road*) provides an excellent example of the ways in which the new novel can involve itself with issues at once personal and political. *The Flanders Road* has the additional merit of demonstrating the difficulties inherent in attempting to break free of fictional and intellectual traditions dating from the Enlightenment era. For these reasons chapter 4 is devoted to this novel.

The impetus for the Group 47 and the new novelists was the realization that, however temporarily, literature had reached a limit. Germany's efforts to get beyond this limit involved a simple prose style and a story line closely related to everyday experience, while the French opted for structural complexity linked to the raising of questions that were primarily epistemological. Both movements eventually petered out, each a victim of its own achievement.

When at the Princeton meeting of 1966 Peter Handke excoriated the writing of the Group 47 as "idiotic, inadequate and banal" (in Lettau, 244), he was at the very least indicating that contemporary German fiction had become so accessible that it no longer had the ability to challenge its complacent audience of *Wirtschaftswunderkinder* (the children of Germany's industrial miracle). Meanwhile, as Handke was turning his eyes in admiration toward Paris, the French were raising their eyebrows in frustration at the increasing unreadableness of the new novel. During a period when, according to Handke, the Germans were beginning to write "popular" literature in the worst sense of the term, the French were busy churning out volumes for the sole delight of academics, principally American ones. Whatever the "limit of literature," the question appeared to have been forgotten as each group settled into its particular and relatively profitable mode of expression.

Even granting the weaknesses or eventual ossification of the Group 47 and the new novel, they both contributed greatly to the rethinking of literature in the postwar period. Part of this rethinking involved identifying the precise audience for the literary text. The Germans clearly opted for Everyman, while the French equally obviously were aiming at an intellectual elite. One possible explanation for the demise of both movements is that each misjudged its audience. Readership in any age is bound to be constituted by a minority of citizens, and this is especially apparent in a century when the written word must attempt to compete with the more immediate delights of radio and film. Nevertheless prose fiction has always had an audience, one which could range from a war veteran we will soon meet, who is content to discover his past in *The Flanders Road,* to the university professor who builds a career upon subtle examinations of complicated novels. It also includes the myriad varieties of people from different educational backgrounds who find pleasure, fascination, and occasional enlightenment in the act of reading.

The minority constituting the reading public is sufficiently large to create the phenomenon known as "bestsellers," a term with negative connotations that are not always deserved. A novel may achieve the bestseller status because of a preponderance of sex, violence, trendy mysticism, or sheer escapism, but it may also sell impressively because it addresses important issues in a serious yet accessible manner. The implications of World War II for the present are surely one such issue, and after the chapter devoted to *The Flanders Road,* I deal in each of the five succeeding chapters with one work that engaged an aspect or aspects of this question in ways that proved challenging to a rather large readership. The books I discuss are neither as transparent as the works associated with Group 47 nor as obscure as those of the new novelists frequently are.[1] They are, however, innovative texts that display clear breaks with the fiction of the immediate postwar period and, in a more nuanced way, with the limitations perceived in the initial efforts to revitalize the writing of literature.

Memory and the Collapse of Culture: Claude Simon's *The Flanders Road*

4 At the famous *colloque* held in Cerisy-la-Salle during July of 1971 and dedicated to the *nouveau roman,* a curious incident occurred. One of the conference organizers, Françoise van Rossum-Guyon, quoted a passage from a letter Claude Simon had received from a World War II veteran concerning *The Flanders Road:* "How is it possible? How were you able to see that? It's exactly what I experienced!" (*NR,* 1:29). The former soldier's question seemed rather old-fashioned to the conference participants, whose reactions, best exemplified by Jean Ricardou, were appropriately dismissive: "When the subject is theory, letters from a former cavalry officer, I have to admit do not mean much to me" (*NR,* 1:29).

Ricardou, his colleagues, and the various *nouveaux romanciers* whose works they discussed at Cerisy were extremely sensitive to the need to break with earlier literary and intellectual traditions, which from the perspective of 1971 appeared bankrupt. Hence the soldier's question, focusing on the past rather than the present, proved of little interest to them. What mattered to the participants at Cerisy was not reviving former times but, in terms of literary creation, finding new ways of articulating the present and thus preparing the future. Although many years have passed since the 1971 *colloque* and the subsequent one held in 1974, which was devoted exclusively to Claude Simon, the general tendency in criticism concerning the *noveau roman* remains to stress its innovative qualities and its departures from established literary practice.[1] Commenting in 1988 on a famous passage in *The Flanders Road* (about destruction of the Leipzig library), Lucien Dällenbach details the variety of factors that necessitated radical changes in thinking and artistic expression for the *nouveaux romanciers:*

What one reads there, as well as in other passages where book learning is attacked in the name of experience . . . and where proceedings are initiated against the homage paid by Rousseau to Reason and Virtue, is a recognition of the bankruptcy of twenty centuries of Western culture, since this culture proved useless in the face of Auschwitz and the Gulag. Along with this acknowledgment, the feeling exists that the liberating, modernist Enlightenment project has led to an impasse; that human perfectibility is an illusion; that there is no more virtue in Progress than progress in Virtue; that one must mourn the Revolution; and that traditional humanism (of which absurdist and "engaged" literature are reincarnations) is to be discarded. Briefly, one senses that we are at point zero in every area. (*Claude Simon*, 12)

Dällenbach goes on to argue that in the face of this multifaceted debacle, Simon's art has its origins in an effort "to start out again—to reconstruct—on completely new bases, which offer more solid foundations" (12).

Few would deny the accuracy of Dällenbach's description of the reasons for Simon's disillusionment (and that of many of his colleagues) with the traditional novel form. Nor would one want to question Simon's desire (once again shared by his fellow nouveaux romanciers) to find new bases for the writing of fiction. I would, however, like to propose an approach to *The Flanders Road* that is closer in spirit to the soldier's question than to the tenor of the discussions at the Cerisy colloques, since my argument deals more with the persistence of traditions inherited from the past than with the literary innovations of the present. In this chapter I want to analyze the ways in which Claude Simon casts the novel's main character, Georges, as an example of a failed new novelist, whose efforts to break with his bourgeois class values and Enlightenment heritage paradoxically confirm the lingering power of a social and intellectual tradition that, however moribund, continues to affect his attitudes and writing. This enduring and unwanted tradition remains an obstacle to Georges' understanding of the present, the elusive nature of which I propose Corinne represents. To focus my argument I begin by noting the ways in which Georges *appears* to reject the very values that I then maintain he continues to embody.

In his recently published *Lire Claude Simon: la polyphonie du monde* (Reading Claude Simon: The polyphony of the world, 1995), Patrick Longuet points to the traumatic influence World War II had on the writings of Claude Simon: "The war has . . . the effect of the Copernican revolution on human consciousness: it deprives it of a center" (21).[2] The early pages of *The Flanders Road* vividly illustrate the effect of this decentering. Georges finds himself "in the middle of this collapse of everything as if not an army but the world itself the whole world and not only in its physical reality but even in the representation the mind can make of it" (16). Georges at least senses the intellectual as well as the practical consequences of the defeat, but this is not the case with the French civilians attempting to flee the victorious Germans with the odds and ends of their households, "probably just so as not to be wandering around empty-handed, to have the impression the illusion of taking something of possessing something as long as there could be attached to it . . . the arbitrary notion of price, of value" (17). Georges' attitude contrasts markedly with that of his compatriots; he understands that something has been lost, perhaps forever. This refusal to deny the fundamental changes in intellectual and moral sensibility that emerged in the postwar era is central to Simon's creative activities, and initially it would appear to characterize Georges' attitudes as well. In *Flanders Road,* it seems to engender in Georges "a radical suspicion of customs and language. His eyes opened by the series of corpses that the war produces with indifference, the narrator questions the symbols of the tradition that culminated in this degree of monstrosity" (Longuet, *Lire,* 12). Among the traditions that appear open to question in this novel is the Enlightenment heritage.

One can read Georges' narrative in *Flanders Road* in terms of his growing awareness that Enlightenment aspirations have no place in the world wherein he finds himself. Ernst Cassirer's *The Philosophy of the Enlightenment* remains one of the most influential assessments of Enlightenment beliefs. According to Cassirer: "If there is one formula by which the period of the Enlightenment can be characterized . . . it would seem to be that it is an era of pure intellectualism" (165). The Enlightenment was imbued for Cassirer "with a belief in the unity and immutability of reason" (6). Central to Enlightenment thinking, according to Jean-François Lyotard, is "the Idea of the emancipation of humanity." As discussed earlier in chapter 2, Lyotard sees the Enlightenment heritage as recklessly optimistic and, as such, unable to entertain doubts about itself. Yet Lyotard then continues in *Le Postmoderne expliqué aux enfants* to explain why these ideals, which gave birth to "all the political currents of the last two centuries" (129), are "declining in the general opinion of countries termed 'developed': It is not the absence of progress, but on the contrary developments in the technical sciences, the arts, the economy and politics which have made possible total warfare and totalitarianism" (130). For Lyotard, Enlightenment idealism, its confidence in rationality, led to a very different reality than was intended by the thinkers whose ideas Cassirer describes.

Early in the novel Georges interrupts his friend Blum's efforts to make sense out of de Reixach's death. As Blum is in mid-sentence ("Maybe it would have been smarter on his part if—"), Georges interjects: "No: listen . . . Smarter! God what do you think smart . . . " (19). The English translator has rendered the French word "*Intelligent*" as "Smarter," and then when Simon writes "*intell . . . ,*" the translator recreates the break in the word by "smart."[3] This ellipsis that Simon places in the middle of *intelligence* serves to represent for Georges an initial disavowal of the value of searching for rational explanations. This tendency rapidly increases: "he had gradually stopped being surprised, had abandoned once and for all that posture of the mind which consists of seeking a cause or a logical explanation for what you see or for what happens to you" (24). Later, as a prisoner of war crowded with other soldiers in a train, "it was not his intention to philosophize or to tire himself out trying to think of what thought was incapable of achieving or learning, for the problem consisted more simply of trying to get his leg free" (59). In wartime the only real issues are practical ones.

If World War II confirmed Georges' distrust of Enlightenment values, the origins of his disillusionment go back to his father.[4] Georges' father, along with his avatars, de Reixach, the other French officers, and to a degree de Reixach's ancestor, are the physical embodiments of this discredited tradition. The father is obese, bloated with a learning that appears to Georges largely useless. The old man's workplace, a kiosk separated from the main house and "at the end of the row of oaks" (28), is where he diligently pursues what is for Georges purposeless research. The physical placement of the kiosk, removed from the main living space and relegated to an obscure part of the garden, provides a clear image of the extent to which the father's activities have nothing to do with contemporary concerns.

The scene that best exemplifies both the father's values and his son's contempt for them involves, of course, the Allied bombing of the Leipzig library. For the old man, the loss of life, the morally questionable air attack on a civilian target, the war against Nazism of which the bombing was a part are issues that find no echo in his thinking. From the father's perspective: "History will say later what humanity lost the other day in a few minutes, the heritage of several centuries, in the bombing of what was the most precious library in the world, all of which is infinitely sad" (166). *History,* which the father capitalizes in his letter, has no meaning for the son; it is an abstraction, a vacuous term that only obscures the stupid, wartime event it purports to explain. In Georges' narrative, this physically disgusting old man, "elephantine, massive, almost deformed" (166), who had insisted upon his son trying for admission to the *Ecole Normale Supérieure* so that he would be better able to profit from the allegedly "marvellous culture which centuries of thought have bequeathed us" (165), incarnates ideals that are simply obsolete. From Georges' perspective the father represents less a viable intellectual and/or moral position than a ludicrous attempt to uphold outdated, even dangerous abstractions that mask themselves as eternal, humanistic values. The father's words find their physical embodiment in de Reixach's melodramatic posturing, sword in hand on his rearing horse, as the German bullets tear through him. The body language of de Reixach, along with the words of Georges' father, are as woefully inadequate to the situation as was another French officer's characterization of the defeat as "bad business" (124). In the midst of the French retreat Georges describes the world around him as a vast garbage dump, a hodgepodge of broken objects and ideals: "simply detritus, something like a vast public discharge spread over kilometres and kilometres and exuding not the traditional and heroic odour of carrion, but only of ordure, simply stinking" (152). Somewhere in the midst of that stinking junk is, for Georges, the Enlightenment heritage.

The foregoing analysis offers ample justifications for Georges' breaking with a social and intellectual tradition that proved inadequate in the face of World War II. However, the main character's attitudes toward the Enlightenment tradition and bourgeois complacency reflect merely an intellectual understanding of a situation, awareness of a failure of hitherto sacrosanct values. Putting this new apprehension of loss into practice, especially when "practice" involves the act of writing, would prove immensely difficult, as Claude Simon well knew.

Randi Birn cites Simon's comments in relation to "the remnants of inherited ideas and techniques within his work as 'slag which I have endeavored to suppress little by little'" ("The Roads . . . ," 87). Shortly thereafter Birn once again quotes Simon: "It takes time for one to rid himself little by little of his bad habits" (87). Claude Simon was keenly aware that the heritage from the past, however unwanted, does not simply go away. His working title for *La Route des Flandres* was *Matériaux de construction* (Construction materials; Dällenbach, 124). Simon, the accomplished artist, was able to transform these materials into a novel called *The Flanders Road*, whereas Georges, the aspiring writer, confuses the possession of the materials with the finished product.

Michel Foucault offers a telling analysis of the difficulty inherent in breaking with the Enlightenment, while at the same time he cautions against a simplistic assessment of this heritage. In "What Is Enlightenment?" Foucault maintains that "one does not have to be 'for' or 'against' the Enlightenment" and suggests in fact that we "must try to proceed with the examination of ourselves as beings who are historically determined, to a certain extent, by the Enlightenment" (43). No matter how traumatic the experiences of World War II and its aftermath, especially the revelations about the Nazi Final Solution and the efforts to assess the moral implications of the atomic bombing of Japan, those who sought to respond to these events were doing so with intellectual tools that were to some degree forged in the Enlightenment. Foucault goes on to make a distinction between "humanism" and "Enlightenment," two terms often used synonymously and which Dällenbach criticizes as equally suspect. For Foucault these words indicate very different things: "Humanism . . . is a theme or rather, a set of themes that have reappeared . . . over time . . . in several European societies" (44). These themes are "always tied to value judgments" (44). What characterizes Enlightenment is something more fundamental than value judgments: "the principle of critique and a permanent creation of ourselves in our autonomy" (44). From the

Foucaldian standpoint humanism is the articulation of commonly held positions at a particular historical moment, while Enlightenment refers to a general methodological stance that at times would lead to the expression of a humanistic tenet. Because of the distinction he draws, the French philosopher was "inclined to see Enlightenment and humanism in a state of tension rather than identity" (44).

In *Flanders Road* Georges rejects certain values because of the critique he makes of them. In this respect he abandons a certain version of humanism, but he unconsciously remains faithful to the analytical tradition inherited from the Enlightenment. He realizes, among other things, that education is not necessarily transformative in a moral sense and that the possibility of establishing meaningful, universally recognized truth is a pipe dream. The disapproval he voices toward his father, his scorn for the "heroism" of de Reixach, his impatience with obfuscating language reflect his refusal to accept the sets of values underlying these words and gestures. The irony, of course, is that the very acuity of the analysis leading to these conclusions demonstrates the lingering power of Enlightenment critique.

Georges' criticism of his elders' beliefs nonetheless fails to free him from their intellectual universe. His narrative remains imbued with the literary allusions, the class values, and even attitudes toward women that mark him very much as his father's son. When the peasant soldier Wack announces that "the dogs have eaten the mud," Georges remarks that "I had never heard the expression" (9). This banal incident points to the major flaw in Georges' analysis and the implicit values that govern it: the words he does understand, and the ideas they express, are inextricably associated with the class-bound intellectual tradition he ostensibly seeks to escape.[5]

Georges' admiration and respect for Blum stem in part from his friend's being Jewish. Because of his origins "Blum possessed by heredity a knowledge (intelligence . . . but it wasn't only that: still more: the intimate atavistic experience, which had passed to the reflex stage, of human stupidity and wickedness)" (126). Blum's knowledge, according to Georges, "was worth a good three times what a young man of good family could have gained from the study of the classical French, Latin and Greek authors" (126–27).

Georges' comments appear to acknowledge the potential superiority of Blum's perceptions over his own, but while that may be true, Georges proves incapable of accepting either his friend's judgments about his lingering adherence to an allegedly moribund tradition or the counternarrative Blum offers concerning the death of de Reixach's (and Georges') ancestor. In both instances Georges' failure to respond to Blum's analysis reflects the lingering adherence of this "young man of good family" to cultural and class values he believes himself to have rejected.

At one point Blum announces to Georges, "You've read too many books" (99), and later he adds, "But you're talking like a book!" (165). The issue, of course, is not how much or how little Georges has read but that his perceptions and consequently his narrative are influenced by his literary culture. Georges might have intended to be ironic when he described his father's confidence in words: "After all words are at least good for something. . . . he can probably convince himself that by putting them together in every possible way you can at least sometimes manage with a little luck to tell the truth" (77). Whatever Georges' precise intent in writing these lines, he shares in large measure, as his own choice to compose a narrative indicates, his father's perhaps naive confidence not simply in language but in forms of language that are closely akin to those of his parent. However greatly Georges may desire to break with his lineage, his way of "combining words" is remarkably similar to that of his predecessors. Two tendencies characterize Georges' narrative and mark him clearly as a member of the well-educated bourgeoisie: his penchant for literary allusions and his concern for propriety when someone from a different social background discusses matters related to his own family.

As an individual soldier slogging along the Flanders road Georges may find no value in attempting to turn his particular experience into anything meaningful by placing it in some sort of literary continuum. Yet as a writer this is precisely what he does: "I've already read in Latin what's happened to me, so that I wasn't too surprised and even to a certain extent reassured to know that it had already been written down" (77). These words, mentally addressed to his father, are doubtless intended as ironic, and Georges may not really believe that cultural fragments from the past can offer any protection against his ruin, but the fact remains that Georges' narrative makes ample use of literary analogues. Stuart Sykes cites references to "Leda, Vulcan, *The Golden Ass,* Molière, Shakespeare" (*Les Romans de Claude Simon,* 83), and that list is only partial.

Something Sykes fails to mention, but which is germane to the present argument, is that the literary allusions are often placed in the text in a very self-conscious fashion; they are clearly intended as literary markings, as indications that the narrator (Georges), unlike the author (Simon), is unconsciously anxious to call attention both to his education and to the traditional proclivity of the culturally informed to use learning to invest an incident with a potentially greater significance than it may indeed possess.[6] Consider Georges' deployment of a reference to Don Quixote. His fantasy concerning Corinne at an elegant racetrack amid well-dressed people suddenly switches back to himself on the Flanders road, watching the refugees pass by: "there was no grandstand, no elegant public to look at us (Quixotic shapes diminished by the light that gnawed, corroded the outlines)" (22). Is the reader to imagine that the refugees are in some obscure sense comparable to Cervantes's hero or rather, by extension, is the adjective "Quixotic" an allusion to Quixote's horse, Rocinante, an image suggested by the earlier description of the racetrack? Whatever the intent of the reference, it really does not have any serious purpose except demonstrating Georges' literary education. Don Quixote was an idealist, however benighted, and in his own mind at least his quest was meaningful and had a fixed end (the liberation of Dulcinea). The refugees, on the contrary, are simply seeking to escape an onrushing army. Perhaps one might argue that, in the tradition of modernism, the allusion invites the reader to experience the dichotomy between Don Quixote's heroic undertaking and the pathetic twentieth-century equivalent. Yet even if one were to place this sort of reference in a modernist context, it would still remain an indication of Georges' adherence to an older literary heritage, the very "modernist project" that Dällenbach argued had contributed to the "impasse" affecting contemporary literature (*Claude Simon,* 12, cited in full above). Finally, whatever interpretation one chooses to give to this allusion, its most obvious function is to fill the scene with an aura of portentousness that the refugees' activities hardly warrant.

To mention the quantity of literary references in *Flanders Road* is not to imply that in Georges' conscious mind they have any redemptive function. Rather they show that however disillusioned the narrator might be, he is incapable of voicing this disillusionment in terms other than those that reflect the education his father provided and which he claims to despise. This literary heritage might well be dead or dying, but like the destroyed horses that litter the Flanders road, its lingering presence, even in decay, remains very much in evidence.

Georges' attachment to the values of his social class, especially to a version of *bienséance* (decorum), is most evident in the contrast between his version of the death of de Reixach's ancestor and the one proposed by Blum. Georges' family is related to de Reixach's through his mother. If Georges rejects his father's intellectual legacy, while at the same time retaining significant aspects of it, his professed contempt for his mother obscures his similarity with her. He associates his mother with "chatter" (42) and scorns the importance she ascribes to the family tradition.[7] Yet his own description of the ancestor's death, which follows his mother's account, remains relentlessly heroic: "de Reixach had so to speak forfeited his noble status during the famous night of August fourth, . . . he had later held a seat in the Convention, voted for the king's death, then, probably because of his military learning, been assigned to the armies to get himself beaten at last by the Spanish and then, disavowing himself a second time, had blown his brains out with a pistol" (46). As a young man Georges believed that the family portrait of the ancestor actually showed the blood dripping from the self-inflicted wound, whereas what appeared to be blood "was actually only the reddish-brown preparation of the canvas revealed by a long crack in the paint's surface" (46). This misapprehension sets the stage for what Blum's counternarrative suggests is an even greater misapprehension.

Georges' version of the ancestor's demise provides a tragic dimension to the occurrence; it is an account of a man who takes his life because of a loss of confidence in "the idyllic and sentimental reign of Reason and Virtue" (150). Blum's story is otherwise. If tragedy is "a farce without humour" (147), Blum's version is pure farce. According to Blum, the ancestor returned unexpectedly to find his wife's lover, "the coachman, the groom, the dazed bumpkin" (147), hidden in the family closet. This discovery earns the ancestor a bullet in the head. Georges' reaction to his friend's account marks one of the few moments in the novel where he is truly at a loss for words; he can only mutter: "No" (151).

Blum's narrative is inadmissible not because it is either true or false; there is no means of knowing whether the friend's or the mother's story possesses any significant degree of veracity. Blum's version is unacceptable because it is farce, and as such it defies the canons of dignity by which the bourgeoisie defines itself. Georges' mother's language might well constitute "chatter," and her concern with "tradition" pure pretension, but hers is the only version her well-brought-up son can possibly acknowledge.[8] If any truth emerges from Georges' belief that his Jewish friend, by virtue of centuries of marginalization and persecution, can possess a deeper understanding of life, it is that Blum can accept human existence as a chaotic, meaningless farce, while Georges' education and class values compel him to manufacture significant meaning at all costs. That he is frustrated in the endeavor does not prevent Georges from ceaselessly attempting to achieve this end.

The most enigmatic figure in *The Flanders Road* is de Reixach's wife, Corinne. Blum maintains that the Corinne Georges constantly discusses is "invented . . . fabricated during the long months of war, of captivity, of forced continence" (171). To the extent that Corinne is an invention, a product of the imagination, the imagination in question is certainly male but not uniquely Georges'. For the groom, Iglésia, who had much more prolonged contact with de Reixach's wife than Georges ever did, Corinne was "something like a host (that is, something unreal, melting, something that can be known, tasted and possessed only by the tongue)" (105); she was, for this otherwise simple soldier, "the most Woman of all women he had ever seen, even in fantasy: 'Even in films'" (106). Patrick Longuet provides a neat summary of the predominant male attitude toward Corinne: "A mixture of temptress, baby doll and sex symbol, Corinne is a pure fantasy, the object of male desire such as one finds 'magnified' in the movies" (*Lire,* 24).

The beginning of an explanation for Corinne's enigmatic quality may be that she appears primarily in *Flanders Road* through different men's perceptions of her, and she rarely speaks. Bernard Andrès notes the effect of her abrupt departure: "Corinne disappears from *Flanders Road* the morning after a night of love, leaving perplexed both the frustrated lover and the dissatisfied reader" (*Profils,* 155). Given the brevity of Corinne's appearances, the paucity of her words, and the rapidity of her exit, one might well be tempted to share Blum's puzzlement about Georges' obsession with Corinne and to wonder, along with Blum, why Georges cannot see what everyone else seems to recognize in the sundry versions of

Corinne's relationship with de Reixach and Iglésia: "an everyday piece of sex between a whore and two fools" (138).

Blum's assessment of Corinne, however, is as simplistic as it is vulgar; unfortunately for Georges' literary aspirations, his own appreciation of this woman will prove to be little better. Just as Corinne is a sexual fantasy for the soldiers in *Flanders Road,* in the context of the novel she is the symbolic embodiment of part of what Georges aspires to be but fails to become: Corinne is the negation of the cultural, social, and moral values that proved incapable of preventing the war. Whereas Georges' *words* argue against his father's beliefs and his mother's concern about lineage, Corinne's *acts* demonstrate her contempt for bourgeois conventionality. She sleeps with whom she likes, when and where she wishes; she is blithely indifferent to the social origins of her lovers or the restraints of the marriage bond. More tellingly, when she married de Reixach she insisted he resign his military commission (54). She was demanding a clean break with the past and a movement into a present with values that remained to be discovered. De Reixach was incapable of doing this socially, just as later Georges would be unable to do so intellectually. De Reixach's motives for wanting to marry her are obscure; sexual desire was certainly a factor, but so was his love for her, and perhaps in this love was an ill-defined sense that Corinne had something to offer him that could improve his life. Georges' obsession with Corinne is similar; she bespeaks a freedom from the past, which he desires to achieve but ultimately hesitates to pursue. When he is with her after the war, his rapport with her is stereotypically masculine: he possesses Corinne's body. He fails, however, to master, or even begin to understand, what she represents. At the end of their lovemaking Corinne accuses him of seeing her merely as "a soldier's girl" (204). For Corinne, Georges is yet another example of a man who, whatever his pretensions to the contrary, can only relate to a woman on a sexual level. Georges disputes this description of his attitude toward her, but he cannot find the words he needs to convince her, perhaps because he was never completely sure what he was looking for, what she might have been able to give to him.

Randi Birn sees Corinne as "the catalytic agent of *The Flanders Road*" ("The Road . . . ," 99). I agree with this assessment, albeit for very different reasons.[9] From my perspective Georges' failure with Corinne, in all ways except sexual, marks his inability to come to terms with the contemporary

world both as a thinker and as a writer. Corinne is the tentative representation of the postwar mentality that has truly broken with tradition; she
embodies what Georges can only claim to be. Hence his attraction to her,
as well as his failure to remain with her. Corinne's ideas remain largely
unexpressed because they have yet to be determined; she acts out of
defiance of a seemingly moribund heritage even before she can articulate
what the new postwar cultural and personal standards will be. By rejecting a tradition that in *Flanders Road* is decidedly male, while at the same
time failing to articulate what the alternatives might be, she symbolizes a
new, inchoate desire for freedom as well as the moral and intellectual
emptiness that would characterize the immediate aftermath of World War
II. When Blum, speaking about Corinne, told Georges that "you don't
even know her" (47), he was only half right. Georges at least sensed what
Corinne was about, but he proved incapable of turning this instinct into
an understanding of an admittedly difficult subject. Pat O'Kane makes
the intriguing suggestion that Georges' "own quest for knowledge
through Corinne exactly mirrors that of his father through books" ("La
Route . . . ," 97). In a sense Corinne is the contemporary text that Georges
is incapable of deciphering; his inability to "read the present" points to his
greater failure to create a truly contemporary work of art.

To the degree that writing involves a passage from an instinct to its
verbal expression, Georges, as a postwar writer, is a failure. Still, it is in
this failure that Georges achieves, albeit in parodic form, the outmoded
tragic dimension he sought to reject but the pursuit of which he had
never really abandoned.

Georges' inability to relinquish another set of values he claims to despise is also apparent, again in parodic form, as the novel draws to a close.
During the war Georges' language expressed considerable contempt for
the Enlightenment heritage. Yet after the conflict he displays no interest
in entering a profession that would permit his participation in the political and intellectual changes characterizing the postwar era. Much like
Rousseau at the end of his life, he deserts the city for the country, the
hectic present for a putatively idyllic past. Georges becomes a farmer and
plows the fields, which like his father's kiosk, are in back of the house.

As *The Flanders Road* draws to a close, Blum's query concerning what
Georges has understood about the events they supposedly witnessed in
the war—"But what do you know about it?" (206)—undergoes a subtle

transformation in Georges' mind: "but how can you tell, how can you tell?" (218). This question is repeated several times (226, 228, 230). The reiterated question, with its obvious echo of Montaigne's "que sais-je?" (what do I know?) provides yet another example of Georges' anchoring his inquiry in a well-established tradition of French thought. Yet it is also one reformulation of the question asked by *les nouveaux romanciers*. The war raised the demand for a new approach to literature, a new epistemology that could reevaluate and in some instances discard traditional questions. A great merit of *The Flanders Road* is that it demonstrates, through Simon's description of Georges as a failed new novelist, how difficult that enterprise would be.[10] A rejected literary and intellectual tradition remained nevertheless the tradition that had formed those artists who sought to free themselves from it. As a novel, new or otherwise, *Flanders Road* is certainly not a failure, but it is a novel about failure. As such it provides an illustration of an aspect of the nouveau roman that is frequently overlooked: the power of a work like *The Flanders Road* not simply to illuminate the present but also to indicate the enduring, possibly malignant, yet nevertheless lingering heritage of the past: "If the 'new novel' has a *political* function, it resides at once in the power certain books have to make apparent (*lisibles*) the ideological context of which they are part, the society that produces them, and the subversive force (the power to negate existing literary values) of their own writing" (Raymond Jean, *NR*, 1:367, emphasis in text).

Women Writing War: Christa Wolf's *Patterns of Childhood*

5

Do you think I'm not writing about the present?

Christa Wolf, in an interview

It may well be true that the victors write the history of a war, but that is not the case in literature. Both winners and losers are quick to produce poetry, plays, and novels, yet the authors on both sides of the conflict usually do have one thing in common: they are men. It would be relatively easy for an educated person with an interest in the literature surrounding World War II to make a list of worthwhile novels dealing with the subject and composed by German or French men, but asked to name women authors, the same person would probably find the task more difficult. One is apt to hear something like "Didn't Simone de Beauvoir? . . ." or "I think Marguerite Duras. . . ." A native German might experience a certain satisfaction in suddenly recalling "Oh yes, Anna Seghers, *The Seventh Cross.*" The fact is, French and German women did write about World War II, but often in a very different fashion from their male counterparts. This chapter centers on one woman's extremely successful and original treatment of the war: Christa Wolf's *Patterns of Childhood* (1976). For better appreciation of Wolf's achievement, I begin with a discussion of the condition of German women writers before and during the war and the types of texts they initially had some success publishing. I then focus on the evolution of German women's writing in the postwar period in order to show the parallels between their efforts and those of their French colleagues. Finally, in my analysis of *Patterns of Childhood,* I hope to show that the importance of this novel to any study of the literature surrounding World War II stems from the ways it brings together so many of the concerns of women writing fiction in the postwar context.

Nazism was, of course, a brutal experience for German culture. Many German artists, male and female, went into voluntary exile abroad; others opted for what is termed "interior emigration," meaning that talented men and women chose to stay in Germany but remained silent during the war years. Perhaps the most famous of this latter group was the painter Emil Nolde, who is in part the model for Max Ludwig Nansen, the harried artist at the center of Siegfried Lenz's *The German Lesson.*

The fate of authors who actually chose to leave Germany and live in exile was particularly difficult. As Sylvia Patsch explains, in the 1930s these politically dissenting writers, both the men and the women, had their books banned and burned; it was essentially impossible to find any of their texts in "cleaned" (*gesäuberten*) bookstores. Their work, if discussed at all, was termed "asphalt literature" (*Asphaltliteratur*), literature presumably fit only for the gutter ("Everything is strange here," in Brinkler-Gabler, *Deutsche Literatur von Frauen,* 305).[1]

Among the women writers whose careers would be severely and even irreparably damaged by exile were many who had only begun to make names for themselves. Patsch offers as examples Vicki Baum, Irmgard Keun, Anna Seghers, and Hilde Spiel (301). It is a measure of the loss to German letters that except for Anna Seghers, these names are largely unknown today outside the area of German literary scholarship.

As can easily be imagined, it was extremely difficult for any author, male or female, to publish in German as an exile in a foreign country during World War II. These writers were greeted with suspicion by their host nations as potential Fifth Columns (306), and publication rights to the translations of their works, when granted at all, were accorded more readily to well-established male authors such as Thomas Mann, Bertolt Brecht, and Stefan Zweig.

Patsch maintains that despite the real difficulty of publication, German women were moved by their experiences as exiles in foreign countries to write about "the unheard of, the injustice that had so altered their lives" (306). Be that as it may, the titles of some of their works are revealing. Marta Feuchtwanger, the wife of the novelist Leon Feuchtwanger, wrote an autobiographical portrait, *Only a Wife,* and Friederike Maria Zweig authored *Stefan Zweig, How I Knew Him.* To find a reading public, the woman writer often had to concentrate on her more famous spouse. As Patsch remarks, "Exile literature by women emphasizes 'great men' in exile" (306).

Patsch uses Martine Wied as a typical example of a woman whose career never recovered from the exile experience. During her years abroad, Weid wrote in German, hence for the desk drawer (*für die Schublade*) (307). When she died in 1957, none of her books was available in German bookstores. The principal reason for this neglect was that many readers no longer wished to remember the *Kriegszeit,* especially as recounted by those who had spent the war years far away in enemy countries such as England (312–13). Unwillingness on the part of Germans to read about the war affected male writers as well, but this general hostility had an especially crippling effect on women whose careers were just being launched in the 1930s.

Patsch concludes her essay about German women writers in exile with the admonition that one must recognize that the texts written by women were not simply documentary accounts of their experiences. Novels, plays, and poems were doubtless part of their output. However, until someone gains access to those *Schubladen,* the world will remain deprived of some potentially important books.

In the postwar era German women writers gained inspiration from an unlikely source. May 1968 left its mark on Germany as well as France. Rita Thalmann argues that the diverse forms of German women's opposition, even resistance, to the Nazi regime were seldom expressed before the 1960s and that the student revolt, along with the beginnings of the women's liberation movement, created a resurgence in female self-expression ("From Non-Conformity to Resistance," in Brinkler-Gabler, *Literatur von Frauen,* 301). As Barbara Kosta puts it: "In Germany, the politicization of the personal, an effect of the woman's movement and an aftereffect of the 1968 student movement, provided an impetus for the sudden circulation of self-exploratory narratives" (*Recasting Autobiography,* 6). In a footnote Kosta adds, "The lack of autobiographical writings during the 1950s reflects the difficulty many Germans experienced in writing about a past that was preferably left repressed" (6). The writings that began to appear after 1968 often took the form of diaries, memoirs, and collections of testimonials (Thalmann, 301).

Such autobiographical reminiscences are generally characteristic of German women's writings about World War II. According to Annemarie Tröger, "what postwar generations in Germany have learned about the impact of World War II has come primarily through the narratives of their mothers and grandmothers" ("German Women's Memories of World War II," in Higonnet et al., *Behind the Lines,* 286). Still, as powerful as these witness testimonials can be, Tröger claims they suffer from the same problem that besets the accounts of concentration camp survivors: "Close examination of these narratives . . . reveals that their message is not one-dimensional or direct, but contradictory and ambivalent" (286). In the writings Tröger studies there is no single, powerful perspective, no convenient means of pigeonholing the putative "woman's perception" of the war.

The real issue, of course, has nothing to do with the fact that these witness narratives may be "contradictory and ambivalent" or that there is no consistently maintained "woman's perception" (who would want or expect such a thing?). What is troublesome is that until relatively recently scholars have been slow to explore women's involvement in World War II. In the preface to her *Frauen: German Women Recall the Third Reich,* Alison Owings explains that when she first got interested in this topic, she was encouraged by the distinguished German historian Gordon Craig, who "confirmed that, in general, the testimony of few 'average' German women had been published, in English or in German" (xii). Owings added that "as of this writing, nearly ten years later, the situation is almost the same" (xii). *Frauen* was published in 1993.

German women artists, both during and after the war, tended to avoid long fictional accounts set in the conflict. This is not to say, however, that such novels do not exist. Anna Seghers published in 1942 *The Seventh Cross,* a book that attracted considerable attention and was even made into an American film. This novel, written during the war and dealing with anti-Nazi Germans' efforts to escape from a concentration camp, is obviously more caught up with the immediate historical situation rather than with the war's implications for the future. Hence it is outside the scope of this study.

One of the best-known contemporary novels by a German woman that discusses matters associated with warfare is Christa Wolf's *Cassandra* (1983). This is a retelling of the Trojan War from a woman's perspective.

For Wolf the Trojan War becomes a conflict literally fought over nothing, since the pawn in the power struggle, Helen, never even arrives in Troy. It is a story of one civilization destroyed and another severely compromised because women's voices are either ignored or suppressed. The strength of *Cassandra* is not, however, confined to its portrayal of male obtuseness; its depictions of women's efforts at mutual understanding and eventual bonding are among the most fascinating aspects of the book.

Any novel written about warfare by a German artist of the postwar era either directly or subliminally alludes to World War II, but it would be a mistake to assume that *Cassandra*'s principal subject was that conflict. In this novel warfare becomes less a historical reality than a metaphor for male-female tensions, with particular attention drawn to their effect on women. In this respect *Cassandra* is an example of a tendency among German women authors to see war, any war, as the most overt example of the male silencing of the female voice.

As Rita Thalmann and Barbara Kosta have pointed out, after May 1968 and with the rise of feminism, German women began to write about World War II from a vantage point markedly different from that of their male counterparts. When Ingeborg Bachmann described her planned trilogy concerning the origins of fascism, she explained that she intended her focus to be on the parallels between fascism and male-female relationships: "It doesn't start with the first bombs that are dropped; it doesn't start with the terror one can read about in every newspaper. It starts with the relationship between people. Fascism is the first thing in the relationship between a man and a woman, and I have attempted to say . . . that in this society there isn't war and peace, there's only war" (*Thirty Years,* xv). Death prevented Bachmann from bringing the projected trilogy to completion.

French women who wrote about World War II chose forms of expression remarkably similar to those of their German colleagues. They preferred to express themselves through memoirs, be they of ordeals in concentration camps or of daily struggles during the Occupation or in the Resistance. Rarely did a French woman attempt a large-scale novel about the war and its aftermath.

Edith Thomas was a moderately successful novelist and political activist who published six works of fiction between 1934 and 1945, but none deals directly with World War II. During the Occupation she was a member of the Resistance. Eventually she turned her wartime experiences into fiction with the publication of *Les Pétroleuses* (The fiery feminists) in 1963. In this novel the Occupied France of the 1940s becomes the Paris of 1871 during the Commune, "also a period of violence and revolt after a traumatic defeat by Germany had ushered in a repressive regime" (Kaufmann, "Uncovering a Woman's Life," 64). This novel has had little impact on either audiences or critics.

A more interesting and certainly more direct account of Thomas's wartime career is her recently published (1995) memoir of the Resistance period, *Le Témoin compromis* (The compromised witness). The editor of this volume, Dorothy Kaufmann, describes the text as "a political memoir, a completed book-length manuscript which looks back at her itinerary from the vantage point of 1952" (17). *Le Témoin Compromis* is Thomas's major work on the war, one she chose to cast in memoir form. Thomas explains her decision to write a memoir rather than a novel in the very first entry: "I'm tired of novels, mine as well as those of others. What's the point of using imaginary characters, when one is writing only to give oneself a little more solidity and sense of being alive (*d'existence*), this one achieves to the extent one exists in the conscience of others?" (29). Thomas's impatience with fiction reflects in part her desire to engage in a more direct dialogue with her readers in order to speak specifically about her experience. However, as a novelist who happened to be a woman, she was quite aware of the tendency among critics not to dismiss her literary efforts but to belittle them in the guise of classifying them: "Literary critics like to group together novels written by women in order to account for them, as if there were a feminine and a masculine literature, while there is only good and bad literature, whatever the author's sex" (*Témoin*, 118). As her words indicate, Thomas was far from imagining the possibility of a distinct form of "women's writing," but both her statement and her choice of the memoir form demonstrate her need to find a means of expression that would give the fullest account of her perception of reality as a woman artist, social activist, and member of the Resistance.

Sarah Kofman is well-known in philosophical circles for her work on Nietzsche, Derrida, and aesthetic theory in general. In 1994 she published a short book entitled *Rue Ordener, Rue Labat* (Ordener Street, Labat Street). This is a memoir of her experiences as a young Jewish girl hiding from the Nazis in Occupied Paris. If Kofman's situation was typical of that of many Jews in comparable circumstances, her account certainly is not; indeed her life under the Occupation cries out for a fictional treatment. After her father, a rabbi, was sent from his home in the rue Ordener to Auschwitz, where he was eventually killed for refusing to work on the Sabbath, her mother did her best to hide her frail and high-strung daughter from the Nazis. Eventually the young Sarah found shelter in the apartment of a Gentile woman, "la dame de la rue Labat" (43), whose rather frivolous lifestyle offended the girl's mother. Sarah, for her part, was fascinated by this woman, who despite a degree of anti-Semitism—"Jewish food is bad for health" (57)—courageously protected her Jewish guests. The joyfulness of "la dame" eventually alienated Sarah from her mother and the latter's somber view of Judaism. From "la dame" she heard for the first time of Spinoza, Bergson, Einstein, and Marx, "those names which are so familiar to me today" (57). At the Liberation, Sarah did not want to go back to rue Ordener and her family's strict Orthodox existence; her mother was forced to sue for the daughter's return. When Sarah's family lost the court case, Jewish toughs had to kidnap the girl and bring her home. At the beginning of this amazing memoir, Kofman explains that "my numerous books have perhaps been routes I had to travel (*voies de traverse obligées*) to be able to recount 'that' (*ça*)" (9). If a novel ever emerges from this memoir, it will not be written by Sarah Kofman. She committed suicide in October of 1994, thus joining the growing list (Primo Levi, Tadeusz Borowski, Jean Améry, etc.) of "survivors" who eventually succumbed to their memories.[2]

Although Simone de Beauvoir is better known for her autobiographical writing and essays than for her fiction, she did attempt a novel about World War II. *The Blood of Others* was begun in 1941, but since it dealt in part with Resistance activities, it could not be published until 1945. The novel initially sold well and garnered some favorable reviews as an example of Resistance writing, but this story, which deals largely with the intellectual passage of a young bourgeois from middle-class complacency to Communism and active opposition to Nazism, suffers from a didactic tone and an abundance of philosophical asides. Maurice Blanchot exposed the novel's fundamental weakness when he called it a thesis novel. Catherine Brosman explains that for Blanchot, de Beauvoir's text was a thesis novel "not because it dealt with meanings—he recognizes that all serious fiction does—but because it shows less than it states and because its statements form a single, closed conclusion that imposes itself on the reader" (Brosman, *Simone de Beauvoir Revisited,* 63). After the initial outburst of enthusiasm *The Blood of Others* provoked in newly liberated France, it largely dropped from view. It was a work so anchored in de Beauvoir's prewar philosophical concerns as to offer little that proved enduring or challenging for a postwar audience.

Marguerite Duras was also active in the Resistance and eventually published her account of that period in *The War: A Memoir* (1985). The title of the English translation is somewhat misleading. In French it is simply *La Douleur* (The pain); this painful "memoir" at times takes the form of autobiographical stories. Even though Duras refers to this book as "one of the most important things in my life" (4), the writing is uneven, and for a long time Duras hesitated to publish it. Lawrence Kitzman offers a general assessment of Duras' unease in transforming history into fiction: "For Duras . . . literature demonstrates its inadequacies in representing history, for as a discursive practice it can only utter the unspeakable horrors of historical reality in austere ways and transcribe this crisis as a form of fiction" ("Duras' War," 63). However, the best explanation for the unevenness of this deeply felt text is Duras' own: "It can't really be called writing . . . I found myself confronted with a tremendous chaos of thought and feeling that I could not bring myself to tamper with, and beside which literature was something of which I felt ashamed" (4). Duras' words echo Adorno's initial unease at the idea of creating poetry after Auschwitz.

There is no simple and satisfying answer to why French and German women rarely attempted substantial fictional works concentrating on World War II. One can, however, indulge in some speculation. Women's experience of World War II was in crucial ways radically different from that of men. They were rarely active participants in the actual fighting; most often they were denied this involvement because of their sex and all the suppositions that traditionally surround being a woman. Edith Thomas recounts in her memoirs that she was at first refused the right to be a war correspondent in the Spanish Civil War because she was not "physically" up to the task (*Témoin,* 66). Her subsequent work in Spain and in the Resistance presumably did little to alter that perception. Nevertheless, if women were forbidden male, soldierly roles, World War II, like all wars, preserved their status as victims. They were the constant victims of the battles, bombings, the loss of loved ones, and the deprivation of food, heating, and other physical necessities for living.

In *Three Guineas* (1936–37) Virginia Woolf asserts that if men reserve warfare for themselves, it is because for men "war is a profession; a source of happiness and excitement; and it is also an outlet for manly qualities, without which men would deteriorate" (6). This is not, of course, women's experience of warfare, since as Woolf observes, men are fighting "to gratify a sex instinct I cannot share" (108). Woolf suggests that men's and women's different perceptions of warfare have their origins in something more complex than active involvement (male) versus passive acceptance (female). She maintains that the male identity requires the experience of violence to establish itself, and thus warfare is, on a psychological level, more inherently interesting to men than to women. From this perspective warfare becomes yet another form of patriarchal oppression, something women are exposed to, subjected to, and required to react to in ways men have deemed proper to women.

For Virginia Woolf, a woman's effort to constitute herself, to achieve an identity, and to establish her *female* voice are much more complicated than the clearly demarcated steps that lead to the achievement of maleness. Writing in the aftermath of World War II, Ingeborg Bachmann famously linked male-female relationships to fascism, but she was hardly the first to make such an argument. As Marie-Luise Gättens points out, Woolf maintained in *Three Guineas* not only that "gender relationships could potentially produce fascism, but that men's power over women was a form of fascistic rule" (*Women Writers,* 9).

If by virtue of their gender men inherit a history that asserts their predominant role in human activities, women's history, which for Woolf is radically different from that of men, must be "invented—both discovered and made up," as paraphrased by Peggy Kamuf.

The creation of women's history that will rival and challenge the version of events long since created by men would require a type of writing that would not always fit comfortably within established literary forms. In the closing pages of *Three Guineas* Virginia Woolf insisted to her fictitious male correspondent that women can best serve the cause of peace as well as establish their own voices "not by repeating your words and following your methods but by finding new words and creating new methods" (143), and, for Gättens, Woolf sought the articulation of such a new perspective in "an imaginative act that makes the borderline between fiction and history fluid" (*Women Writers*, 35).[3]

I would suggest that the choice of the memoir, favored by many women writing about World War II, reflects an effort—not necessarily consciously undertaken—to write women's history in a way that maintains a certain distance from the literary form favored by men, namely the novel. A memoir is not a work of pure fiction, but it certainly provides the author with ample opportunity to avail herself of some of the freedom the novel allows. No memoir can seriously claim to confine itself to the pure "facts." A memoir is a mixture of remembrances, events, assumptions, hopes, and fears, all recorded after a relatively long passage of time and written down by a person who is no longer exactly the individual being described. It is a literary form that needs to make no pretense about establishing a parity between truth and memory, since the memoirist is recalling lived experience, what she saw, underwent, and heard then and what those events mean to her now. The lapses of precise recollection, the uncertainty about the exact truth of a particular incident, and the effect of subsequent occurrences on one's sense of the past can all legitimately figure in a memoir. Furthermore, the writing of a memoir turns a woman's manipulation during wartime by forces over which she had no control into an active response to this imposed subjugation. By choosing the memoir over the novel, she is asserting her real, historical presence during the events she describes. Her different experience of warfare can account in part for the decision of many women to write in a more straightforward, autobiographical manner than fiction permits without having to forgo the imaginative flights that the novel allows. If the memoir was by far the preferred means of expression, it was perhaps ultimately because the author could limit herself to retelling as directly as possible personal experiences, however painful, yet with all the ambiguity and lacunae that memory implies. From this perspective the memoir becomes a search for truth without the guarantee that it will be found; it is an ongoing effort at the discovery of a personal and political past. In addition, the impetus that feminism provided for many women to write about World War II allowed these authors to associate the war with more immediate issues, ones that contained the possibility of challenging and even changing the present, rather than simply reliving the past.

This description of the possibilities inherent in the memoir form finds full expression in Christa Wolf's 1976 *Kindheitsmuster* (*Patterns of Childhood*). This text, which defies easy classification as either novel or memoir, constitutes, to the best of my knowledge, the most successful and sustained effort to combine elements from two literary forms in order to offer a viewpoint on World War II that is at once original and distinctly that of a woman whose postwar present is inextricably bound up with her past.

In *Patterns of Childhood*, Christa Wolf manipulates the memoir form to provide not simply a woman's perspective on World War II but, much more importantly and specifically, a German woman's perspective. At one point in her text Wolf has a character describe a family as "an agglomeration of people of different ages and sexes united to conceal mutually shared embarrassing secrets" (78). This family is, of course, the German nation, both during and after the Hitler period. Wolf sees the Germans as either suffering from, or anxious to suffer from, a form of collective amnesia: "A nation of know-nothings who will later, when called upon to account, assert as one man, out of millions of mouths, that they remember nothing" (141). Yet whatever Christa Wolf's distaste for this stance, these people are her people, and she is very much part of the generation that allowed itself to be led into the war. "Fascism as a concept," the Polish writer Kazimierz Brandys ruefully observed, "is larger than the Germans. But they have become its classic example" (*Patterns*, 36). Wolf is keenly aware of this fact, and it doubtless contributed to her difficulty in starting her book.

Along with her German origins, Christa Wolf had to deal with the reality of the passage of time and the tricks of memory: "You are not only separated . . . by forty years; you are hampered by your unreliable memory" (*Patterns*, 7). After several unsuccessful efforts to launch her book, she hit upon a solution that would permit her to deal with her personal, ongoing history as a German woman and writer, with the war years, and with the differences between the present and the past, the now and the then. Wolf opted for two narratives. The second person singular (*du* in German, for which "thou" is the obsolete English equivalent) reflects the thoughts and feelings of a middle-aged German writer whose life and family circumstances echo those of Christa Wolf. She returns to her childhood home in what is now part of Poland with her husband, H., her daughter, Lenka, and her younger brother, Lutz. The third-person narrative (she) tells the story of Nelly Jordan and her family. Nelly is a German girl coming of age in the 1930s, whose youth and early adulthood parallel the experiences of the adolescent Christa Wolf as well as the rise of National Socialism, World War II, and the Nazi defeat. Nelly lives in the then German, now Polish town that the German woman author (the character/autobiographical voice that provides the "du" narration) is visiting in the 1970s. In *Patterns of Childhood* there is a constant shifting from one narrative perspective to the other and by extension from one phase of Christa Wolf's life to another.

When the West German edition of *Patterns of Childhood* was published, Wolf added the word "novel" to the title (Kuhn, *Wolf's Utopian Vision*, 107), but she remained keenly aware of the amorphous nature of the work. In an interview she noted:

> I don't think that I ever hide the fact that the book is, so to speak, auto-biographical. I admit this. But this "so to speak" is very important because I do not feel an identity with my character. There is, and this is perhaps one of the peculiarities of my life story, though others of my age may have the same experience, a sense of alienation from this period. . . . I no longer feel that it was I who had thought said or done those things.
>
> And that is what I wanted to express through the third person. ("A Model of Experience" in *The Author's Dimension*, 45)

In light of the foregoing discussion and Wolf's own choices concerning the framing of this text, I would suggest that *Patterns of Childhood* might best be read as a memoir in the form of a novel, rather than a novel in the form of a memoir. Such a distinction would distance the book from the traditional category of the novel and move it into the less clearly demarcated area of the memoir, where fictional elements are implicit in the memory of recollected experience. Read as a memoir-novel, *Patterns of Childhood* would become an example of an attempt to write women's history partially by inventing it—both discovering it and making it up, to paraphrase Peggy Kamuf (in Gättens, *Women Writers*, 34).[4]

In what amounts to a brief preface to *Patterns of Childhood,* Wolf publishes an ostensible disclaimer that really serves to alert the reader to the deeply ironic and complex text about to be read. The first paragraph is as follows:

All characters in this book are the invention of the narrator. None is identical with any person living or dead. Neither do any of the described episodes coincide with actual events.

If this were the extent of the author's statement, the reader's task would be considerably simpler. *Patterns of Childhood* would be a novel telling a story that took place during the *Hitlerzeit*, and while the broad historical background (the Nazi period, the war) corresponds to real occurrences, the characters and the particular events that shape their lives are nonetheless entirely fictional. The second paragraph, however, constitutes a critique of the first:

Anyone believing that he detects a similarity between a character in the narrative and either himself or anyone else should consider the strange lack of individuality of many contemporaries. Generally recognizable behavior patterns should be blamed on circumstances.

While it may be perfectly understandable for an author to separate her narrative from real individuals living or dead (indeed publishers might insist on such a statement), it is another matter to do so because the generation she describes produced no individuals. If this has the makings of a rather odd novel, it suggests an even more bizarre autobiography, since the emphasis in autobiographical writing is usually "on the uniqueness of the individual" (Kuhn, *Wolf's Utopian Vision,* 106). To the extent that this short preface creates a dilemma, Wolf's title resolves it in large measure.

There has been some scholarly discussion concerning the English equivalent of *Kindheitsmuster.* Instead of *Patterns of Childhood,* some specialists have preferred *A Model Childhood,* believing that this title underscores the irony of a young girl and her generation conforming faithfully to all the rules set before them, only to discover themselves minor players and victims in one of the twentieth century's most horrific scenarios. If today the commonly agreed-upon translation is *Patterns of Childhood,* this is largely due to a desire to be literally faithful to the German original than to any disagreement with the interpretative reasons offered on behalf of *A Model Childhood.* As Barbara Kosta explains, the "designation 'patterns' . . . emphasizes sameness, rather than the singularity of experience that the critic of autobiography Georges Gusdorf insists on in his delimitation of autobiographical representation as 'a conscious awareness of the singularity of each individual life'" (*Recasting Autobiography,* 59).

Whether one opts for *Patterns of Childhood* or *A Model Childhood, Kindheitsmuster* is about the pressure on a specific group of people, indeed an entire generation, to conform to predetermined behavioral structures. This pressure is exercised on both men and women, but the "patterns" or "models" created for women have always been more rigid and constraining.[5] This general truth was accentuated during the Nazi period when "education in school and youth movement was strictly gender segregated and reflected the Nazis' belief in an inherent biological difference as the determining factor of each gender's social function. The education of girls was supposed to turn them into 'mothers of the nation'"; given the Nazis' aim, it is not surprising that "a girl's relation to her body was clearly not her own private matter" (Gättens, *Women Writers,* 91). To be a good girl, "ein echt deutsches Mädel," was to conform as strictly as possible to a stereotype. For instance, when Nelly is overcome by cold and exhaustion during a Hitler Youth rally, she bursts into tears. This is, however, a rare occurrence since Nelly knows perfectly well that a "German girl does not cry" (*Patterns,* 130).

If *Patterns of Childhood* is a memoir lacking individuals, it is because Wolf intended this text to be a memoir of a generation, or more properly of a major segment of a generation, the women who were never permitted to forge their individual identities. Although men figure in the book, the emphasis is on the experience of women alive at a particular historical moment when, more than is traditionally the case, they are forbidden the right to self-definition at the same time as they must suffer the consequences of their association by nationality with a political structure responsible for some of history's most heinous crimes.

One major goal of autobiography, the overcoming of self-alienation caused by earlier experiences, does *not* occur in *Patterns of Childhood:* "What is past is not dead; it is not even past. We cut ourselves off from it; we pretend to be strangers" (*Patterns,* 3). The two narrative voices represent a girl's co-optation by the Nazis in the past and the lingering resentment the memory of this experience continues to evoke in a middle-aged

German woman writer.[6] Hence the two narrative tracks. If the adult who composes this memoir can now lay claim to a certain individuality, this is not necessarily the case for the generation of young women she describes. Yet these women have their collective story, and however typical it might be, it remains nevertheless not the story that their male contemporaries can tell.

Anna Kuhn stresses the various ways Nelly's "war" was specific to women's experience: "The war, from the perspective of an adolescent female civilian, signified the absence and possible death of Nelly's father; his infrequent home leaves; her mother's struggle to maintain the shop; bombings and air raid shelters; and most significantly the trek west" (*Wolf's Utopian Vision,* 117). Kuhn maintains that *Patterns of Childhood* "differs from most German war narratives in describing the flight from the Red Army in terms of experiences specific to old people, children, and (particularly) women" (117).

Certainly the "trek west," the women's effort to avoid falling into the hands of the Russians, is of major importance in Nelly's story: "Few descriptions exist of the 'flight'. Why? Because the young men who later wrote books about their experiences had been soldiers? Or because there's something dubious about the subject?" (*Patterns,* 321). The flight is so significant in this memoir not simply because it is a woman's rather than a man's experience. It is one of the few instances in *Patterns of Childhood* where women play an active role, although their actions are largely controlled by the exigencies of the situation. Starting with Nelly's mother's initial refusal to flee the approaching Red Army and moving to the decisions about sleeping arrangements, the foraging for food, and the dealing with personal animosities, the women take some small control over their lives. It took a bloody war and the accompanying breakdown of the social norm to allow women this derisory freedom. Perhaps no other portion of the story conveys so powerfully and ironically the suppression of women in traditional society. Only a nation's collapse permits them a modicum of liberty in determining their fate, and this "liberty" expresses itself in their efforts to cope with their unwanted roles as victims of the destruction of Germany's social fabric. The description of Nelly's flight provides more than a tale of German women escaping an onrushing army. In a narration dealing with the victimization of women, it becomes the embodiment of both this victimization and the perhaps heroic, but certainly circumscribed, attempts of women to react to this victimization.[7]

Quite aside from the drama inherent in the trek west, *Patterns of Childhood* has much to tell about the daily lives of women during the Third Reich. Nevertheless, to read this text merely in terms of the information it supplies about German women during World War II would be to misunderstand the book and to misjudge its achievement. *Patterns of Childhood* is at least as much about a woman's effort to evolve a means of writing about herself and the women of her generation as it is about the events she and they experienced. Christa Wolf has few illusions about the difficulty of this task. The passage of time and the faultiness of memory are obvious obstacles: "You'll have to ask what would become of us if we allowed the locked spaces in our memories to open and spill their contents. But memory's recall—which incidentally varies markedly in people who seem to have had the same experience—may not be universally a matter of choice. If this were not so, people's assertions would be accurate: documents could not be surpassed; the narrator would therefore be superfluous" (69).

The reference to "documents" is particularly noteworthy, because in *Patterns of Childhood* such documents did and do exist. Nelly keeps a diary that begins before the war, and throughout the narrative the middle-aged writer refers to the newspapers of the period she has consulted to refresh her memory. Yet any archival material gleaned from these sources would be of limited value. The newspapers, for example, reflect the heavy censorship of the Nazi regime; their accounts may stir memories, but these accounts must be heavily interpreted. Nelly's diaries are totally useless because she was forced to burn them just before the family's flight from the advancing Russian Army. Yet even if, by some miracle, they survived the war, what would they contain? The immediate, hence imperfect apprehension of experience from the viewpoint of an intelligent, albeit frightened adolescent.[8]

Besides the issue of flawed or lost documentary evidence, there is the question of time's passage. The memories that haunt Christa Wolf are obviously from the distant past, but they also contain traces of subsequent occurrences. The choice of a narrative voice (the "du") reflects the author's apprehension of the impossibility of totally accurate recall. Although the narrator resembles Wolf in so many ways, the slight distance created by the fictional alter ego recognizes that space caused by time and memory that can never be completely bridged. Yet for her middle-aged narrator even to begin to come to terms with the past, she must do so from the vantage point of the present, must evolve a form of expression that permits her current concerns to dialogue with her remembrances of a child she might once have been, but whom she can no longer perfectly recall, and to whom she experiences some difficulty relating. This explains both the middle-aged narrator and the adolescent Nelly. They provide two perspectives, both from women, who together attempt to articulate the concerns of a generation of women who were never permitted voices of their own. The memoir form, as deployed by Christa Wolf, with its inextricable mixture of fact and fiction, past and present, reflects a woman's effort to extract from history her story and that of her female contemporaries.

Toward the end of *Patterns of Childhood,* Nelly encounters a Communist recently liberated from a concentration camp. When Nelly's mother naively suggests that being a Communist is no reason to be put in such a place, the man, "no longer able to show anger, or perplexity, or mere astonishment," simply replies, "Where on earth have you all been living?" Nelly says that while she never forgot that sentence, "only later, years later, did it become some kind of motto to her" (332). The Nelly of years later is the middle-aged narrator who in significant ways is an auto-portrait of Christa Wolf, a writer who has arguably spent most of her life living in the wrong places. The setting for much of *Patterns of Childhood* might well have been the archetypal wrong place, but as this memoir-novel vividly indicates, by the time Christa Wolf wrote the book she certainly knew where she had lived and what had been done to her and the women of her generation.

Céline and the Act of Reading: The War Trilogy

6

The contemporary French novelist Le Clézio once wrote an essay called "On ne peut pas ne pas lire Céline" (One cannot not read Céline). This rather bizarre title encapsulates the problems raised by the work and the life of Dr. Louis-Ferdinand Destouches, a.k.a. Céline. Of the six novelists I discuss here in detail, Céline is arguably the most brilliant and certainly the most controversial. A collaborator in World War II, a professed anti-Semite—it would initially seem quite justified to wonder why anyone would want to read his lengthy war trilogy, which comprises almost one thousand pages in the French Pléiade edition. *From Castle to Castle, North,* and *Rigadoon* could easily be seen as three self-indulgent novels, replete with whining asides, personal attacks, and occasionally boring passages—all the product of an unsavory individual who, not content with his well-founded reputation as a Jew hater, decided to add attacks on Orientals and blacks as well.

Given Céline's personality, as well as his political and racist convictions, it is certainly possible that many early readers of the trilogy purchased the books hoping to find interesting gossip about the Vichy leadership forced into German exile, to read vivid descriptions of the plight of more insignificant collaborators, and to enjoy the spectacle of France's most despised writer ranting about the imagined injustice of his situation. To the extent that these were indeed their expectations, readers were not disappointed, but the fact

86   remains that fifty years after the end of World War II, Céline's trilogy continues to attract popular interest, both in France—a country still very much in the process of coming to grips with its wartime history—and in the international scholarly community.

The attempt to explain the enduring fascination with Céline's writing, especially when the discussion focuses upon the sprawling canvas of the war trilogy, is a complex matter, involving several elements. Principal among them is the author's famous *style émotif parlé* (emotive spoken style), and if there is a single theme that pervades the following pages, it is the meanings and implications of this technique. Therefore, in the interest of clarity I begin my analysis with an explanation of the style émotif and then divide the rest of the chapter into sections treating the relationship between the narrator (Céline) and the main character (Céline); the role of the chronicler; the image of the doctor; and finally the use and abuse of symbolism.

The mechanical elements constituting the style émotif are several: the use of ellipsis, the abundance of slang, and, in the trilogy, the presence of a character named Céline. The essence of this style is, however, emotion, the ability to "*Re-sensitize the language so that it pulses more than it reasons*" (Hindus, *Crippled Giant,* 93, emphasis in text), thereby simulating the rawness of lived experience. This is what Céline sought and most often achieved: "I return to my great attack against the Word. You know, in the Scriptures, it is written: 'In the beginning was the Word.' No! In the beginning was emotion" ("Louis-Ferdinand Céline vous parle," *Romans II*, 933).

The style émotif has its origins in an intense sensitivity to the spoken word: "Emotion is rediscovered, and with enormous difficulty, only in 'the spoken' . . . emotion only can be caught in 'the spoken'" (*Entretiens avec le Professeur Y,* 25). Céline's manipulation of the style émotif permitted him to use words to disconcert and constantly unbalance his reader and to describe people and events in a way that precluded titillating incidents and reassuring conclusions. With particular regard to the trilogy, Céline found in warfare yet another example of the chaos of human existence, but probably so did many others. His peculiar genius stemmed from his ability to convey the emotional content of this chaos.

The style émotif is an elusive phenomenon, and there is a temptation among those discussing it to tend to recreate it rather than to describe its workings and effect. Thus, in an effort to provide a clearer sense of the style émotif, as well as of the variety of reactions it provokes in the reader, I have chosen to isolate and examine one scene in *North:* the picnic attended by the main characters, in which Isis attempts to seduce the narrator in order to persuade him to use his medical license to buy the drugs necessary to kill her husband. Something I hope will be evident from the following discussion is that, despite Céline's claims to the contrary, the style émotif is not devoid of intellectual content.

The section begins with a parody of Gide's famous dictum, "They tell me it's completely out of date to write: 'At ten o'clock the countess's char-à-banc drove up'" (265). Gide had written that an omnisciently narrated phrase such as "the countess's char-à-banc drove up" no longer had a place in modern literature, but as well-taken as Gide's point might have been, the sad, unfashionable truth is that this is exactly what is happening in this scene. Céline and his friends are setting out with a countess in her coach for a *déjeuner sur l'herbe* in the middle of a war zone; "the earth was still rumbling, the whole plain, no worse but no less" (265). From the outset the reader has to confront the disparity between literary fashion and what appears to be happening, while at the same time having no choice but to be aware of the absurdity of the situation.

Shortly after the scene is set, the narrator indulges in one of his numerous, seemingly irrelevant asides. He refers to a memory from World War I, talks about how the author René Duhamel might have described his war experience, and then mentions how Duhamel's prose has become a fixture in the conservative newspaper, *Le Figaro* (267). According to Céline, Duhamel's success, the strength of his narrative, came from what he chose to emphasize: "big calves, high arches, the cult of big or little tits" (267). For his literary accomplishments Duhamel had been invited to join various academies, whereas the narrator remains an outcast, a figure of universal contempt who is constantly challenged to prove his assertions (268).

The effect of this digression upon readers is to push them to examine why they continue to read this book. Is it because of prurient interest in a seduction narrative, a somewhat idiosyncratic style, the narrator's possibly jealous whining or the burgeoning suspicion that the standards for recognizing great literature are themselves in need of reassessment?

An integral part of the style émotif involves the narrator's constant play upon readers' sensibilities as he tries to disturb readerly equilibrium and move them out of the passive, absorbent mode that characterizes most people's way of reading. While Céline is waiting for the picnic to begin, he notices some German women calling to his wife Lili, who is over near some trees. Whatever the reader's expectations, it probably comes as a shock to learn that "they've been peeing" (270). This unnecessary bit of verisimilitude is immediately followed by the hypocritical disclaimer "I assure you, I'm not talking about peeing for the hell of it" (270). The purpose of this gratuitous incident in the text is to further discountenance readers and perhaps make them question their own involvement in this act of reading.

The central moment in this scene deals with Isis's attempt to seduce Céline, but what governs the reader's reaction to the actual seduction is something that occurs shortly before. While discussing some of the highlights of the Parisian social calendar with the aged Countess Tulff-Tcheppe, the starving narrator has been frantically stuffing sandwiches in his pockets: "while she's busy with her emotion I stuff my pockets . . . have I got pockets! . . . ten! twelve on each side" (271). When Isis beckons him to rise and follow her, the mayonnaise on the sandwiches begins to run down his legs. Isis is aware of this but much more so is the reader, because in everything that ensues, the ostensibly erotic nature of the scene is undercut by the reader's image of the condiment sliding down Céline's legs. The result is the direct opposite of Duhamel's "big or small tits," even though the narrator details the charms of Isis's body. In place of sexual excitement, adultery, or possible murder, the dominant motif is one of buffoonery.

The style émotif functions on several levels. It is an attempt to recreate the simulacrum of the spoken word, to provide the impression that the author is speaking: "Not simply in her ear! . . . no . . . in the depth of her nerves, right into her nervous system! in her own head . . . like someone playing to her as he wants, on the harp of her own nerves!" (*Professeur Y,* 122–23). It aims, thus, to imitate the immediacy of an event without the distance that a literary text traditionally provides. At the same time the purpose is to maintain readers in a constant state of imbalance, forever having to adjust their attitudes to the text and their ways of reading.

Céline's development of his style émotif reflects his clear understanding that in the twentieth century, literature's role is no longer to disseminate information readily available from other sources: "the novel no longer has the mission it had; it is no longer a source of information" ("Louis-Ferdinand," 932). In the same interview he stresses the importance of style and implicitly contrasts his efforts in that domain with what has become the classic form of French prose, examples of which he finds cited in the baccalaureate exam that a French student must pass to enter the university and also in newspapers, public speeches, etc. (932). For him this language might possess a certain eloquence, but it lacks emotion. In his concluding comments he imagines how an established nineteenth-century painter might have reacted in a conversation with an Impressionist to a work as unusual and original as Van Gogh's view of the church at Auvers: "But this is a horror; he's a criminal, they ought to kill him" (932).

To the extent that an individual is interested in historical information or perfect reproductions of the physical world, the twentieth century can provide better referents than the contemporary novel. To make matters worse, the very greatness of traditional French prose, its clarity, smoothness, and balanced periods, have become obstacles to an accurate perception of the contemporary situation. In the works of Gide, Camus, and even Sartre (except perhaps for *Nausea,* which the author admits owes much to Céline), whatever the subject matter, the eloquence of style tends to ease the reader into a passive state, however difficult the incidents described. In an essay in praise of Céline, the painter Jean Dubuffet described the phenomenon of "beautiful writing" and its dangerous implications: "The myth of beautiful writing is an essential aspect of the bourgeois defense. If you want to strike at the heart of this evil caste, hit its subjunctives, its celebration of beautiful, hollow language, its simpering aesthetics" ("Céline Pilote," in *L'Homme du commun,* 240).

Traditional French prose is often replete with moralizing tendencies, something Céline abhorred and labored to avoid in his own writing: "Camus . . . he's nothing . . . a moralist . . . always busy telling people what is good and what's bad, what they ought to do, and what they ought not do" (Interview with Robert Stromberg, in Dauphin and Godard, *Cahiers Céline,* 2:175; hereafter cited as *Cahiers*). The style émotif is Céline's device for avoiding the complacency that often underpins an ethically uplifting tone.

Céline's comments concerning the role the novel used to play end with references to Impressionism and Van Gogh. His choices are illuminating and add to the understanding of the style émotif. The Impressionists were never concerned with conveying purely subjective impressions; their goal was a more accurate and nuanced depiction of the physical world through the use of highly refined techniques of seeing. If Van Gogh is most often considered a Post-Impressionist painter, it is because his innovations are not purely technical. Anyone looking at a Van Gogh painting has to realize that the contorted images are themselves content. His highly charged style projects a vision of a world that is suffused with emotion. Philippe Muray scolds critics for taking too seriously Céline's oft-repeated insistence that he is merely a stylist. Muray argues convincingly that these critics want to keep Céline "unreadable" by forever praising a style in a way that makes it devoid of content (*Céline,* 73–74). Muray's point is well taken and underscores the fact that the style émotif is as much a vision of reality as is a Van Gogh painting.

In his writing Céline was attempting something comparable to Van Gogh's effort. He sought a form of expression that permitted at once a description of a person and/or event along with a sense of the emotions informing the particular experience described. In this respect his frequently reiterated contempt for ideas is comparable to his rejection of traditional French prose, the verbal equivalent of nineteenth-century academic painting. Just as the measured periods of the "masters" fail to capture what is happening in the contemporary world, so too what commonly passes for "deep thinking" is, for Céline, equally outmoded. When he directs his readers to hypothetical sources of intellectual stimulation, he tends to refer them to that great Enlightenment creation, the *Encyclopedia*: "Ideas, nothing is more vulgar. The encyclopedia is filled with ideas. There are forty volumes, enormous, stuffed with ideas" ("Louis-Ferdinand," 934). Similarly, for readers looking for that vulgarization of thought which is an author's "message," he counsels an even more ancient source: "There aren't any messages in my books, that's the Church's business" (Stromberg interview, in *Cahiers,* 2:175–76). In both cases, the encyclopedia and the Church, Céline mentions depositories of learning, the putative collective wisdom of which has to a considerable extent formed and developed modern Western society. Regardless of whether individuals are religious or even aware of the Enlightenment, their educations have molded them in these two traditions. It is irrelevant that these two traditions are frequently at odds; what matters is that both are essentially optimistic—one arguing for a paradise in this life and the other in the next. Céline has little use for either. When he said in an interview that "if one spoke of life as one knows it to be, one would not get out of prison" (Pierre Audinet, in *Cahiers,* 2:205), he was doing more than whining about his own situation. He was suggesting that contemporary experience provides little comfort or hope. This negative assessment of human existence appears throughout Céline's writings, and the vehicle he uses to express such a judgment is the style émotif.

Céline Author, Céline Fiction

From the outset one of the most perplexing problems that the reader of the trilogy confronts is the highly ambiguous relationship between Céline, the author of the three novels, and Céline, the main character. They resemble each other so greatly that there is a temptation to dismiss the issue and proclaim what might easily appear obvious: that the two Célines are in fact one. With regard to this issue, John Weightman's comments are all too typical. Speaking about *From Castle to Castle,* he testily remarks: "Actually, Céline is a novelist only in the limited sense that he produces imaginative variations on his autobiography" (*Concept of the Avant-Garde,* 265). Several matters prevent such a facile judgment. The trilogy is published as novels (*romans*), not autobiography. The author is thus inviting the reader at least to entertain the possibility that a rift exists between the man who wrote the books and the narrator who tells the story. The second aspect is associated with the fictional nature of the trilogy. The author Céline manipulates and controls a narrative featuring a main character, Céline, who constantly demonstrates a near-total incapacity to control anything. These are the obvious justifications for insisting that the dichotomy between author and character be maintained, but a more significant reason emerges in the course of my discussion.

The narrator of the trilogy would appear to go out of his way to be as offensive and alienating as possible. At the beginning of *From Castle to Castle* he makes sure the reader understands that he was a collaborator during the war, that he was imprisoned for his activities, and that this experience colored his view of humanity. He appears to praise Pétain's courage and dignity precisely at a historical moment when the disgraced general has become a source of national embarrassment to the French (*Castle,* 161). In *North* he lambastes the supposed achievements of Western culture: "the genius of this Civilization is to have found justifications for the most paranoid slaughters" (203). *Rigadoon* provides gratuitously negative comments on religion and on the alleged power of Western literature: "The Bible . . . the world's most widely read book . . . more obscene, more racist, more sadistic than twenty centuries of lion's dens . . . racism, massacres, genocides, butcheries of the vanquished that make our worst atrocities look pink and blue, like thrillers for kindergartens. . . . next to the Bible everything . . . Racine, Sophocles, or what have you . . . is candy bars" (15). In the event his anti-Semitism has not proven sufficiently antagonizing, he offers some general, more sweeping racist predictions: "the white race has never existed . . . your real, honest-to-God man is black and yellow" (*Rigadoon,* 2), and "in the year 2000 there won't be any whites left . . . nothing to get excited about" (*Rigadoon,* 243). The narrator does not talk to his readers but, so to speak, at them, challenging their beliefs as well as their intelligence: "Public opinion is always right, especially when it's really idiotic" (*Castle,* 132).

Henri Godard, the editor of the Céline Pléiade edition, sums up the narrative stance toward the reader: "The reader finds himself confronted by a man who appears to have nothing but words of bitterness, indeed of disgust and hatred with regard to his fellows" (xxi–xxii). Godard then goes on to suggest a reason for such a seemingly bizarre narrative stance: "The essential is that there be created between the reader and the narrator a current, be it positive or negative, which is in Céline's eyes the condition necessary to transmit the story" (xxii). Few would question Godard's description, but the issue of the dichotomy between author and narrator, as well as the antagonistic stance toward the reader, remains far from settled.

The beginning of a response to these issues involves a consideration of the commonly held distinction between fiction as a form of make-believe and truth as something that can be objectively grasped. Although some people might succumb to the temptation to plead mitigating circumstances, few would deny that Céline's activities during the war were those of a collaborator and racist. Yet are these the only elements that constitute the true portrait of the man, Céline, to whom the narrator frequently alludes?

At various moments in the three novels the narrator plays on the anger the very word *Céline* provokes. He interrupts his narrative for a digression about the "real" Céline, the author. The narrator notes bitterly that the author has been called a drunk, a fornicator, the model anti-Semite, and someone who sold out France for German money. These rantings against sundry accusers culminate in *North:* "The little triumph of my existence, my tour de force, is getting them all . . . right, left, center, sacristies and lodges, cells and charnel houses, Comte de Paris, Joséphine, my Aunt Odile, Kroukroubezeff, and Abbé Piggybank . . . to agree that I'm the foremost living stinker!" (344). For the narrator it is apparently irrelevant to others that the author was a teetotaler practically all his life; that throughout the war period and beyond he was a faithful husband; that Sartre was certainly exaggerating when he used Céline as the model for the typical anti-Semite and just plain wrong when he claimed the author was in the pay of the Germans. The real Céline, as he is perceived by others, is as much a mixture of fact and fiction as is the narrator of the trilogy. Separating truth from fiction is as difficult to do in life as it is in art, and the uncertain relation between author and narrator establishes the ambiguity of truth, the impossibility of ever possessing it fully, as one of the major motifs in the trilogy.

The ambiguous nature of truth is constantly thrust upon the reader. Despite the narrator's frequently reiterated insistence that he tells the truth—"you'll say I'm making it up . . . not at all! . . . faithful chronicler! . . . of course, you had to be there . . . " (*North*, 6)—such statements inspire little confidence and doubtless were intended as such. Not even the allegedly truthful statements in the trilogy are devoid of hyperbole, and thus they contribute, together with the nakedly offensive remarks, to the overall effect of assaulting the reader. The continuous exaggeration, the abrupt shifting back and forth between Céline author and Céline fiction transform the reading of the trilogy into an extremely active experience, in which the reader must constantly sift through the various and at times contradictory pronouncements. What compels a reader to do so is that despite the trilogy's unpleasant and aggressive facade, the reader who perseveres begins to discover a vision of the war and its implications that possesses a startling originality. Disentangling this vision involves an examination of the role of the chronicler, and more generally of the meaning of History, in these three texts.

The Chronicler and History

The three books that constitute the trilogy were all published under the rubric of *roman* (novel), but throughout these works the narrator insists he is writing a *chronique* (chronicle). Hayden White describes chronicles as "open-ended. In principle they have no *inaugurations;* they simply "begin" when the chronicler starts recording events. And they have no culminations or resolutions; they can go on indefinitely" (*Metahistory,* 6). The structure of Céline's texts would in general seem to conform to this description. They begin abruptly and essentially end for no apparent reason.

From a more specifically Gallic perspective, the word *chronique* brings to the mind of an educated French reader the quasihistorical narratives of medieval writers such as Villehardouin, Joinville, and Froissart. Céline exploits this association: "I consider myself a memoir writer, a guy like Joinville or Froissart" ("Interview with André Parinaud," in *Cahiers,* 2:76). Like his medieval predecessors, the author provides purportedly eyewitness accounts of wartime experience in which prominent people figure.

Critics have not, however, been unanimous in supporting Céline's judgment. J. H. Matthews argues that Céline's emphasis is not that of the traditional chronicle: "Céline's chronicle novels place more stress on the tone and character of the narrator's testimony than on the incidents related. The novelist selects episodes that most of the time draw attention away from the major historical events, so as to depict a microcosmic world of horror, cruelty, suffering, and death" (*The Inner Dream,* 179).

Despite the value of these comments, it remains worthwhile to follow Céline in his insistence that he is writing chronicles. In *Rigadoon* he asserts: "I could invent, transpose . . . that's what they all did, the lot of them . . . in Old French it went over . . . Joinville, Villehardouin had it easy, they took full advantage, but our French today, so anemic, so strict and finicky, academized almost to death" (161). The narrator praises the old chroniclers because they had no qualms about manipulating experience and because they were writing a French that had real power; theirs was not a language in which force had been debilitated through excessive formalization and centuries of accumulated rules and grammatical niceties. Also, like Céline, the chroniclers had no pretenses about being intellectuals writing for other intellectuals; they claimed, somewhat disingenuously, that they were simply recounting what happened. From Céline's perspective the relatively unsophisticated prose of the chroniclers came closer to the rawness of experience. More significant still, by insisting on the role of invention in his own books, he underscores what can easily be overlooked. The medieval chronicles were not the historical documents their authors maintained them to be, since the writers of these texts described themselves as objective witnesses of events they could not possibly have seen. In the guise of being historians, the chroniclers were actually writing, just like Céline, a form of fiction in which they doctored occurrences to make them conform to some predetermined pattern.

Hayden White inaugurated a heated scholarly debate when he argued in *Metahistory* that to the extent that historians employed narrative in their accounts, they were involved to some degree in the writing of fiction. The trilogy assumes a more extreme stance concerning the possibility of objective history. In *Rigadoon* the narrator inserts an article by a literary critic who praises Céline's novels in an elegant style—academic writing at its finest—while earlier, in *Nord,* the narrator cites an article from *Le Figaro* describing a diplomatic meeting between Gromyko and the French foreign minister, Couve de Murville (215). Ian Noble offers an illuminating interpretation of the significance of these two interpolations. For him each of these passages is a means of recording history, one of taste and one of fact, but both are controlled in some measure by literary conventions. Noble proposes that the trilogy is yet another approach to history writing, a quite radical one: "by alluding to the variety of discourses claiming to represent contemporary events or history, the text invites us to question the possibility of representing history" (*Language and Narration,* 161).

Noble remarks that for the Célinean narrator, "history is either linear or circular, but never dialectical" (136). History teaches nothing because there is nobody willing to learn. Despite the cataclysmic events that frame the major portions of the narrative, the proclivity for self-serving fictions prevents people from understanding what takes place right in front of them. During the war the reality of impending defeat only heightens the desire for escapist fantasies, but as will be seen, peacetime does little to alter the need for self-delusion.

In *North* the narrator describes the château life as "an opera, the comic kind," (10), while in *From Castle to Castle* he provides details. The buffo pieces in this latter novel detail the amalgamation of orgies, hatreds, self-interests, and intense, meaningless conversations at Siegmaringen: "they blocked the stairs, complete bottleneck . . . if you tried to buck the current, you'd be crushed, rolled thin! . . . because they were ripping mad in addition, they wanted everything and right away! to sleep, to eat, to drink, to piss! . . . and they were all yelling" (*Castle,* 230). A passage in *From Castle to Castle* crystallizes this ambience: "the Chancellery of the Greater Reich had worked out a certain mode of existence for the French in Siegmaringen, neither absolutely fictitious nor absolutely real . . . a fictitious status, half way between quarantine and operetta" (262).

This is the wartime experience: a world of frenzy, make-believe, and backbiting, but life is little different in peacetime. In postwar France sick people demand the services of Dr. Destouches while they vilify the writer Céline; ambitious journalists of all political stripes seek to further their careers by insisting on interviews with the former collaborator. The expression "postwar" is really a misnomer, since conflict remains an omnipresent reality of concern to nobody, especially the authorities:

> The wars raging on seven fronts and all the oceans don't interfere with their caviar . . . the super-squashery . . . Z-bomb, sling, fly-swatter . . . will always respect the *delikatessen* of the high and mighty. . . . You won't see Kroukrouzof eating monkey meat in this world! Or Nixon feeding on noodles or Millamac on raw carrots . . . the tables of the high and mighty are a 'Reason of State'. (*North,* 4–5)

Finally, the making and breaking of literary reputations by the editorial board at the Editions Gallimard in "postwar" France displays a penchant for frenzy and chaos equal to any orgy at Siegmaringen (*North,* 378–83).

Given this context, it is not surprising that History continues to engender fictions catering to the political exigencies of the moment: "The movement of History demands that France and Germany become brothers" (*Rigadoon,* 6). According to the narrator, literature proves equally adept at providing delusions, since the literary form most cherished by his contemporaries is "Comics, heavens alive! . . . more important than the atom bomb! . . . the super-sensation of the day! . . . Renaissance, bah! . . . The *quattrocento* is out . . . phooey! . . . *comics! comics!*" (*North,* 219, emphasis in text). In the trilogy the juxtaposition of scenes from the present with those of the past illustrates that the only difference between past and present is an essentially meaningless passage of time.

This notion gives meaning to *rigadoon,* the word chosen for the title of the last volume of the trilogy. While the term has multiple significance in French, referring also to the bull's eye of a target and a drum and bugle roll in the army, the most pertinent meaning concerns a dance. Céline's wife, herself a professional dancer, describes it: "a rigadoon is danced to a tune in duple [sic] time, on the spot, *without moving forward or backwards, or to the side*" (Noble, *Language and Narration,* 136, emphasis mine). A rigadoon is motion without direction or progress; it is repetition in the guise of movement. When one applies this dance metaphor to the trilogy, it becomes apparent that for Céline nothing is gained, nothing is learned from the unfolding of events, except perhaps that "the meaning of history is . . . a continual repetition of insanity, viciousness, and cataclysms" (Thiher, *Céline,* 180). In such a universe there is a certain logic to the fact that the obsessive concern of the narrator is to flee.

In James Ensor's crowded canvas "The Entry of Christ into Brussels," the gaudily dressed citizens of the Belgian capital are marching in a parade, ostensibly with the purpose of welcoming Christ into their city. The Savior is lost in the crowd; what predominates are the faces of the marchers. All wear masks; in some instances the demarcation between mask and face is apparent, but in others the masks and faces form an inseparable whole. In these latter instances the bearers and their masks have become one.

In the grimly operatic world of the trilogy, masks constitute one means of avoiding the reality of historical events. In some cases the masks are literal. The narrator and his entourage carry gas masks at all times, but the more significant mask is figurative. It is the capacity to avoid facing encroaching events through a self-image that, if it fails to fool others, has nonetheless the great benefit of fooling the person who assumes it. There is the collaborator poet, Châteaubriant, who strides around Siegmaringen decked out in a fanciful Tyrolean outfit, proclaiming the value of "a message . . . a stupendous moral bomb" he and like-minded cohorts are about to devise (*Castle,* 269). Less successful is the aged German firefighter, rechristened "Siegfried" by the authorities in an effort to inspire martial, neo-Wagnerian ardor (*Rigadoon,* 96).

The most successful image maker is the narrator's friend, the actor Le Vigan, who deals with stress by assuming the roles he has played in the movies. He becomes at times "the man from nowhere," but his most effective personification has a more prominent model: "Christ on the Mount of Olives . . . ever since his last picture *La Passion*" (*North*, 45). Le Vigan is such a good actor because he does not merely play a role; he manages to delude himself into believing completely that he is the character. At the height of the actor's fantasy the distinction between mask and man disappears; the narrator remarks that at moments like these, Le Vigan is indeed superior to the twentieth century's greatest ham actor: "You're the greatest actor of the century! . . . next to you Adolf's a feeble-minded blowhard!" (*North*, 237).

The narrator's dilemma is neither that he fails to appreciate the utility of a mask nor that he lacks a very convenient one. His problem is that while he has an excellent role to play, he cannot do it to the total satisfaction of his audience.

The Role of the Doctor

The narrator Céline, like his real-life counterpart, is a doctor. Ultimately this fortuitous circumstance will save the lives of his wife, his cat, and himself: "without doctors and medicine I'd never have come through" (*Rigadoon*, 230). Nevertheless, the cause of many of his problems during and after the war was his inability to convince himself and others that he possessed the image appropriate to a member of the medical profession.

In a postwar interview Céline spoke of his lifelong admiration for doctors: "Since my early childhood I have found nothing more venerable than a doctor" ("Entretiens avec Jean Guénot et Jacques Darribehaude," in *Cahiers*, 2:147). When asked precisely what he so admired about doctors, Céline replied that he saw the physician as "a miraculous guy . . . who healed, who did astonishing things with a body. . . . I used to find him, absolutely, a magician" (159).

The narrator-doctor lacks all these qualities. At the beginning of *From Castle to Castle* Céline is back in Medun, trying to make a living as a physician in postwar France, but his efforts have been only marginally successful. His greatest problem is the disparity between people's image of a doctor and the narrator's wretched situation: "a doctor without a maid, without a housekeeper, without a car, who hauls his own garbage" (11).

His socially anomalous role is exacerbated by other factors. It is bad enough that he lacks the social prerequisites of his profession, but he is also a doctor who "to top it off writes books . . . and who's been in prison" (11). With habitual exaggeration the narrator styles himself "the doctor more monstrous than Pétiot! more criminal than Bougrat!" (19).

The references to these two physicians are hardly fortuitous. Pétiot was indeed an awful man, a person who exploited and murdered Jews during the Occupation. Bougrat's story is another matter. Despite his protestations of innocence, he was accused of murder in 1925 and sentenced to life in prison on Devil's Island. Somehow he managed to escape and spent the rest of his life in Venezuela, where he became famous for his selfless devotion to treating the poor (see Godard, *Romans II*, 1069). In one case there is no doubt about guilt, but Bougrat's situation is highly ambiguous. Yet in the popular mind the two doctors are one; like the narrator himself, they are symbols of unmitigated evil.

At the end of *From Castle to Castle* there is a scene that neatly summarizes the alleged failures of the doctor-narrator. A woman he tries to help mocks him: "I'm going to call you Dr. Stringbean! . . . It seems you haven't any patients left! . . . Not a single patient!" (342). In French slang *haricot* (bean) has two potential implications, both of which are nastily apposite. *Aller manger des haricots* (to go and eat beans) calls to mind the common expression "c'est la fin des haricots," which has the sense of "that's it— there's nothing left," and suggests that the doctor will be forever without clients. *Les haricots verts* (string beans) may be an allusion to the gray-green German uniforms of the occupying army. Whatever the complex truth of the matter, in this woman's eyes, the narrator is nothing other than an impoverished, thus ineffective doctor, a jailbird, and a collaborator.

Céline remarks apropos of the elderly woman who hurled this last insult at him that "she wasn't the kind of woman you could contradict" (345). Nothing will change her mind, nor the attitudes of his fellow citizens toward him, even though some of these people shared Céline's opinions during the war. Yet the narrator knows that whatever the mixture of fantasy and truth in the image others have of him, the real cause of his failure as a doctor lies elsewhere. Baldly stated, he cannot succeed in his profession because people expect too much of the physician in the contemporary world: "If I were a quack, I'd do all right. . . . that would be a way . . . and not a bad one. . . . I'd turn my office in semi-Bellevue into a refriskyment center! . . . a 'new look' Lourdes . . . Lisieux on the Seine . . . but the catch! . . . I'm just a plain doctor" (*Castle,* 20). Despite popular myths surrounding the medical profession, this doctor knows he is no miracle worker and that the solace he has to offer is at once limited and temporary. Initially evoked in the opening pages of *From Castle to Castle,* the image of the doctor is developed throughout the trilogy.

The sickness of the Nazi-cum-collaborator world is physically manifest at Siegmaringen. "Doctor, doctor, save me!" (*Castle,* 164) resounds in the château's corridors, but not entirely due to his own fault, Dr. Destouches' response is pitifully inadequate. The only "effective" drugs at his disposal, and both are in short supply, are cyanide and morphine. Cyanide provides relief through death and thus "I was always being asked for cyanide" (285). It is the drug of the most clearheaded of the collaborators, those able to face the full disaster of their situation and foresee the only possible escape. Although the narrator refuses many people's demands for it, he does promise some to two leading collaborators, Bichelonne, the Vichy minister of industrial production, and Pierre Laval.

The more popular drug, preferred by those unwilling to abandon their fantasies of an eventual Nazi victory, is "morphine! . . . morphine! . . . My head on the block! the worst stratagems! for the exercise of my art and the last resource of the dying! morphine! . . . morphine! " (*Castle,* 186–87). Morphine masks a pain but cannot cure the disease that provoked it. It is a chemical that makes reality bearable by inducing a distorted mental state that has little regard for truth. In this respect the doctor's wartime problem is no different from what he encounters after the war: patients who want him to treat a symptom because in most cases they are unable to confront the cause.

Although the narrator-doctor violated medical ethics in providing two collaborators with cyanide, he does refuse in *North* to get the drugs Isis needs to kill her husband. This latter refusal may be praiseworthy, but it underscores the doctor's inconsistency, which contributes to his failure in playing the medical role demanded of him. The trilogy has portraits of numerous doctors who, with two exceptions, prove themselves perversely consistent in the performance of their nefarious tasks.

At Siegmaringen a deranged surgeon is intent upon eviscerating his screaming patient (*Castle,* 168). When Céline complains to the Vichy minister Brion, he is blithely informed: "Oh, you know, a crazy doctor . . . he's not the only one. . . . We know that of twelve French doctors, supposedly French, supposedly refugees, ten are insane . . . really insane, escaped from asylums" (168). What Brion did not mention was that madness can be an asset in a madhouse.

The successful doctors in the trilogy all have the strength of *idiots savants.* The German physician Haupt in *Rigadoon* is a would-be Nietzschean whose addled theories about the survival of the fittest lead him to expose people overnight in freezing temperatures (743). Werner Göring, the psychiatrist cousin of the better-known Hermann, makes a brief appearance at the end of *North.* This seemingly affable and intelligent man is nonetheless the doctor responsible for treating the mental disorders of the Reich's leadership. However flagrantly obvious his failure in this endeavor, he remains totally untroubled by the behavior of his charges and by the destruction their activities have unleashed upon Europe.

In *From Castle to Castle* appears Dr. Gebhardt, who is a source of wonderment to many: "another character! . . . a general on the Russian front for six months . . . in command of a *panzer* team . . . and for six months he'd been chief surgeon of the enormous S.S. hospital in Hohenlychen, East Prussia" (282). This very flattering assessment is not, however, that of the narrator, who views Gebhardt with the bitterest irony: "he staged football games with one-legged teams . . . war cripples . . . he was cracked like the supermen of the Renaissance" (282). This Nazi overachiever was the surgeon in charge when, during a relatively simple medical procedure, the Vichy minister Bichelonne lost his life. The narrator hints strongly that the Frenchman was murdered, but the German doctor remains an admired and respected figure.

Aside from Destouches, the most important physician in the trilogy is Dr. Harras. Like Dr. Göring he appears to be a pleasant and well-educated person, who proves extremely helpful to the narrator and his entourage. However, as head of the Nazi Health Bureau (*Reichsgesund*) he is implicitly responsible for all sorts of unnamed obscenities; he is the embodiment of the medical arts in the service of madness. In his last appearance toward the end of *Rigadoon,* Harras' dress, full S.S. uniform with Mauser and hand grenades on the hips, transforms the youthful Céline's image of doctor as magician into doctor as warlock.

It is not by chance that the one of the doctors who is an important exception to the pattern I have delineated is a Greek named Proseïdon, who treats lepers. This physician represents an ironic remnant of the Hippocratic ideal, the notion, clearly antiquated in the trilogy, that the medical doctor is a principled individual unselfishly devoted to alleviating human suffering. For the most part, Dr. Destouches attempts to uphold this ideal as well, but the Greek is more fortunate than the Frenchman with regard to the illnesses he treats. Even though leprosy continues to exist in the twentieth century, in the context of the trilogy it is a disease associated with an earlier age, when the problems doctors handled were more clearly demarcated and the ethical issues less ambiguous. Proseïdon is an anachronistic figure who deals with an illness that can be successfully cared for, if not always cured.

The sickness that the narrator-doctor confronts is much more than physical. If Dr. Destouches has a literary ancestor, it is Kafka's physician in "The Country Doctor." This man, like Destouches, wants to be of service and true to his professional ideals, but he is progressively stripped of his medical dignity as he struggles against a sickness that makes a mockery of his expertise. The diseases he is expected to treat are the physical manifestations of a much greater spiritual malaise. Toward the end of the story, Kafka's narrator-doctor is deprived of his expensive clothing and forced to lie naked next to his dying patient. When he finally leaves the patient's house, he is alone and shivering in a coach drawn by suddenly slowed horses: "Naked, exposed to the frost of this most unhappy of ages, with an earthly vehicle, unearthly horses, old man that I am, I wander astray. . . . Betrayed! Betrayed! A false alarm on the night bell once answered—it cannot be made good, not ever" (143).

Kafka's doctor was ruined and humiliated because he foolishly responded to an emergency that far exceeded his skills. The complexity of the problem was perhaps due to the fact that what appeared to be an illness, a deviation from the norm, had become so established as a condition of daily life that it was nothing other than the human condition. However, once the response was made, the doctor had no recourse except to experience the full weight of his inadequacy. He would have been wiser to stay at home, oblivious to problems of the world, content with his fancy clothing and his flattering self-image.

The narrator-doctor Céline made similar mistakes. Had he restricted himself to practicing medicine and writing the occasional novel, he might eventually have captured the Goncourt Prize or even a Nobel Prize. Instead, like the country doctor he responded to a call he ought not to have heeded, became embroiled in the political tensions of his age, engaged in activities beyond his control and in excess of his knowledge, and ultimately found himself wandering within a fearful and threatening landscape. However vast the metaphysical anxiety that haunts Kafka's fiction sometimes appears, the demon that menaces Dr. Destouches is no less grand. It is the inexorable decay of Western civilization, exacerbated by the war but by no means limited to it. This is the sense of Philippe Muray's comment concerning the trilogy: "What a mistake to have believed that it was merely a chronicle of the Second World War" (*Céline,* 209). The war is simply an instance of a much greater malaise, and the devolution described in the three novels is portrayed as continuing to unfold in the present as it did in the past.

The narrator's assertion that he would not have escaped from Germany were it not for his medical training (*Rigadoon,* 900) requires some additional clarification. In fact he would not have succeeded in getting to Denmark without a group of Down's syndrome children he befriended. When a Danish Red Cross train is preparing to leave Germany for Copenhagen, the narrator dons his Red Cross armband from Bezons in France and manages to persuade a sympathetic Danish doctor that the children are Danish nationals whom his wife and he have been attempting to get out of the war zone. The ruse is transparent, but it works, largely due to the decency of the Danish doctor. Nevertheless the children were the essential ingredient in the plan.

In a trilogy replete with irony, the Down's syndrome children constitute one of the most ironic elements. As Ian Noble points out, even the gibberish these youngsters speak has a corollary with what is occurring around them: "The undifferentiated language of the orphans is the linguistic correlative of the physical world, disintegrating under Allied bombings" (*Language and Narration,* 158). The children "are emblematic of the dissolution of order and meaning, a dissolution which is never far away. They form the opposite pole to civilized language, used as a weapon to keep people in their place" (158).

The retardation of these young people stems from birth defects; it is genetic and as such in no way the result of anything they have done. This retardation with its attendant innocence contrasts sharply with the madness of the normal men and women the narrator encounters. The members of this latter group are not functional and mad; they are functional because they are mad. To the extent that these people do survive, it is in part because they manage to create fantasy worlds filled with simple and simplistic alternatives that shield them against reality. Some turn to drugs, others to glorified self-images or imitations of film heroes.

The Down's syndrome children initially appear to stand in sharp contrast to the legions of connivers and self-servers who abound in the trilogy. These children are totally helpless, and it is by sheer good luck that they manage not to get hit by a bullet or a bomb, not to be burned alive or asphyxiated by the fire and smoke they encounter in Hamburg. Nevertheless there is an important parallel between these "cretins" (197) and the people who surround them in *Rigadoon.*

The adults' situation is quite similar to that of the children. They are equally vulnerable to destruction from the instruments and results of modern warfare, and their "intelligence" rarely provides them with any better physical protection. The children survive by chance; this can also be said of those adults who cheat death in the trilogy. In *Rigadoon* the narrator is injured by an errant brick that might just as easily have killed him. The train in which he is traveling with his young charges somehow avoids a direct hit from Allied bombers, and by sheer luck the weight of the train does not buckle a bridge they are crossing. The narrator stumbles upon food when he follows the children through the rubble of Hamburg. During all these incidents there is no sense that he has the slightest control over what is happening.

When the narrator does assert some initiative with his flagrantly contrived story about overseeing the children, he has the good fortune to tell it to one of the few decent people in the trilogy. If for the narrator-doctor wartime is peacetime writ large, then these idiot children are what normal people become when reality intensifies and forces them into situations that defy their control.

Symbolism

A curious corollary of *le style émotif* in the trilogy is the assault on literary symbolism, which is employed in an obvious and vulgar way to demonstrate the possible irrelevancy of this device to the writing of postwar literature. When the actual Céline had to flee France, he eventually wound up with other collaborators at a château named Sigmaringen. This place becomes Siegmaringen in the novels, the slight adjustment of nomenclature turning the meaningless "Sig" into "Sieg," the German word for "victory," which is also a crucial portion of the infamous Nazi salute, "Sieg Heil." In *North* the narrator and his entourage stay briefly in a hotel called the Brenner, a word which alludes to the German infinitive "brennen" (to burn). Later they take refuge in a town named Zornhof (court of scorn), a name that aptly sums up the attitude of the locals toward the newly arrived French. In the Berlin subway the narrator and his group are rescued from zealous *Hitlerjugend* by a French prisoner with the unlikely name of Picpus. In Paris there is a cemetery (another sort of underground) called Picpus, which is reserved for nobles executed during the French Revolution and their descendants.

In a more mythological vein, Isis, the woman who attempts to seduce the narrator in *Nord,* has a name recalling the Egyptian goddess, whose efforts to restore her murdered husband to life contrast sharply with the activities of the Célinean character. To the extent that Dr. Proseïdon's name is an allusion to the sea god Poseidon, who favored the Trojans over the Greeks in the Trojan War, this reference might be an ironic homage to a man who defended a bunch of losers. Also in *North,* the enraged prostitutes who murder the *Rittermeister* might be compared to the avenging Furies of Greek myth. In *Rigadoon,* the narrator's sojourn in the Phenix Hotel is perhaps a tribute to his ability to survive the numerous efforts to destroy him. Finally, there is the association of Le Vigan and Christ.

This list is by no means exhaustive, but it is sufficient to show that the trilogy abounds in symbolism of a particularly clumsy sort. This appearance of clumsiness was probably intentional and meant to serve as a parody of literature's use of symbolic analogy. The only constant in the examples I have cited is the obvious dichotomy between the prototype and the contemporary embodiment. For instance, if for a moment the reader were to take seriously the possibility that the whores represented the Furies, what then was the crime of the benighted old man they so brutally murdered? Or, on a more elaborate level, were the reader to imagine some correlation between the narrator's peregrinations in war-torn Germany and Dante's journey through Hell, what could be gained from such a comparison, except perhaps that the goals, as well as the moral states of the protagonists, were entirely different?

It is more sensible to ascribe other aims to the symbolism in the trilogy, aims that may clarify different aspects of the style émotif. Céline's way of writing cannot provoke only horror, outrage, and disgust but also evokes laughter at human stupidity. Le Vigan as Christ is a joke, Isis as a goddess an absurdity. When, at the end of *North,* amid the frenzied preparations for the flight from Zornhof, the psychiatrist Werner Göring indulges a nostalgia for his youthful visits to the village, his reference to "the embarkation for Cytherea" (436) does not evoke wistful images from Watteau or even Baudelaire. Rather, the reader is overwhelmed by how little place reality holds in the mind of this student of the human psyche.

One traditional function of symbolic analogy is to place an event, group, or individual in a timeless context in order to add a greater dimension to what is being described. This technique has certainly been often parodied in the twentieth century, perhaps most influentially by Eliot in *The Waste Land,* where throughout the poem the author marks the difference between the West's cultural models and their contemporary embodiments. In the trilogy Céline goes further. If he makes anything appear timeless, it is human stupidity, and if he indulges in symbolism, it is only to show how unnecessary it is. World War II had no need of a Dante to indicate that what was occurring was hellish, and in cases like Zornhof and Siegmaringen, readers without the slightest knowledge of German would surely get the point.

Symbolism in the trilogy is like a vestigial organ; it is there as a leftover from the past, but it serves no useful function except to force upon the reader an awareness of its uselessness. More than any other stratagem in the trilogy, this parody of symbolism helps explain Céline's easily misunderstood insistence on the absence of ideas in his writing. The purpose of his hyperbolic pronouncement was to distance himself from other authors whose dependence upon allegedly distinguished literary techniques served only to mask a lack of content: "What Céline whispers is what our age whispers to us, and it is essential. If he was always so severe with his contemporaries, so scornful toward other writers, it is because he saw them ceaselessly in their babblings trying to *divert the conversation*" (Muray, *Céline,* 71, emphasis in text).

Ending

Julia Kristeva has argued that "without the war it is hard to imagine a Célinian scription; the war appears to trigger it off, to be its very condition" (*Powers of Horror,* 152). Kristeva is referring to World War I as the cathartic event that determined Céline's worldview and influenced all his fiction. Probably this is true, but by the time of World War II, warfare had become a symptom for Céline, not a cause of the contemporary state of affairs. A reader of the trilogy today is not involved in an exercise of historical recreation of events that began and ended over fifty years ago. One is instead participating in a vision of an ongoing present where ugliness predominates, a place where literary activity, as Céline envisioned it, becomes a form of vengeance, a reaction at once angry and pathetic against a world that escapes rational control. This may have been what Pol Vandromme had in mind when he wrote concerning the trilogy: "For the first time, the war speaks in a book with the voice of the twentieth century" (*Céline,* 91).

There is no closure to the trilogy; it simply stops. Even if Céline had lived long enough to undertake another revision of *Rigadoon,* it is doubtful whether there would have been a smoother ending. Nothing in these novels suggests a final synthesis, a polite bringing together of the disparate rantings, asides, and fragmented narratives. A reader of the trilogy might well enjoy the dark humor, the gossip, and even the self-pity, but these are not reasons enough to warrant reading these books. The ultimate effect of the style émotif is to awaken in the reader the darkest suspicions about the course of history and its nefarious influence upon twentieth-century society. Céline explains nothing; he simply recreates contemporary experience in a manner that appears to be terrifyingly accurate. For this reason the reader is at times repulsed by these novels, at times impatient with them, yet always compelled to keep reading them. Still, to live with the Célinian vision of the world is another matter. Le Clézio, with whose essay title I began this chapter, offers a powerfully ambiguous acknowledgment of the force of Céline's prose: "Céline is among those it is necessary to forget in order to be able to live" (in Dauphin, *Critiques de notre temps,* 184).

Günter Grass's *The Tin Drum:*
Hiding from the Black Cook

7

At the 1958 meeting of the Gruppe 47, in Grossholzleute, a relatively unknown poet and sculptor, Günter Grass, read a portion of his novel-in-progress. Hans Werner Richter describes the reaction: "Marcel Reich-Ranicki stops taking notes, some listen with mouths agape, and Joachim Kaiser shakes his head, quietly laughing. And I know, this is the beginning of one of the great successes for the Group 47" (Broadcast, 136). Richter's words proved prophetic, as *The Tin Drum* became, and remains, the best-known work of postwar German fiction. Given the novel's fame, as well as the seemingly massive role the *Nazizeit* plays in it, the question I am about to pose may well seem at best naive and at worst ridiculous, namely: What is *The Tin Drum* about?

Michael Hollington provides an example of what might be considered the standard response when he states that Grass's aim is "to put the reader in question about his past, his involvement in and responsibility for the crimes committed by the National Socialists" (*Günter Grass,* 30). Although this summation contains a great deal of truth, such a concentration on the Nazi experience obscures the fact that the novel covers much more historical and political ground (World War I, the Polish experience in Danzig, the post–World War II German industrial miracle), and while guilt is a leitmotif in the book, as the Onion Cellar section indicates, guilt is not limited to what occurred during the war; people go to the Onion Cellar to cry over all sorts of things. At the same time the novel engages in a constant reflection on the meaning and limitations of art in the modern world. It is perhaps the emphasis accorded to the wartime sections of *The Tin Drum* that has prompted the dissatisfaction of the writer-critic Hans Magnus Enzensberger with the novel's subsequent sections: "The only weak parts of the book are those where the action moves into the Present" (*Einzelheiten,* 225). Yet there remains another possibility, one that recalls elements I have already mentioned in the Céline chapter: that the novel's main concern is with a phenomenon accentuated by warfare but which existed beforehand and continues afterward.

At the center of this novel is not Hitler, or even Oskar Matzerath, but the hovering presence of *die schwarze Köchin,* the black female cook (in Ralph Mannheim's otherwise excellent translation, the black cook becomes the "black witch"; I have stayed with the literal translation). At the end of *The Tin Drum,* Oskar claims that only recently had he come to be wary of the Black Cook (581), a comment as open to question as any of Oskar's utterances and one that stands in clear contradiction to his earlier admission that the Black Cook "gave me an occasional fright in my childhood days" (533–34). The fact is that in her sundry embodiments, the Black Cook pervades the novel. She first appears in a children's rhyme (64); she has a vague sexual connotation through association on two occasions with girls' faces (98, 386). Henri Plard sees the Niobe figure sculpted on the ship's prow, which becomes the source of Herbert's ecstatic self-immolation in the museum, as "one of the incarnations of the Black Cook" ("Une Source," 284), and in postwar Germany Oskar admits to being more aware of her than ever before (534). The novel's last words are the doggerel rhyme about the Black Cook.

The Black Cook has been the subject of considerable critical speculation. Constantin Ponornareff suggests that she has a "moral function, the power to energize the writer's sense of social responsibility" (*Silenced Vision,* 41). The problem with this reading is that the novel's narrator, Oskar, spends most of his time fleeing social responsibility, and unlike the Céline of the war trilogy, he is not fleeing for his life but rather from life, an existential situation he deems meaningless in itself, yet one made increasingly frightening because of the presence of other human beings, coupled with the political situations they create. In this context, what is more important than Oskar's famous first words, "Granted, I am an inmate in a mental hospital" (15), is that in the asylum he speaks of his bed as his "goal" (womb?), wishing its bars were higher "to prevent anyone from coming too close to me" (15).

Glenn Guidry has explored the psychological implications of the cook (witch), explaining that she represents for Oskar "the dark side of his personality. . . . The Black Witch is a projection of the infantilism of Oskar, who in turn is a projection of the psychological disposition of his readers. The implication . . . is that German society faces the same challenge that Oskar does: to purge itself of its infantile drives" ("Theoretical Reflections," 140).

This type of broad psychological reading purports to explain a great deal, but in fact it clarifies little. Childish behavior is certainly a motif in *The Tin Drum,* but it would be simplistic in the extreme to dismiss Oskar and his compatriots in terms of this single concept, which seems so associated with activities during the Third Reich. As noted, the novel is not limited to the war years. Yet even if it were, what would be gained by talking about Germany's suffering from the vantage point of a national infantilism, of which Oskar is the particular embodiment? If such an approach were to be taken seriously, might it not also be applied to the French adventures in Algeria or Indochina or the American debacle in Vietnam?

A more modest but useful suggestion is proposed by Bernard McElroy, who describes "an Oskar who is a terrified Oskar, aware of his powerlessness and aware that the issue ultimately at stake is his survival in a monstrously threatening world whose spirit haunts him in the person of the Black Cook" ("Lunatic, Child," 320). McElroy adds that Oskar essentially has two choices: "either to find some way of controlling events or to find some impregnable refuge" (320). I am in agreement with McElroy and think that *The Tin Drum* is about fear, a visceral fear of life itself that the war experience accentuates but does not create. From this perspective Oskar's story details the various means—artistic, social, and culinary—that people employ to cope with this emotion.

Cooking is essentially an act of transformation, on its simplest level from the raw to the cooked. Sometimes this transformation requires little obvious alteration. To take a vegetable dear to Oskar and his grandmother, a superficial glance at a potato might not reveal at once whether it was raw or baked. However, cooking can certainly involve a total transformation, and few people would confuse an uncooked or baked potato with its mashed equivalent. Still, whatever the nature of the altered state, baked or mashed, the basic element, the potato, remains the same.

In *The Tin Drum* the basic element is fear of life's complexity. Whether this fear is overt or subdued, existential or political, like a strong kitchen odor, it permeates its environment, in this case the novel, and just about all the characters and social groups are engaged in transforming this emotion into something more palatable. The transformation can take place on a personal and harmless level (Matzerath in the kitchen), on a sexual level (Agnes and Jan in bed), on a political-social level (the Third Reich), or on an artistic level (Oskar the singer-drummer-writer). Behind all of these transformations is a desire to protect the individual or the group from life in all its chaotic rawness, to offset the suspicion suffusing the novel that human existence is "an activity without meaning, purpose or sane unifying principle" (Cunliffe, *Günter Grass*, 52).

Now all of these transformations, be they anodyne, evil, or aesthetic, have one thing in common: they are simplifications. The Black Cook can occasionally be muted, but only for a time; she never goes away for good, and if the novel's ending is to be believed, she is making her presence increasingly felt in the modern world.

The Tin Drum begins on a note of fear. Joseph Koljaiczek's fear is not of the existential variety; it stems instead from his difficulties in eluding the two policemen who are chasing him. Nevertheless, his actions establish a pattern that will become predominant later in the novel and that has its contemporary embodiment in Oskar's flight from his pursuers at the end of the story. Koljaiczek escapes his pursuers by hiding under Anna Bronski's four skirts and finding literal solace in her womb. The rest of Joseph's life involves a constant hiding, a fear of his true identity being revealed, and his ultimate disappearance, slipping under the water as logs close atop him, suggests yet another return to the womb. Anna's nephew, Jan, is constantly afraid, but the embodiment of fear in its purest, most existential form is Anna's grandson, Oskar.

His concerns about the travails of human existence began even before birth—"he lost his enthusiasm even before this life beneath the light bulbs had begun" (49)—and the longing to return to the womb accompanies him, in myriad forms, throughout the novel. This desire for the womb bespeaks an effort to transform fear into forgetfulness, an attempt that yields at best partial and temporary successes. The womb can be, as it was for Joseph, under Anna's skirts, but it can also be under tables, in closets, in short in any enclosed space that offers the semblance of escape, however illusory. At his mother's funeral Oskar wants to join her in the pit (165), and despite the comforts of his hospital bed, he still laments: "Who will take me under her skirts today" (169)?

Oskar's decision to remain the size of a three year old separates him from the grownup world, but only in appearance. If Oskar is an intelligent adult who looks like a retarded child, grownups are bigger people who most often blithely behave like little children. The Cristal Night is the cruelest of childish games, something Oskar emphasizes when he notes that the S.A. members who trash Markus's store "in their characteristic way . . . were playing with the toys" (202). Intellectually too, the grownups rarely get beyond the childish. Grownups, Oskar says, "simply have to have their explanations for things" (63), and so he orchestrates his falling down the stairs to justify his lack of growth. Oskar correctly perceives that adults do not necessarily want the truth; they just want an explanation, some excuse for not having to look too deeply into an issue. According to Oskar, even the greatest of grownup inventions, the clock, has its infantile aspect: "There is something very strange and childish in the way grownups feel about their clocks . . . they have no sooner created some epoch-making invention that they become a slave to it" (67).

During the war, Oskar's attraction to the gang of boys called the Dusters has nothing to do with politics. He sees them instead as kindred spirits whose quarrel is with those who thrust them into life: "We have nothing to do with parties. . . . Our fight is against our parents and all other grownups, regardless of what they may be for or against" (374). Oskar's refusal to grow, his conscious decision to remain ostensibly a child, is the most obvious form of his protest against those compelling him to live life.

Oskar considers his attraction to nurses as "a kind of sickness" (482), but perhaps there is more to it than that. The existence of nurses attests to the reality of sickness, existential as well as physical. They, like the Dusters, are kindred spirits who have at least the potential to understand his own discomfort with life. His keeper in the asylum, Bruno, explains to him that whereas "your male nurse takes conscientious care of his patient and sometimes cures him, his female counterpart, woman that she is, beguiles the patient, sometimes into recovery, sometimes into a death pleasantly seasoned with eroticism" (482). It is the beguilement, or failing that, the "death pleasantly seasoned with eroticism," that attracts Oskar. His attempted seduction-rape of Sister Dorothea illustrates his complicated fascination with female nurses. Her room is "a repulsive tomb" (492), which Oskar would prefer to avoid. When he attacks her he has her lying on the four-layered carpet in the hallway, which recalls his grandmother's four skirts. His ensuing impotence is more than a sexual failure; it is the confirmation of his deepest, darkest suspicion: the impossibility of forcing his way back into the womb. However great his fear of life, Oskar has no choice but to live, and to do so he must employ his various talents to keep the Black Cook at bay.

Joseph Matzerath would appear to have no fear of the Black Cook; he does his own cooking. Yet what Matzerath—who "always had to wave when other people were waving, to shout, laugh, and clap when other people were shouting, laughing, and clapping" (152)—and others like him help concoct is the twentieth century's most unpalatable mess: the Third Reich. While *The Tin Drum* deals with much more than Germany's wartime experiences, it remains nevertheless true that this section of the novel lingers longest with readers and critics. I think Helmut Koopmann provides a brilliant explanation for the power and originality of these passages. Koopmann argues that to analyze Nazism, earlier German treatments of the Hitler period and the war (Brecht, the Mann brothers) tended to seek elaborate historical parallels from the past (Caesar's efforts at industrialization for Brecht, the career of Henry of Navarre for Heinrich Mann) or psychological explanations (Freudianism for Thomas Mann). Grass, for his part, avoids any attempt at analysis, profound or otherwise, and offers in its place "eine Frontalansicht des Kleinbürgertums, der Wohnküchenkultur und ihrer Bewohner" (a frontal view of the petite bourgeoisie, of their apartment-kitchen culture and inhabitants) ("Der Faschismus als Kleinbürgetum und was das wurde" in Görtz, *Günter Grass*, 103). Koopmann maintains that in *The Tin Drum* the boredom of the lower middle class was assuaged by the rhetoric and pageantry of National Socialism (105) and that in place of analysis, Grass contents himself with representation (*Darstellung*). What distinguishes this novel most clearly from earlier treatments is the fact that so little is asked about the basis for the rise of the brown-shirted movement (Röhm's S.A., the early version of the Nazi Party). In the past those were really the questions that authors were asking; now those sorts of things have become practically meaningless. Not only are historical parallels and attempts at psychological explanations lacking, but also the representation of the history of that time to a large extent does not need the questioning of the whys and wherefores. (107–8)

Historical parallels were simply too grandiose to explore specifics, and as I argue in the first chapter of this book, the war itself sapped confidence in the veracity of the psychological structures currently at hand. Finally, the posing of the same old questions in anticipation of the usual responses was becoming tiresome.

Fear, especially the sort of fear that Oskar experiences, can certainly be a psychological phenomenon, but in insisting on its importance in the novel, I have carefully avoided psychological labelings (Freudian, Jungian, Lacanian), because in Oskar, Grass depicts a symptomatic fear of existence without providing any means of ascribing to it a cause more concrete, more open to psychological analysis, than life itself.

The *Langeweile* (boredom) Koopmann attributes to the lower middle class in *The Tin Drum* is not so removed from fear as Matzerath's complacency in the kitchen might suppose. Fear, outside of the kind resulting from perceived danger, requires a degree of imagination, whereas boredom frequently stems from the lack of same. Yet both fear and boredom share a sense of dissatisfaction, the former perceived consciously and the latter muted by obtuseness. When Agnes is sickened by the sight of eels emerging from the dead horse's head, Jan and Oskar are initially both at a loss concerning what to do. Although Matzerath loves his wife deeply, his eventual reaction is simply to buy the eels and insist on cooking them for dinner. He is incapable of penetrating even slightly the surface of his emotions and acknowledging his real concern. Complacency and routine protect him from his feelings. In a comparable manner, boredom can alleviate anxiety by discouraging self-examination. Boredom, and its attendant vague dissatisfaction, can cloak many things, among them fear.

Certainly World War II manages to turn German boredom into terror. In terms of the novel, the war transforms the latent fear of life, experienced consciously only by a few, into a practical fear of death shared by everyone. Just as when Hitler came to power the vacuum cleaner began to replace carpet racks (175), life in general began to move at a faster, more mechanized pace, and Germany's Nazi leadership would prove particularly adept at cleansing the *Vaterland* of its unwanted elements. The war accentuated the latent and turns vague dissatisfaction into real horror. Much as in Céline's war trilogy, warfare in this novel is no deviation from the norm but merely the bursting of social, moral, and psychological restraints; it is human existence writ large.

Oskar's search for methods of coping with life began before birth, and despite the impact of the war sections in *The Tin Drum,* it should be remembered that the fine advice he gets from Bebra occurs in a scene that takes place years before World War II starts: "Our kind has no place in the audience. We must perform, we must run the show. If we don't, it's the others that run us. . . . Always take care to be sitting on the rostrum and never be standing out in front of it" (114). Bebra is referring to the plight of "little people," but "little" here is at least as metaphoric as it is literal. After all, Bebra and Oskar are small by choice; their size is a form of cunning, a way of protecting themselves from big bodies attached to baby brains. Bebra's point is that an intelligent person has to be able to avoid vulnerability by asserting control, and control does not always depend upon physical strength. Oskar's size provides him with options; he can be an adult with the Dusters and a child to the S.A. or the invading Russians. The situation dictates the mask he will wear to dominate a group or to extricate himself from danger.

Size is one means Oskar has for protecting himself against life, but its efficacy is limited in time. After the war the world changes, and so does Oskar. He had earlier and prophetically remarked that when Markus died "he took all the toys in the world with him away with him out of this world" (206). Postwar Europe was in intellectual and moral, as well as physical, ruin. Largely because of the wartime genocide, traditional assumptions about "natural goodness" and the continual amelioration of human nature were missing and presumed dead. People had changed despite themselves, and society was in search of new values and complacencies. Oskar was no exception, although his change was essentially physical. He no longer resembles a retarded child; he is now a hunchbacked dwarf. His hunchback may be the result of his guilt feelings for complicity in Matzerath's death; it may represent the guilt of the German people or the disfigurement of their partitioned nation. Whatever the symbolic ramifications of his new physical appearance, in practical terms he is now perceived as a grownup.

In addition to size, Oskar had three other means of protecting himself: his voice, his drum, and his fountain pen. His voice was his only overt instrument of aggression. He used it to destroy glass in order to warn grownups to keep their distance, or to enact vengeance, as when he breaks the windows in the Danzig theater because he is angered at his mother's adulterous relationship with Jan. During the war he employs his vocal pyrotechnics to distract German soldiers from their serious and ill-fated business. However, as a grownup in postwar Germany, he no longer has that power. In a sense, Oskar's diminished singing skills do not constitute a serious impediment because it is hard to imagine people trying to dig out of the wartime rubble being particularly intimidated or amused by a little man who can shatter whatever unbroken glass remains to be found.

The drum is another matter. Essentially he uses it to conjure up the past. His drum can evoke memories, both in himself and in others. In the postwar world it becomes the basis for his short-lived, albeit brilliant, career as a cabaret and concert artist. On a level more subtle than anything he ever did with his voice, Oskar also makes use of his drum for revenge. Whether he is playing in the Onion Cellar or in one of his concerts, he forces his audience to share his greatest fear, that of the Black Cook. The results are at once predictable and indicative that he really no longer needs his vocal powers: "fifteen hundred crusty old miners, who had lived through cave-ins, explosions, flooded pits, strikes and unemployment, let out the most bloodcurdling screams. . . . Their screams . . . demolished several windows" (555–56). This fear is deeper than any wartime memories; it is the fear of life itself.

Just as the importance of the war sections in *The Tin Drum* have been somewhat exaggerated, the drum device—with its associations with Hitler, *der Trommler* (the drummer), and postwar rubble, *die Trümmer,* as well as the new literature associated with it, *die Trümmerliteratur*—has been accorded more significance than it deserves. Oskar's drumming is riveting and affecting, but its scope is limited to reawakening memories. His true artistic talent, although it too has its limitations, is literary.

It is through the words he confides to the "virgin" paper Bruno provides for him that Oskar creates his elaborate, intersecting vision of past, present, and future. Writing also protects him; not, however, by supplying some grandiose synthesis that wrests order out of chaos. Rather, much more modestly, the act of writing takes his mind off the Black Cook for extended periods.

Like most writers talking about their own literary activities, Oskar cannot always be believed. He begins his story of his life and times with a discussion of possible ways of writing about contemporary experience:

> You can begin a story in the middle and create confusion by striking out boldly, backward and forward. You can be modern, put aside all mention of time and distance and, when the whole thing is done, proclaim, or let someone else proclaim, that you have finally, at the last moment, solved the space-time problem. Or you can declare at the very start that it's impossible to write a novel nowadays, but then, behind your own back so to speak, give birth to a whopper, a novel to end all novels. I have also been told that it makes a good impression, an impression of modesty so to speak, if you begin by saying that a novel can't have a hero any more because there are no more individualists, because individuality is a thing of the past, because man, each man and all men together—is alone in his loneliness . . . and all men lumped together make up a "lonely mass." . . . And so to you personally, dear reader, . . . I introduce Oskar's maternal grandmother. (17–18)

With these words Oskar leaves the impression that he will not attempt a Homeric epic, a *nouveau roman,* or a Teutonic version of *The Lonely Crowd.* All this is doubtless true, but neither his story nor its telling will be simple or straightforward. He is going to attempt something quite innovative and, as the invocation to the reader suggests, something in which his audience will be actively involved. Despite Oskar's calm and apparently friendly tone toward the reader, his narrative, once again much like Céline's, is a prolonged attack on his audience's sensibilities. Just as early in his narrative Oskar refused to provide his readers with a pat Hollywood ending to his grandfather's efforts to escape detection as a boatman—"We know the scene from the movies: the reconciliation between two enemy brothers, brilliantly performed" (32)—nowhere in the rest of his tale does he offer his audience a means of escape. His story may enlighten, and it certainly does shock, but its goal, with regard to others, is to force the reader to acknowledge that the Black Cook is indeed there.

Oskar's major innovation, which in the context of postwar Germany, is also the major innovation of *The Tin Drum,* is to write humorously of fearful things: of fear of life, and of Germany's frightening activities during and after the war, when economic success became a metaphor for moral recovery. The comic narrative produces a curious situation for the reader. Humor frequently achieves its effect through a twofold movement. The first involves distancing—creating a gap between the comic situation and the audience. Although one can laugh *with* someone else, quite often we laugh *at* them. When this latter occurs, a complicity between the person recounting the humorous situation and his listener usually takes place. This is the second movement, which unites teller and audience in a shared pleasure at the discomfort of others, a phenomenon for which the German language has an exact term, *Schadenfreude.* For the most part, this is the form that humor takes in *The Tin Drum.* The reader discovers himself delighting in Oskar's sardonic viewpoints, ironic analyses, and gleeful depictions of human stupidity—a situation compelling readers to acknowledge that their own way of thinking, despite appearances, is not very far removed from that of the bizarre little man with the tin drum.

The reader's uncomfortable position is compounded by Oskar's occasional assertions that his own narrative at times escapes his control: "Oskar hopes to be forgiven for his poetic effects" (251). This creates doubts about the veracity of the narration, a suspicion Oskar confirms when, after his bravura description of the assault on the Polish Post Office, he sums up his accomplishment: "I have just reread the last paragraph. I am not too well satisfied, but Oskar's pen ought to be, for writing tersely and succinctly, it has managed, as terse accounts so often do, to exaggerate and mislead, if not to lie" (246). Oskar not only dismisses one of his account's major passages as a fabrication but even offers a stylistic analysis, stressing terseness and succinctness, which may not at all correspond to his audience's sense of what they just have read.

Oskar at times indulges in a flagrantly awful use of symbolism worthy of Céline, whose purpose is to destabilize the reader. As Matzerath is being machine-gunned while he chokes to death on his Nazi badge, Oskar crushes a louse (394). The juxtaposition of the two events obviously suggests that Oskar considers the shopkeeper to be little more than vermin. That is, of course, not the case, as Oskar's collapse at Matzerath's funeral demonstrates. His attitude toward this one of his putative fathers is much more complicated, and the supposed symbol only simplifies the matter, something that should be apparent to the reader.

Oskar's recourse to literary and religious analogies is also intentionally simplistic. Oskar is no more Jesus than he is Hitler; he is no more Parsifal than Vittlar is either John the Baptist or Judas. Oskar explodes this traditional literary technique toward the end of the novel when he presents the reader with Vittlar as the Snake in Paradise. Vittlar, sitting in a tree, slams home his latest persona: "You might mistake me for the Snake" (562). "Allegorical rubbish," Oskar replies. Of course, these associations are more than that. They have a place in *The Tin Drum;* they are cultural props that are now quite useless but cannot be completely disregarded because of the memories they evoke, just like the old drums Oskar refuses to discard.

During the postwar period Oskar mentions that he always asked Maria to keep his old, broken-down drums (209). They served no purpose, but they were part of his past that he was unable to abandon. Oskar preserves the vestiges of his culture and religion for much the same reasons. Christianity, for example, is a major aspect of his background, and so it is normal that when forced to leave the asylum at age thirty, he should compare himself to Christ. However, if the comparison is inevitable, its only function is to emphasize the disparity between the heroic prototype and his contemporary avatar; difference rather than similarity emerges from the allusion. Christ wanted disciples; Oskar emphatically does not (556). Christ thought in terms of the eternal; Oskar's obsession with his age as he prepares to leave the asylum suggests rather that, like the adults he decried as a youth (67), he too has become a slave to time.

References such as this are part of a heritage that is no longer viable but is not as yet forgotten. They clutter Oskar's intellectual and artistic landscape in much the same way as the Trümmer disfigure the cities of Germany. However, if the Germans are anxious to get rid of the physical rubble and by doing so attempt to minimize the souvenirs of the events that provoked it, Oskar keeps his wreckage before his reader's eyes, as a concrete reminder of what once had force in Western society but is now at best a memory or at worst a source of irony. A reader might debate the merits of Oskar as Hamlet, or Oskar as Yorick, but the possibility of either analogy leading to great new insights seems scarcely promising. What matters and what remains is that with or without literary predecessors, Oskar is a brooding, intelligent clown who turns horror and fear into a form of entertainment that is as disquieting as it is amusing.

Oskar's challenges to his readers are part of his effort to find a means of writing about the experiences not of Everyman but of an intelligent German with "an encyclopedic half-knowledge" (170), someone who has lived through the cataclysmic events of the first half of the twentieth century. A large part of *The Tin Drum* is preoccupied with the question of evolving strategies for writing about the war. As discussed earlier, World War II precipitated a crisis for German artists. The old aesthetic devices no longer seemed appropriate to the postwar world, but it was difficult for artists, young and old, to break with traditions. Oskar's employment as a model for painters and sculptors places him in the center of this controversy. The art teacher, Professor Kuchen—whose name, so close to *Küche* (kitchen) eerily evokes *die schwarzen Köchin*—captures the rhetorical stance of the day: "Art is accusation, expression, passion" (462). This sounds fairly radical, but when Kuchen gets to specifics, his language reflects a nostalgia for the past: "I don't want you to sketch this cripple, this freak of nature, I want you to slaughter him, crucify him, to nail him to your paper with charcoal" (463). Despite the events and revelations of the war years, the professor can still evoke *the* religious prototype, of which Oskar is a sorry deviation, and speak of pain and suffering in the language of the Cross. The war has brought into serious question the notion of "an ideal for humanity" as well as the survival of the Christian message as a moral force in the modern world. Oskar's physical presence, his sexuality, and his attitude toward his fellows all make him a living reproof to the concept of an ideal nature, and a foray he makes into literary parody indicates that he considers Christianity's bequest to the twentieth century to be just so much as yet undiscarded trash.

Oskar admits that his description of the Cristal Night is indebted to Paul's First Epistle to the Corinthians (209). In this letter Paul urged unanimity of opinion among his followers, that they avoid quarreling and trust "not . . . in the wisdom of men but in the power of God" (May and Metzer, *New Oxford Annotated Bible with the Apocrypha*, 1381). Once secure in his faith, the Christian "judges all things, but is himself judged by no one" (1382). The Christian is thus above the secular law that constrains others, and the essence of his religion is force: "For the kingdom of

God does not consist in talk but in power" (1383). The considerations that affect nonbelievers should be of no concern to the faithful because "the wisdom of the world is folly with God" (1383). Replace God with Hitler, and the result is the mindset of the mindless S.A., Nazism's ill-fated predecessors to the S.S., who destroyed the homes, stores, synagogues, and lives of countless German Jews. Paul, like Hitler, was a zealot, intolerant of opposing opinion and animated by the certainty of his convictions. Paul believed he was preparing the world for the Second Coming, just as Hitler thought he was creating a new and purer Germany. Yet just as Hitler was a pathetic individual with delusions of grandeur, for Oskar Paul was never anyone other than Saul, "who told the people of Corinth about some priceless sausages that he called faith, hope and love, which he advertised as easily digestible and which to this day, still Saul though forever changing in form, he palms off on mankind" (205). Oskar's point is not that Christianity has been misunderstood but that it reflects a mentality that has little interest in thinking and questioning. It enjoins its adherents to follow the Leader, and although throughout history the particular identity of both the Leader and his message have changed, the proclivity to follow remains the same and invites disastrous consequences. In the next chapter we meet Abel Tiffauges, who in *The Ogre* provides a fine example of the "follower" mentality and its dire consequences.

Another approach to art that Oskar encounters is embodied in a painter nicknamed Raskolnikov because "he never stopped talking of crime and punishment, guilt and atonement" (472). This man's masterpiece consists of Oskar sitting on a female model's naked thigh; "she was the Madonna while I sat still for Jesus" (472). Raskolnikov, like the art teacher Kuchen and other postwar German artists, addresses the issue of guilt through recourse to Christian iconography. Oskar's approach to religious reference as a literary device is far more modern and original. He says almost nothing about it, because he does not have to. He carries no cross because he already has a burden on his back, and whether his hunchback is a unique reference to Matzerath's death or to the German actions in the war is ultimately irrelevant. As a German who lived through those times, whatever his active participation, the guilt is there, even though some Germans believe they can limit its scope. After the war Oskar becomes a frequent visitor to the British Center where he "discussed collective guilt with Protestants and Catholics alike and shared the guilt feelings of all those who said to themselves: 'Let's do our stint now; when things begin to look up we'll have it over with and our consciences will be all right'" (436). A person can set aside a cross but not the sort of physical deformity Oskar bears. Oskar's approach to war guilt, aside from this ironic description of getting rid of it, is to say almost nothing. The self-evident does not require explanation and the hump he carries for all Germans of that generation does not go away.

Like everything else about him, Oskar's choice of an artistic prototype is irreverent: "your incorrigible partisan, who undermines what he has just set up, is closest to the artist because he consistently rejects what he has just created" (423). Thus Bruno describes "Mr. Matzerath's" artistic philosophy. Oskar realizes that in the modern world all efforts at establishing coherence, while they must be attempted, must also be questioned. This is why when he began his story he discussed how to tell it primarily in terms of fiction. He instinctively knew that he needed a form that could structure his experience without any claims to total truth. Oskar is no Dostoyevskian guilt monger, a neo-Raskolnikov obsessed with crime and punishment, nor is he an Olympian man of letters, a new Thomas Mann, for example; he is a person possessed of "encyclopedic half-knowledge" (170), someone who sees the world and writes about it but without any conviction that either his knowledge or his talent is sufficient to provide the whole picture. He writes for but also against his readers; his aim is reaction, not acquiescence, because the latter only breeds complacency. Writing about the orgy of "guilt for awhile" sweeping postwar Germany, he remarks: "I know that a postwar binge is only a binge and therefore followed by a hangover, and one symptom of this hangover is that the deeds and misdeeds which only yesterday were fresh and alive and real, are reduced to history and explained as such" (436–37).

The image of the partisan is well chosen because the partisan, although opposed to the status quo, is nonetheless a political figure, and in the modern world the fear the Black Cook engenders is profoundly political. The partisan, like the artist, may not always know what is right, but for Oskar he certainly knows what is wrong. Like the partisan, the artist is constantly struggling, against an evil political system when necessary but always against his own limitations. Early in his story he mentions his debt to Rasputin and Goethe: "The conflicting harmony between these two was to shape or influence my whole life, at least what life I have tried to live apart from my drum" (90). As a young man Oskar saw his personality as somehow oscillating between a demonic and a sublime figure. This explanation is as appealing as it is simplistic, yet no more so than trying to see "the German character" imaged in the portraits of Hitler and Beethoven in Matzerath's living room glaring at each other in mutual disapproval. Interestingly enough, it was only when Oskar played his drum, his earlier form of artistic expression, that he escaped this facile dichotomy. Now, in the postwar era, the man and more mature artist Oskar realizes he must abandon the notion of "an oversimplified world evenly divided between Goethe and Rasputin" (436). Oskar can become a more sophisticated reader relatively easily, but creating an art that can reflect and critique the intricacies of the modern world is another matter. Once when Oskar was under a rostrum at a Nazi rally, he compared himself to Jonah but with one big exception: "Oskar was no prophet" (122). The crucial point here is not the allusion to a biblical figure but rather Oskar's awareness of his personal limitations. Oskar knows he is no omniscient artist, but he also understands how easily people permit themselves to be led. Jonah hid from a destiny that he at least knew was divine; Oskar hides in the sanatorium because he is afraid of humans.

Günter Grass once described Oskar as "a converted stylite" ("*The Tin Drum* in Retrospect or the Author as Dubious Witness," in *On Writing and Politics 1967–1983*, 26). By that he meant an ascetic deprived of the pillar that separated and distanced him from others. This is certainly the grim fate that awaits Oskar at the novel's end. The authorities now know that he did not murder Sister Dorothea, and thus he will have to leave the safety of his asylum.

During the war, Oskar's friend Lankes characterized this century as "barbaric, mystical, bored" (337). The barbarism speaks for itself, and the boredom helped create a climate that facilitated the rise of Nazism. The mysticism bespeaks the desire for "quick fixes," for simplistic, ersatz responses to complicated issues. Aside from the obvious example of Hitlerism, all the examples of quick fixes in the novel are not evil. Oskar's uncle, Vincent, defeated the difficulty of living through a lifelong devotion to confirming "the Virgin Mother's claim to the Polish throne" (26). According to Oskar, the Poles in general have found some solace, given the tenuousness of their geographical and political situation, in evoking the protection of Pan Kichot, a Middle-European version of Don

Quixote, whose heroic and romantic cavalry will save them from German tanks (251). Mr. Fajngold, the Polish Jew who takes over Matzerath's store after the latter's demise, maintains his fragile ability to function in the "real" world through a nonstop dialogue with his family members, every one of whom was murdered at Treblinka. Finally, Leo Schugger's passion for funerals may well be a sign of madness, but he shows more sense than the rest of the Germans by running away from Meyn when he sees him decked out in his S.A. uniform.

Evil or benign, mysticism is the order of the day, and Oskar is in the unfortunate position of being able to provide it. There are already the beginnings of a cult called "Oskarism" (556), a term that, like other of the century's grander delusions, is replete with resonance while short on content. Oskar's mystical powers, such as they are, come from his drum. On his drum he can conjure up the hysteria and terror of the past; for the duration of a concert he can provide a cathartic visit with everyone's childhood Black Cook. However, as Oskar himself realizes, the more fearsome manifestation of the Black Cook is in the present. The German past is the past; it will continue to be reexamined, studied, and mourned. The more immediately important question is not what happened then, but can it happen again now?

Oskar discovered during the Cristal Night that behind Santa Claus's mask lurked the face of the gasman, the murderer of millions, and that for human beings it was an easy transition from faith in the former to obedience to the latter. Hitler and his followers are gone, or in the latter instance at least out of power, but for Oskar it remains unclear "who it is nowadays that hides under the beards of the Santa Clauses" and "what Santa Claus has in his sack" (204). What he does know is that anyone with a bit of talent (the stone mason Korneff calls Oskar's hump his "gas meter" [440]) has the potential to become a new Santa in a world that cries out for one (204). Oskar has more than a bit of talent, and although his drum, with its capacity to offer immediate release through return to the past, is his most marketable tool, he has another one as well: his fountain pen. Writing, and the attendant act of reading, are slower processes, but in Oskar's case they provide more profound visions, capable of linking past and present in a sometimes unhappy continuum. Writing is the source of Oskar's genius, the expression of which is not in a musical note but in a book called *The Tin Drum*.

In a television interview Günter Grass reiterated his concern about fear: "We have grounds to be afraid. This fear does not come from our feelings but from our understanding, our reason. On the basis of our reason we must be afraid; however we must also articulate this fear" (Görtz, *Günter Grass,* 46). For Grass this fear is not simply an emotional reaction to events; nor is it merely the anxiety that attends daily living. These relatively normal sources of concern are accentuated by a clearheaded, rational perception of the modern world. Grappling with these myriad forms of fear is no easy matter. It requires the use of the very attributes that perceived it in the first place: thought and imagination. Heinrich Böll once suggested that when the postwar German authors attempt to confront these issues, "Perhaps humor, or cynicism, or irony was generally the only thing that remained to us" (*Eine deutsche Erinnerung,* 102). Certainly *The Tin Drum* provides ample examples of these qualities. And yet what remains for those less gifted artistically but nonetheless sensitive to the omnipresence of fear, one of the more recent incarnations of which concerns the problems raised by the war and the way the past continues to impinge upon the present? It would appear that Grass had these people very much in mind when he ended this interview by urging the television audience not to forgo one of the more pedestrian but, in its modest fashion, effective means of confronting the Black Cook in all her embodiments. His last word is: *Read* (47).

The Ogre: Myth as Fiction, Fiction as Myth

Dr. Otto Essig is a ridiculous figure who would appear to play a minor role in Michel Tournier's *The Ogre* (*Le Roi des aulnes*). He is a benighted scientist (an expert of sorts concerning deer antlers), an inept, albeit assiduous sycophant, and if spent bullets count for anything, a pathetic marksman. Yet—and this *yet* goes to the heart of the novel's central irony, the parody of the personal and political use of myth—an errant round fired by Essig manages to strike and kill Candelabra, the most prized buck in a herd carefully selected and developed for the delight of Hermann Göring. How does Dr. Essig accomplish such a feat? His success is due to chance, to stupid blind luck, which for a moment at least makes a champion of a fool. This scene stands practically at the midpoint in the novel, bracketed between Abel Tiffauges' incessant musings on his mythic destiny and the equally imaginative examples of Nazi racial theorizing.

The very first pages of *The Ogre* invite the reader into a mythic universe, replete with mystery and allegedly profound truths:

I do think there's something magical about me, I do think there is a secret collusion, deep down, connecting what happens to me with what happens in general, and enabling my particular history to bend the course of things in its own direction. . . . I do believe I issued from the mists of time. . . . The dizzying antiquity of my origins explains my supernatural power. . . . Old as the world, and as immortal, I have none but putative parents and adopted children. (*The Ogre*, 3–4)

Myth may well be eternal, but one hopes that so too is the memory of Auschwitz. The juxtaposition in *The Ogre* of Abel Tiffauges' mythic musings with the story of his life—which details a bizarre interest in carrying little boys on his shoulders, an obsession with cosmic signs he is forever finding around him, and ultimately collaboration with the Nazis—makes for strange and troubling reading. Jean Améry ("Aesthetics of Barbarism") and Saul Friedländer (*Reflections of Nazism*) were troubled enough by the novel to suggest that it constituted an implicit defense of Nazism, and while this charge has been denied by others, including Tournier himself, the aesthetic dimension of *The Ogre* cannot be studied in isolation from the ethical questions it raises. One cannot divorce a fascination with Abel's conviction that one day "I . . . will spread the great wings I keep under my garage owner's disguise and . . . fly among the stars" (32) from a very exact awareness of what he does while still on earth.

A powerful sense of quotidian reality pervades Michael Worton's incisive account of the workings of myth in *The Ogre*. Worton focuses upon Abel Tiffauges' highly selective use of myth: "Most of the evocations are of but one aspect of various mythic figures" ("Myth-Reference," 300). Abel chooses the part of the mythic prototype he wants, when and where he wants it; he distorts the mythic figure to suit his purposes. At the same time, this arbitrary recourse to myth is constantly offset, as Worton emphasizes, by the novel's meticulous attention to historical detail, which works against the mythmaking process. Abel Tiffauges' selective use of myth, as well as his refusal to confront directly the historical situation in which he finds himself, are both typical of a mentality that Roland Barthes ascribes to the bourgeoisie.

In his *Writing Degree Zero,* Barthes remarks that "it is where History is denied that it is most unmistakably at work" (2). His subject here is literary language, but later he was to apply his thesis that history cannot be denied to what is often considered the most ahistorical of phenomena, the world of myth. In *Mythologies,* and specifically in the essay, "Myth Today," Barthes offers a theory of the structure of myth and its relationship to social class, a theory that proves extremely germane to the workings of myth in *The Ogre.*

One day Barthes is sitting in a barbershop when someone gives him a copy of *Paris-Match.* On the cover is a photo of a black African soldier saluting the French flag. Using ideas borrowed from Saussure's semiological system, Barthes exposes the mythic subtext contained within this seemingly innocuous picture.

As Barthes explains it, for Saussure language (*langue*) is divided into three elements. The *signifier* is the acoustic image, which is mental; the *signified* is the concept, and the *sign* is the relation between the concept and the image (the word, for instance), which is a concrete entity ("Myth Today," 113). With regard to myth Barthes calls this semiological structuration "the *object-language* because it is the language which myth gets hold of in order to build its own system" (115, emphasis in text). Myth itself is "*metalanguage,* because it is a second language, *in which* one speaks about the first" (115, emphasis in text). Metalanguage takes the literal meaning of "object-language" and builds its mythic significance upon this. Barthes clarifies this distinction by slightly altering the terminology. In myth the signifier becomes the form, the signified remains the concept, and the sign becomes the signification.

Turning back to the photo, the form is the black soldier saluting; the concept is something akin to everyone is equal and loyal in the French empire, regardless of color; and the signification is the presence of the concept through the form (116). What is implicit in this analysis of the photo is that the myth it projects is false but also powerful, because it reassures and justifies a social group disinterested in exploring the reality of French colonialism.

The function of the form, as Barthes explains it, is not to deny literal meaning—that is, that the black soldier is a black soldier—but to hold that meaning in abeyance: "The form does not suppress meaning, it only impoverishes it, it puts it at a distance" (118). When signifier becomes form, the literal meaning becomes less important; the soldier as an individual, isolated entity who may have very personal reasons for doing what he does (patriotism, professional advancement, a delight in being photographed, etc.), is no longer the focus of attention.

The concept, for its part, has little use for anything unique or personal about the form—that is, in this instance, the soldier. It replaces his particular history, "which drains out of the form" (118), and creates "a whole new history which is implanted in the myth" (119). The concept contains knowledge but of a special sort. It is "confused, made of yielding, shapeless associations . . . it is not at all an abstract, purified essence; it is a formless, unstable nebulous condensation, whose unity and coherence are above all due to its function" (119). Barthes insists that "the fundamental character of the mythical concept is to be *appropriated*" (119, emphasis in text); the concept derived from the form serves to fulfill a particular function. In the case of the soldier the concept becomes a justification of French imperialism.

In the correlation between the form and the concept, the two entities are at once independent and associated: "However paradoxical it may seem, *myth hides nothing:* its function is to distort, not to make disappear" (121, emphasis in text). This means that the form and concept have a constantly shifting relationship; depending upon the mythmaker's needs, the form can cease to be a mythic form and can function simply as a word or an object. Thus, when circumstances so demand, the black soldier is merely a black soldier. Should this occur, the concept disappears. However, in different circumstances the form can reassume its function and the mythic process reconstitutes itself, thereby making the black soldier saluting the flag a symbol of France's supposed lack of racism. In *The Ogre* tanks appear on several occasions. Depending upon Abel's state of mind, they can merely be tanks or be examples of "*the overturning of the phoria by malign inversion*" (292, emphasis in text).

Just as in Saussure's system the third term (the sign) is merely the synthesis of the first two, in the mythic framework "the signification is the myth itself" (121); the myth is the end product of the union of the form and the concept. However, since myth is a double system that builds its metalanguage meaning on object-language, the possibility always exists that this metalanguage can be disassociated from object-language and then reassociated with it according to whether a "mythic" significance is needed: "The signification of myth is constituted by a sort of constantly moving turnstile which presents alternatively the meaning of the signifier and its form, an object-language and a metalanguage, a purely signifying and a purely imagining consciousness. This alternation is . . . gathered up in the concept, which uses it like an ambiguous signifier, at once intellective and imaginary, arbitrary and natural" (123). In short, myth comes into being when the mythmaker requires it.

At this point Barthes touches upon the moral implications of the mythic mechanism and compares myth to a limitless alibi: "Myth is a value, truth is no guarantee for it; nothing prevents it from being a perpetual alibi. . . . The meaning is always there to *present* the form; the form is always there to *outdistance* the meaning. . . . There never is any contradiction, conflict, or split between the meaning and the form: they are never at the same place" (123, emphasis in text). Barthes illustrates this point through the analogy of his looking out of a car window. Depending upon his focus, he can see either the passing landscape or the window pane. There is a remarkably similar situation in *The Ogre*. Abel is staring out of a casement window at the German landscape. Initially all he notices are scenes of daily life, "a bit of road . . . an old woman pulling a baby along on a sled" (179), but the vividness of these images arouses his mythic consciousness, and suddenly: "Now he knew what it was he had come to see so far to the northeast: in the cold and penetrating hyperborean light, all symbols shone with unparalleled brilliance" (179). Part of the enormous appeal of myth for Abel Tiffauges is that it permits him to pass at will from object-language to metalanguage.

Barthes maintains that myth is "defined by its intention"—justification of French imperialism—much more than by its "literal sense"—the black soldier saluting (124). Yet the literal sense is always there and constitutes a challenge to the myth. For this reason myth must have an "imperative, buttonholing character" (124) that forces its presence and meaning upon the audience. Whereas in a language the sign is arbitrary, "nothing compels the acoustic image *tree* 'naturally' to mean the concept *tree*" (126, emphasis in text); the mythical signification, at least to someone like Abel, is never arbitrary (126). Its meaning is motivated in accordance with the requirements of the mythmaker.

For Roland Barthes myth is a complicated and volatile structure in which the mythic level is grafted onto the literal and can be replaced by the latter according to the whim of the mythmaker. Barthes' form, which is the myth's first stage, always has the possibility of being downgraded to the purely literal level, should circumstances so require. The African military man as a triumphant example of France's beneficent imperialism always has the potential to revert to being a black guy with a gun. Myth therefore demands a certain collusion with its inventor, an all too willing suspension of disbelief, if it is to be effective. The mythmaker invents the signification by supplying the appropriate content to the form and the concept. This understanding of myth, which emphasizes human rather than divine origins while accounting at the same time for myth's manipulative aspects, helps expose Abel Tiffauges' cosmic aspirations for the self-deceptions they are.

There are numerous mythic figures mentioned in *The Ogre* (Nestor, St. Christopher, Telamon) as well as geographic locations invested with mythic import (Canada, Germany), but the principal mythic referent in the novel, the one that dominates the others, is the phoria.

On a literal level the phoria is anodyne enough to figure in a Hallmark card: it involves a man carrying a child, usually but not always on his shoulders. However, as Abel describes it, this otherwise innocuous experience seems to be sexual in nature: "It was then something swooped down on me of unbearable and heart-rending sweetness. I was struck by a bolt of benediction from on high. My eyes fixed on the limp body in my arms, on one side the gaunt bloodstained face under its tufts of brown hair, and on the other the thin pair of knees and the heavy boots dangling clumsily in the air. . . . 'I'd never have believed,' I said, 'that to carry a child was such a wonderful thing!'" (78–79).

In saying that the phoria seems to be of a sexual nature, I am not indulging in some form of discretion through avoidance. Whatever the erotic or emotional implications of the phoria, they are never made clear. Nevertheless, the meaning of Abel's existence is inextricably tied up, at least in his own mind, with the significance of the phoria, and it is precisely this meaning that his mythic meanderings only serve to obscure. In *The Ogre* it is less important to know that the phoria is highly erotically charged than to realize that the mythic connotations Abel ascribes to it only obfuscate whatever the phoria might mean. Abel's musings about the phoria constitute the most bizarre yet telling example in the novel of his penchant for avoiding, through his deployment of myth, the attempt at either concrete knowledge of his surroundings or self-knowledge.

Abel's sex life certainly does not resemble anything that passes for standard practices in a Hollywood movie. His girlfriend, Rachel, who calls him "an ogre" (3), claims he makes love like a "like a canary" (7); he mentions on several occasions that he has an abnormally small phallus, and when he was a schoolboy, licking another boy's cut knee provoked an orgasm, "I was seized with a fit of shuddering, convulsions even" (15), which he later realized he liked (348). However different this combination of attitudes and attributes makes Abel, they do not in themselves *explain* either his actions or his identity. Yet coupled with his opaque, mythic explanations of the phoria, his personal, obscurely described sexuality enhances the ominous aura he creates around himself. Abel confronts his sexuality as obliquely as he confronts the phoria, and yet, given the evidence the novel provides, to explain and dismiss him as some sort of sexual pervert is to indulge in a form of totalizing mythmaking worthy of Abel himself.

In the mythic schema the act of carrying a child becomes the form to which Abel quickly adds the concept: "a shaft of light suddenly falls on my past, present and, who knows, perhaps my future. For the fundamental idea of portage, of *phoria,* is also found in the name of Christopher, the giant Child-Bearer; . . . and yet again it is embodied in the cars to which I reluctantly give the best of myself, but which even in their triviality are nonetheless instruments for the bearing of men, anthropomorphic and therefore *phoric* par excellence. . . . This series of revelations is making my eyes smart" (80).

In a manner that conforms to Barthes' explanation of the concept, the knowledge here is confused. Something significant appears to have been said, but what it is remains unclear. For example, what does one learn from the "revelation" that St. Christopher and automobiles have carried children? That Abel Tiffauges is a motorized saint? Subsequent associations of Abel with moving vehicles strongly suggest otherwise. In any case the carrying of the child is always present, but its precise meaning is deformed by the process of mythmaking. The concept's "unity and coherence," which is "due to its function" (Barthes, *Writing,* 119), exists in Abel's mind only when the myth's purpose is to exalt the cosmic at the expense of the concrete. The carrying of the child and its clear sexual overtones are not hidden, but just what is revealed remains moot.

The signification is the phoria itself. The turnstile effect Barthes describes is always there, since on one level all Abel does is carry boys, but as the novel progresses, the notion of "alibi" becomes increasingly important. As Abel rides through the Prussian countryside requisitioning boys for the Nazi training school, the *napola,* he imagines himself fulfilling his vaguely articulated destiny. In fact he is participating in the collection of cannon fodder for Hitler's war machine. Abel is aware of this, but none-theless allows his "phoric" obligation to obscure a true sense of what he is doing. The greater significance of his activities constantly "outdistances" the literal import of his hunting boys. As the Reich collapses, his searches become more frenzied in much the same way as the Nazis redoubled the slaughtering of Jews as the war came to an end. The "imperative" of his mythic destiny parallels the Nazi madness.

This occurs despite ample warnings of the terrible error Abel is making. At one point the Nazi chief of the napola, Stefan Raufeisen, discusses tanks with his young charges: "A tank is deaf and half blind" (341). This instrument of destruction, one of the main causes of the boys' deaths when the Russians arrive at the napola, has a quite personal parallel with Abel himself, who, as he explained earlier, is "slightly deaf, slightly short-sighted" (21). In addition the tank, which carries children on its back, is a mirror image of Abel, the boy bearer. Ostensibly a great decipherer of signs, Abel fails to make these obvious connections.

The tank also provides an example of myth's ability to obscure in the guise of clarifying. Abel is troubled to see the boys riding on the tanks as if they were toys. In his system, children should carry toys, but here it would appear that the toys are carrying the children. This enigma, how-ever, is quickly resolved by applying a new concept to the form of carry-ing: "I now touch for the first time on what is probably a phenomenon of the first importance: *the overturning of the phoria by malign inversion*" (292, emphasis in text). The malign inversion is the opposite of the be-nign inversion, which "consists in re-establishing the meaning of the val-ues that malign inversion has previously overturned" (74). Even though the two concepts are at antipodes, they are related and hence part of the same system. Myth may occasionally falter, but it can always adjust.

Myth is Abel's most precious tool, and that is the reason he can survive any confrontation with truth. The self-evident means practically nothing to him. When Abel picks up the body of a boy killed by a mine, he experiences "phoric ecstasy" (344) while noting that the "headless body weighed three or four times its live weight" (344). This, of course, is an allusion to one of Tiffauges' alter egos, St. Christopher, who staggered under the increasing heaviness when carrying the Child Jesus across a stream. But Christopher's efforts led to his exaltation and salvation. Eventually his soul rose to heaven. Abel's fate is the contrary; at the novel's end, after having contributed to the deaths of hundreds of boys, he sinks into the mud.

In the final pages of *The Ogre* Abel's mythic universe would appear to dissolve. He discovers, through the revelations of a Jewish boy, the full horror of the Nazi experience. He learns, among other things, that his mythical Canada has its equivalent in the Reich. Canada is the name given to the treasure house at Auschwitz where the Nazis stored the belongings of murdered Jews. The slang name for Auschwitz, Anus Mundi, likewise provides a bitter commentary on and corrective to his own musings about the anal personality he had associated both with horses and himself. The Germany he claimed to understand so well turns out to be quite different from what he had imagined. Reality contradicts Abel Tiffauges on every level, but contradiction is no obstacle to myth, and as Colin Davis indicates, there is nothing about the novel's end to suggest that Abel has abandoned his mythmaking. Commenting on Abel's rather confused lumping together of gypsies and Jews, and his seeing himself as an Abel set off against the Nazi Cains, Davis remarks: "The assertion of mythological fraternity between Jew and gypsy is at best problematical, at worst nonsense; and the invocation of Cain and Abel is of little help in explaining the historical circumstances which made the death camps possible. . . . Myth provides a powerful means of making sense; but here as elsewhere . . . Tiffauges's mythological grid seems inadequate to his historical material" (*Michel Tournier*, 48).

Abel's mythological grid is inadequate because it is much more rooted in his social origins than he wishes to believe. His mother was a gypsy (31), but that fact has no interest for him; "I never had the curiosity to look into her family background" (31). His father is a greater, if negative influence. A "cold, taciturn presence" (64), incapable of expressing emotion, he embodies at least one trait of France's petite bourgeoisie to the point of caricature. A classic quarrel with his brother over money results in neither sibling having spoken to the other in years, and when the uncle hires Abel, "The warmth of his welcome owed something to his desire to annoy my father" (64).

Abel's attitude toward his girlfriend, Rachel, "that little Hebrew shepherd's head" (8), reflects the passive anti-Semitism of his social class: "She was a Jewess, and I had occasion to notice that all her clients were Jewish too; the explanation being the confidential nature of the documents she dealt with" (7).

In a similar mode, the "Sinister Constitution" that vilifies the abuses of power by the clergy and government officials (72–74) reflects the anger and helplessness of a petit bourgeois social class that exists on the edge of power, pays society's bills, but rarely reaps the benefits for all its sacrifices.

Perhaps more than anything else, Abel's willingness to be led marks him as a member of a social group who know, consciously or unconsciously, that their role is to follow. Following characterizes Abel's activities throughout the novel. Initially Abel follows Nestor, his mentor at the conveniently named school, St. Christopher. He follows Mme Eugénie to witness the ghastly execution of Franz Weidmann, and he docilely marches off to war, mindless of the issues involved. In Germany he follows his German captors and ultimately the orders he receives from the Nazis in the napola. Of course, all of these examples can be explained away as part of his mythic journey of self-discovery; but, the mythic framework aside, what Abel most often does is just what he is told to do.

Although Abel Tiffauges displays traits typical of a subset of a specific social class, the bourgeoisie, he remains largely oblivious to any class identity. For Roland Barthes this lack of class consciousness bespeaks the triumph of the bourgeoisie in France, a class whose influence and values are so pervasive that even those like Abel who believe themselves in opposition to the status quo nonetheless reflect, at times in parodied form, the values of "their betters."

Principal among these values is the transformation of the historical and contingent into the eternal and unchangeable: "The status of the bourgeoisie is particular, historical: man as represented by it is eternal. The bourgeois class has precisely built its power on technical, scientific progress, on an unlimited transformation of nature: bourgeois ideology yields in return an unchangeable nature" (Barthes, *Writing,* 141–42). Despite its posturings of opposition, the petite bourgeoisie, according to Barthes, is really no different because it too accepts "the immobility of Nature" (149). Abel Tiffauges reflects the confusion typical of the lower middle class by changing what is historical and contingent into what is natural and eternal.

Barthes describes the social conflict between the oppressed and the oppressor in terms of language: "The oppressed *makes* the world, he has only an active, transitive (political) language; the oppressor conserves it, his language is plenary, intransitive, gestural, theatrical: it is Myth. The language of the former aims at transforming, of the latter at eternalizing" (149). From this perspective, Abel, despite his claims to the contrary, is clearly not among the oppressors. His language and actions constantly eschew the concrete and the political for the mythic and eternal. His lack of self-knowledge is such that he transforms the reality of his social inferiority into a myth of cosmic superiority.

Barthes believes he can sketch the rhetorical forms of bourgeois myth. Of the seven figures he mentions, with some modifications at least six provide a remarkable reflection of Abel's behavioral patterns. The first he calls *inoculation,* which "consists in admitting the accidental evil of a class-bound institution the better to conceal its principal evil" (150). Abel's recourse to inoculation is particularly apparent when he is a prisoner of war. He excoriates the Nazi scientists, Göring, the Reich, and the ideology of the napola, but by doing so he creates the impression that despite his collaboration with the Nazi war effort, somehow he is not part of what these people and institutions are doing. The very contempt he voices serves to lessen his sense of his own involvement. Also, the distancing he hopes to achieve through expressions of scorn only hide, from himself at least, his begrudging admiration. When he first arrives at Rominten, for example, he thinks "he is entering a magic circle as the protégé of a magician who, though minor, was recognized by the spirits of the place" (195–96). Hermann Göring is the magician.

The second figure is *the privation of History:* "In it, history evaporates. It is a beautiful servant: it prepares all things, brings them, lays them out, the master arrives, it silently disappears: all that is left for one to do is to enjoy the beautiful object without wondering where it comes from. Or even better, it can only come from eternity" (*Writing,* 151). History as the daily unfolding of events that must be dealt with in their particularities is a source of annoyance to Abel. His work is not that of a humble car mechanic or an obscure French citizen. His true vocation is to be like his friend Nestor, a decipherer of signs, since "all is sign." (5). History as such does not matter; it is merely the vehicle through which the eternal reveals the destiny awaiting Abel Tiffauges.

Barthes offers the following description of *identification:* "The petit bourgeois is a man unable to imagine the Other. If he comes face to face with him, he blinds himself, ignores and denies him, or else transforms him into himself. . . . How can one assimilate the Negro, the Russian? There is a figure for emergencies: exoticism. The Other becomes a pure object, a spectacle, a clown. Relegated to the confines of humanity, he no longer threatens the security of the home" (*Writing,* 151–52). The Other is strange and different, someone whose similarity with oneself is denied or severely qualified. To the extent that the Other is at all like oneself, it is only as a caricature: a spectacle or a clown. Abel Tiffauges, whose myopia is figurative as well as literal, attempts to enact this denial by distancing himself from the Nazis around him. Yet quite aside from the obvious, albeit partial, similarities between Abel and Göring and Dr. Blaettchen, the Nazi doctor who experiments on the bodies of Jews and Communists, another character, whom Abel hates, is a near perfect image of the Frenchman.

About two thirds of the way through the novel there is a curious section where the narrative appears to come to a halt, and the commander of the napola, Stefan Raufeisen, tells the story of his childhood, youth, and eventual adherence to the Nazi Party. Like Tiffauges, Raufeisen comes from a lower-middle-class family. Although he becomes a butcher like his father (Abel followed his father's profession as well), Raufeisen claims, as does Tiffauges, to reject the values of his class: "We threw back into our fathers' faces the sordid heritage they were trying to fasten on us" (268). He joined a hiking club, the *Wandervögel,* "a sort of freemasonry of the young" (269) that lacked any coherent ideology; "we understood one another too well to need a doctrine" (269). This looseknit organization was soon absorbed by a Nazi youth group, the "League of Vagabonds," which "possessed . . . a revolutionary strength that directly threatened the social edifice" (269).

Raufeisen bonds with other boys who share the dissatisfaction typical of the generation coming of age in Germany after the defeat in World War I. This is initially not Abel's situation. In Paris he was a loner and an outsider, whose dissatisfaction had vaguer causes and took no overtly political form. At the end of the first war France experienced no comparable upheaval, and hence the political and social climate was considerably less conducive to Fascist mass movements, although such groups existed. In the post–World War I setting France's extreme right certainly did its best to exploit dissatisfaction and create unrest, but the political vacuum was never so great in France as in Germany. The situation changes for Abel, and brings him physically and mentally closer to Raufeisen, when France's defeat sends him into Germany, where he eventually becomes the head of what amounts to a youth movement in the napola.

The cathartic moment occurred for the young Stefan Raufeisen on October 1, 1932, which was the date of the first Nazi youth rally at Potsdam. Amidst parades and banners, he and his fellows pledged their fidelity to the Führer. Significantly, Hitler was not present at the event; he was the unseen, omniscient presence, hovering over his minions, who promised to pursue his policies to the death.

Nestor played a similar role for Abel. Although not another Hitler, Nestor was a cipher, given to gnomic utterances—"Alpha and omega must be linked with one stroke" (35)—that Abel invested with mythic significance. When Raufeisen and his friends dedicated their lives to the service of the Führer, Hitler was still four months removed from power, and his blustering speeches hardly conveyed the full weight of his future policies. In death Nestor becomes Abel's invisible but guiding presence, whose larger than life existence outside of time gives meaning to Abel's activities. Stefan Raufeisen, far from being the Other detested by Abel Tiffauges, is nothing less than a slightly parodic form of the Frenchman.

Tautology, "this verbal device which consists in defining like by like (*Drama is drama*)" (Barthes, *Writing*, 152) is another rhetorical form of bourgeois myth. In its pristine form it cannot be found in *The Ogre*, but its near equivalent crops up in phrases like "the *overturning of the phoria by malign inversion*," which Abel utters, as previously noted, when he sees boys riding tanks. Abel must maintain the phoria as something good, yet what he sees is bad. Rather than accept the simple fact that there is something wrong with his notion of inversion, he creates another concept, the malign inversion, as an evil counterweight to the benign inversion. This permits him to maintain that the phoria is still the phoria—that is, something good—even if circumstances suggest that for the moment it is not.

The value in mentioning potentially tautological elements in Abel's language is that they highlight the self-enclosed verbal as well as mythological universe in which he lives. He cannot be wrong; everything he says and does must be right: "one takes refuge in tautology . . . when one is at a loss for an explanation" (Barthes, *Writing,* 152). Abel's openness to signs, for example, is merely another way of supplying confirmation for what he wants to believe. In his own view his world is replete with great and startling truths, but unbeknownst to Abel, these truths can only be found at the expense of knowledge. As Barthes puts it: "In tautology, . . . one kills rationality because it resists one" (152).

Closely associated with the tautological aspect of Tiffauges' thinking is his susceptibility to what Barthes calls the *statement of fact:* "Myths tend toward proverbs. Bourgeois ideology invests in this figure interests which are bound to its very essence: universalism, the refusal of any explanation, an unalterable hierarchy of the world" (154). Abel scorns the banal yet complex reality of everyday life in France and prefers instead Germany: "A black and white country . . . a white page covered with black signs" (167). He is more at ease in Nazi Germany because "here I'm always face to face with a *significant reality* which is almost always clear and distinct; or when it does become difficult to read, that's because it's growing more profound and only losing in obviousness what it gains in richness" (260–61, emphasis in text). Such a statement, a simplistic and silly opinion for the uninitiated, is a statement of fact for Abel. It is an arbitrary assemblage of wild conjectures elevated by the speaker to the level of truth.

Early in the novel Abel somewhat sententiously remarks: "Now I know that any human face, however vile, becomes the face of Christ when struck" (26). This pronouncement has the ring of a statement of fact, something eternally true. Yet at the novel's end both the factualness and the eternity of the statement are severely tested when Abel encounters Stefan Raufeisen for the last time. The Nazi officer has been severely beaten by Russian soldiers: "A push sent him flying nearer, and for a moment Tiffauges saw turned toward him a swollen face with one eye running down the cheek in a mixture of blood and aqueous humor. He recognized Raufeisen" (367). It would take an imagination greater even than Tiffauges' to see in the brutalized face of the S.S. commandant of the napola the image of Christ.

Abel Tiffauges prefers quantity over quality. In this respect he illustrates the rhetorical form Barthes calls the *quantification of quality,* which involves "reducing any quality to a quantity" (*Writing,* 153). Abel quantifies little boys: "To have only one child is not to have any. To lack one is to lack them all" (87). His love of photographing children is part of his collector's mania: "Each photograph raises its subject to a degree of abstraction that automatically confers on it all its generality, so that every child photographed is a thousand children possessed" (104). The ultimate quantifying occurs in the napola, where Abel, assuming the role of the departed Dr. Blaettchen, compiles elaborate lists of the boys' physical traits.

Abel's obsession with quantity, like most of his obsessions, has a parallel with a Nazi mania. At the forest retreat in Rominten, Abel witnesses Göring's brutal rabbit hunt, which culminates in the apotheosis of the Reich's minister: "Alone in the middle of this cemetery of softness, Göring, crowned king of the hunt by virtue of his bag of two hundred, posed for his official photographer, belly outthrust, field marshal's baton held aloft in his right hand" (228–29). Throughout *The Ogre,* the slaughter and brutalizing of animals are obvious symbols for the effect of war on human beings. Göring kills many animals needlessly, for sheer pleasure; Abel does not. When he leads the boys in the napola on a rabbit hunt, it is for food. However, at the end of the novel the boys Abel has so carefully collected and quantified assume the role the rabbits played in the forest of Rominten: they become the victims of a pointless slaughter at the hands of the Russians.

In *The Ogre* Abel's mythic consciousness had as little origin in the mists of time as the Third Reich had any serious antecedents in German history. Both are concoctions that reflect in varying degrees social class, personal frustrations, and imaginations unfettered by large doses of knowledge or rationality. However, the Nazis and Abel were both creators of sorts; Abel created a mythic universe with himself at the center, and the Nazis rearranged the past and invented a thousand-year future in which the mythical, Aryan race was intended to become the culmination of Western history. What characterizes the Nazi mentality, as well as Abel's own, is the conviction that what they do is part of an inevitable destiny, where nothing happens by chance.

There is, of course, a vast difference between the individual Tiffauges and the Nazi political and military organization. In normal times Abel Tiffauges' otherwise insignificant existence would have been shattered by the unfounded charge of molesting a little girl. He doubtless would have spent the rest of his days in prison, comforted only by his delusions of grandeur. The war changed all that; it permitted an obscure car mechanic, whose fantasies concerning his hidden destiny were probably not so different from those of many others, to act out his confused and dangerous dreams.

The analogy between Abel Tiffauges and the fifteenth-century mass murderer of children Gilles de Rais, whose castle was named Tiffauges, has often been discussed.[1] More than similarities in names and physiques, what these two figures have in common is the experience of war. In his *Gilles de Rais,* Michel Bataille observes that "in peacetime Gilles would never have had the chance to discover, would never have had the chance to realize, that he had a taste for flowing blood. The war revealed it to him" (189). Abel's situation is comparable. Without World War II, he might have remained nothing other than a frustrated petit bourgeois whose mythic musings would rarely or never have extended beyond the limits of his mind. What freed Abel Tiffauges to become the "ogre of Kaltenborn" was no call of destiny; it was the Nazi war machine.

Abel Tiffauges is capable of two sorts of writing: "one that is 'adroit,' pleasant, social, commercial, reflecting the masked character I pretend to be in the eyes of society; and one that is 'sinister,' distorted by all the 'gaucheness' of genius, full of flashes and cries—in short, inhabited by the spirit of Nestor" (30). Obviously, for Abel his true writing is the "sinister" writing. It is in the sinister writing that he exposes his mythic past and future and maintains that everything that occurs is inevitable and meaningful. However, the thoughts he confides to his secret journal never delve deeply into the possible significance of the phoria; he describes its pleasurable effects but never its implications. Only in the final passages does he begin to discover the sexual aspects of his licking a boy's cut knee, and nowhere in the journal does he assess in any detail the terrible parallel between his own activities and those of the Nazis.

Although Abel's reflections dominate the novel, there is a second narrative voice that offers a perspective lacking in Abel's account. This other voice, a third-person narrative, begins with Abel's mobilization at the beginning of the war. On a structural level, this second voice can appear to be a practical necessity, a means by which the novelist can convey information that the journal could never provide. However, with the exception of Abel's death and the events immediately surrounding it, the third-person narrative offers nothing that could not be placed in the journal.

At first this other voice does little except fill in background and record the thoughts that pass through Abel's head. However, as Tiffauges becomes more and more deeply enmeshed in his mythmaking, the second narrative becomes more ironic, implicitly contrasting Abel's mythic viewpoint with a more down-to-earth perspective: "Germany was always in danger of becoming a theater of grimace and caricature, as demonstrated by her army, a fine collection of gargoyles, from the oxlike sergeant major to the corseted and monocled officer. But for Tiffauges, for whom the heavens, studded with allegories and hieroglyphs, resounded constantly with dim voices and enigmatic cries, Germany was revealing itself as a promised land, the land of pure essences" (179–80).

Irony passes to overt criticism as the deterioration of the Reich and the arrest of the old Count of Kaltenborn give Abel freer rein to act out his fantasies: "Once the old man had gone, Tiffauges gave himself up to the instinct for power, sometimes with farfetched subtleties, as shown in his 'Sinister Writings'" (317).

At the novel's end, the second narrative becomes once again ironic but of the bitterest sort. The revelations of the Jewish boy, Ephraim, concerning Auschwitz ought to have turned Abel's mythic universe on its head. Nevertheless, rather than accepting his own errors, his own collusion with the Nazis, he ponders the destruction of the sons of Abel, "the brothers he felt so close to in heart and soul" (357) by the jackbooted Cains. The narrative comment "The Tiffaugean deduction of the death camps had been achieved" (357) speaks volumes for Abel's inability to assess the self-evident.

As Abel attempts to escape from the besieged *napola* with Ephraim he hears "the cry" (366). For Tiffauges, "he knew he was hearing for the first time in its primitive form the clamor suspended between life and death which was the fundamental sound of his whole destiny" (366). In fact he was hearing the cry of three boys being impaled by the Russians. Abel has heard a similar cry throughout his life. Some instances he mentions in his sinister writings (the shouts that greeted Weidmann's execution, the scream of the little girl being raped), and some are mentioned in the second narrative (the noise of the diving bomber, the shrieks of the deer being slaughtered), and taken together they constitute a pattern more apparent to the reader than to Tiffauges. These are cries of bloodlust and death, the screams of victimizers and victims. Abel cannot make so obvious an association; his commitment to mythic meaning forces him into grandiose and vague conclusions.

Abel's account of his life in his sinister writings gives the impression that he has two identities, the real and the apparent. The real is the ogre from the mists of time and the apparent is the garage mechanic, whose social class and some of whose social attitudes I have here described. There is, however, a third identity, which he terms "the viscous self": "It never understands anything at first. It is a heavy, rancorous, moody self, always weltering in tears and semen, obstinately attached to its habits and its past. . . . I carry it deep inside me like a wound, this innocent and tender being, slightly deaf, slightly shortsighted, so easily taken in, so slow to muster itself against misfortune" (21). This description, with its mixture of real physical traits (deafness, myopia) and equally genuine personal insecurities, is Abel Tiffauges as he would have hated to be seen: as Everyman, a being replete with insecurities and longing for recognition and love. This is the starting point of any human being's effort at personal definition; it is the amorphous substance onto which everyone imposes a frame that will constitute social identity. Abel dealt with this crisis as many people do: badly. It was lingering class values, a refusal to confront the nature of his own desires, and sadly fortuitous political circumstances that led him from St. Christopher's to Kaltenborn. As with many of his generation, particularly in Germany, the Myth he thought he was pursuing turned out to be indeed a myth.

Recapturing the "Deluded Years":
Siegfried Lenz's *The German Lesson*

9 About midway through *Deutschstunde* (*The German Lesson*), the art critic Brent Maltzahn pays an unexpected visit to the painter Max Ludwig Nansen in the latter's studio in the little village of Rugbüll. During the war Maltzahn had written for the Nazi art journal *Art and the People,* in the pages of which he had attacked Nansen's work as a "chamber of horrors" (343). The painter is understandably vexed by the critic's unwanted arrival, but Maltzahn's aim, as he explains to Nansen, is reconciliatory. The critic's earlier work, much to his amazement, had been misunderstood. While of course he did describe Nansen's canvases as "a witches' sabbath in paint" (345), the thrust of his extremely subtle argument had escaped most people, including the painter himself:

But had it not been obvious what he had meant by it? Whom he had been attacking? The sentence as a whole read: "We are surrounded by a witches' sabbath in paint." "We are surrounded"—surely that was clear enough. What he had meant by witches' sabbath was what was going on around one. Nansen had found his own way of depicting that political witches' sabbath. And what he, Maltzahn, had set out to do was to indicate the relationship between the external world and the world of paint—by implication, of course, in discreet ambiguity (345).

Maltzahn characterizes the Nazi era as the "deluded years" (343), a period of admittedly unfortunate personal and social consequences, but one that is very much in the past and as such must be moved beyond. To judge from *The German Lesson,* Siegfried Lenz, like Nansen, does not share the art critic's viewpoint, and in what is arguably the finest German novel about World War II, he sets himself the task of examining these deluded years, not just for what they meant then but for the myriad ways they continue to impinge upon the present.

The German Lesson is Siegfried Lenz's most popular and critically discussed novel. First published in 1968, it had sold 8,500,000 copies in West Germany by 1974 and "nearly two million in the USSR" (Schwarz, *Der Erzähler Siegfried Lenz,* 73). This was an impressive achievement for a novel that purported to be serious, yet the critical response to *The German Lesson* was quite varied and often reflected the political orientation of the commentators. A Marxist critic, Theo Elm, decried the alleged absence of a forceful social commitment and ascribed this weakness to Lenz's "neutrality" (*Siegfried Lenz,* 14). In a chapter entitled "Local Color Instead of Social Criticism," the same author lamented that "the relation between the German petite bourgeoisie and its authoritarian rule, which is no less petite bourgeoise, is scarcely depicted in the text: on the contrary the typical German Philistine . . . is covered over with individual, personal characteristics" (52). A fellow Marxist, Wolfgang Beutin, added that "*The German Lesson* remains apparently still overpowered by the German past. This explains the publication's success" (*Deutschstunde von Siegfried Lenz, Eine Kritik,* 6). For Beutin the novel was a success because it was, in the eyes of the general public, "safe."

Critics of a more conservative bent were likewise ill at ease with *The German Lesson.* Peter Jensen accused Lenz of focusing upon the past at the expense of the present and thereby engaging in a "a punishment exercise that has been turned in too late . . .; Lenz, overwhelmed by the past, has forgotten that neglect takes place daily, neglect that a modern writer has more need to describe than things from the distant past" (*"Deutschstude,"* 151). If *The German Lesson* is not political enough for some, for others it is anchored in a sea of unpleasant political memories.

Critical disapproval extended as well to the treatment of individual characters, especially the strange, adolescent narrator, Siggi Jepsen: "Above all the role of the writer Siggi does not really seem believable: from where, one wonders, does this twenty year old get all these literary tricks?" (Jürgen Wallmann, in Schwarz, *Erzähler,* 161). The "literary" quality of Siggi's narrative, an issue of central importance in this chapter, was also troubling for Peter Härtling: Lenz "permits himself scarcely any crudeness, any jargon; the milieu does not emerge. Siggi writes the same way he combs his hair: straight and orderly . . . the fear, anger and powerlessness of this period remain muted" (in Schwarz, *Erzähler,* 149).

Predictably, those who liked the novel praised the very things others attacked: "Lenz effortlessly manipulates large subjects, without tricks or bravura" (Werner Weber, in Schwarz, *Erzähler,* 161). Paul Hübner admired the fact that "the meaningful and at the same time annoyingly broad flow of the story . . . unfolds without attempts at sensational effects" (in Schwarz, *Erzähler,* 150). For Hamida Bosmajian, the very absence of sensationalism, the studied avoidance of *grand guignol* scenes facilitates the novel's addressing a situation where "the neurosis of history manifests itself on a microcosmic scale" (*Metaphors of Evil,* 58).

The asperity and contradictions of the critical reactions to *The German Lesson* are not surprising. Since 1945 there have been so many novels about the war, in Germany as elsewhere. There has been such a plethora of historical monographs and psychological studies of the Nazi leadership that "Germany in World War II" has become a minor fictional and academic industry. The "World War II market" has been glutted with so many works of often questionable value that the late historian Geoffrey Barraclough once urged his colleagues to avoid writing about Hitler for a ten-year period ("Farewell to Hitler").

German writers are themselves divided about the necessity of continuously resurrecting the Hitlerzeit in their works—about the benefits to be gained, as a character in *The German Lesson* puts it, from "stirring around in all that shit" (162). Among younger novelists, those born during or after the war, a tendency exists to disassociate themselves, *as artists,* from political questions entirely. Peter Handke, in a famous reply to an attack by Gruppe 47 member Jakov Lind on his play *Die Hornissen* (*The Hornets*), rejected the argument that a German artist must be *engagé:* "During my literary work I . . . do not interest myself with criticism of society. I am simply not concerned with this. It would strike me as repulsive to twist criticism of society into a poem. . . . For one to work social commitment into a poem or make literature of it instead of saying things right out, I find hideously phony" (in Mandel, *Group 47,* 73).

Handke's position is certainly understandable. Literature cannot remain affixed to a single past experience, however overwhelming, nor must it always be a forum for political discussion. Other issues exist and different sensibilities respond to different stimuli. Yet for novelists like Lenz, whose lives were radically altered by the war, the question is not whether to write about what happened but rather how to write about a disastrous historical moment, the memory of which remains far from having been exorcised. *The German Lesson* is a novel concerning the difficulty of writing about a past that remains very much a part of the present. It is also a work that argues, more consistently than any of the novels I have discussed so far, for the value of fiction as an imperfect but nevertheless essential analytical tool, as a means not necessarily of answering questions but of demonstrating that certain important issues remain unresolved.

The German Lesson tells the story of Siggi Jepsen, an inmate in a Federal Republic reformatory. Siggi has stolen some paintings done by his friend, the distinguished artist Max Ludwig Nansen. While undergoing rehabilitation in the reform school, Siggi fails to complete an assignment for his German lesson (*seine Deutschstunde*). When asked to write an essay on "Die Freuden der Pflicht" ("The Joys of Duty"), he can only stare at the page. His problem is not that he has nothing to say. It is just the opposite: "What I am being punished for isn't that my memory and imagination let me down. I'm in solitary confinement because, obediently searching for the joys of duty, I suddenly had too much to tell, or at least such a lot that I simply did not know how to start" (12). Siggi's efforts to "do his duty" eventually lead him to recount the story of his early adolescence in Rugbüll, a sleepy North German village largely untouched by the war that raged about it. Yet, as the boy reflects upon the conflict between his father, the Rugbüll policeman, and Nansen, as well as on his own involvement with each, it is not an essay he writes. His struggles to assemble his materials and find a starting place propel him, without his ever being fully conscious of it, into the world of fiction.

Siggi quickly perceives that the failure of his initial attempt at "The Joys of Duty" stemmed from his desire to set down every detail, or at least to avoid having to make a "willkürliche Auswahl" (an arbitrary choice). It is only when he abandons such a simplistic approach and acknowledges the need and difficulty of choosing that his story begins to unfold. The "choice" precipitates his entrance into a more ambiguous realm, but he is still far removed from the writing of fiction since any intelligent historian, for example, must exercise similar judgment in the pursuit of that calling. Nevertheless, Siggi swiftly moves away from a purely historical method, as literary considerations start to influence his handling of the material. He begins to arrange scenes for their maximum dramatic effect. With regard to his framing of the first meeting between his father and Nansen, "I should prefer to delay the encounter a little, because it isn't just any encounter" (29). Obvious occurrences must be forgone in order to high-light more pertinent matters: "The thunderstorm was now directly over the peninsula, and the *obvious thing* would be to describe the various classical types of lightning and go on about squalls and all sorts of thun-der claps. . . . But it is not so much the thunderstorm I remember" (55, emphasis mine). On the other hand, at the behest of his storytelling in-stinct: "I must describe the morning. Even if I find a new meaning with every memory, I must produce a slow dawn now" (89). Also, in the inter-est of the illusion of verisimilitude, certain details must simply be in-vented: "Then he . . . pulled the pointed ends of his cape out from under his belt, and then—this is how I imagine it—cast a final glance at the lighted window before knocking at the studio door" (174).

As Siggi's work progresses, his burgeoning sense of his powers is not without a trace of vanity: "I could get dinner to be served, but I could also, in honor of Doctor Busbeck, design a great sunset" (85). However, he does not allow his abilities to interfere with the developing narrative. In this respect, Siggi does what any good novelist must: he excludes po-tentially interesting scenes, characters, and situations for the sake of the novel as a whole. This is why he does not pursue certain enticing possi-bilities. Who exactly is Theo Busbeck, whom Nansen is clearly protect-ing? What reason did the Nazis have for closing his art gallery? Was he a Jew or a political activist? These questions would be perfectly legitimate if the aim were merely to get the facts straight. And what about Siggi's somber, drug-addicted mother and her relationship with her husband and children? Or his father's apparent gift of "second sight"? Or Siggi's brother Klaas, whose desertion from the army is never fully explained? Doctor Busbeck, Siggi's mother, his father's strange power, and Klaas might all be worthy of novels in themselves, but they are peripheral to the one that, unbeknownst to himself, he is writing.

In *The German Lesson* Siggi's writing stands in contrast to that of an-other author, Wolfgang Mackenroth. Mackenroth's work purports to be scientific and hence objective. He is completing a doctoral dissertation in psychology, the subject being the criminal mind of Siggi Jepsen. Yet despite Mackenroth's diligent research, the envisioned result, "Kunst und Kriminalität" ("Art and Criminality"), will be as much a fictional narrative as "Die Freuden der Pflicht." The difference, however, is that Mackenroth is a bad artist. He is so burdened with psychological theories and jargon that he cannot allow his story to develop: he must push it in directions that reflect the latest academic fashions and toward "discoveries" that conform with what his professors are comfortable hearing. Siggi explains what Mackenroth perceived to be the "line" (84) of his thesis:

What he had in mind was to *defend* me, to *acquit* me, and to *set me up.* My stealing pictures was to be *justified,* and he intended recognizing the founding of my gallery in the old mill as a positive achievement; in general he intended to demonstrate that I was a *borderline case,* and to demand on my behalf that justice be administrated according to as yet nonexistent laws. The quiet-voiced, righteous fanaticism with which he put it all before me made him thoroughly plausible. (84, emphasis in text)

Since Mackenroth's conclusions are implicit in his premises, the entire thrust of his "research exercise" is to reestablish, with some minor and one hopes publishable variations, what is already academically acceptable. At best, such a study will only emphasize the self-evident and obscure the truly puzzling aspects of the subject. Siggi sums up Mackenroth and the type of writer he is in a succinct phrase: "both he and this stuff of his are not of the slightest use to me" (276).

Wolfgang Mackenroth's analysis is as well-intentioned as it is valueless. In *The German Lesson* his work serves as a parody of much German writing about the war. He repeats what has been too often said and offers, in the stilted language of putative scientific objectivity, the sort of prose Beutin calls "Seminardeutsch" (*"Deutschstunde," Siefried Lenz,* 6), the same tired explanations: "Siggi was a precocious, thus alienated child whose loss of parental affection led him into criminal activities" (278). In short, he employs the sorts of bromides that are frequently used to explain the Nazi mentality as well. In addition, Mackenroth does not always get the facts right (275).

As banal as Mackenroth's approach may be, the real problem with his thesis lies deeper. What makes his work dangerous is that the whole tenor of his theorizing helps create a dichotomy between the sick mind of Siggi, and by extension the Nazis, and the mentality of good, well-adjusted German citizens. Siggi and the Nazis are deviations from the norm; they must be classified in a way that permits separating them from the mainstream; then they can either be reintegrated socially through therapy or, failing that, forgotten. In either case the process of social readjustment is essentially quite simple, at least for someone like Wolfgang Mackenroth, who is indulging in the worst form of postwar German fiction.

Hans Wagener makes an illuminating contrast between Mackenroth's and Siggi's writing: "Makenroth is subjective, despite his scientific intention, because he wants to prove something . . . whereas Siggi merely *approaches* the truth" (*Siegfried Lenz,* 66, emphasis in text). Mackenroth deludes himself into believing that he can "prove" something thoroughly and objectively, whereas Siggi, at once more aware of the difficulty that attends writing and the complexity of the issues at stake, confines himself to "approaching" the truth, suggesting some possible causes and intentions motivating an individual's behavior. Mackenroth has total confidence in his methods and literary tools; Siggi is constantly questioning both and experimenting with other techniques. This is why he twice attempts casting scenes in terms of a film scenario or a play (138–44; 450–66), efforts he summarily abandons in favor of prose narrative. Interestingly enough, his second and more extensive effort at theatrical dialogue (450–66) occurs after he has seen his first play ever, Goethe's *Götz von Berlichingen,* a work in which the rhetorical excesses—"Zounds, and Gadzooks, and Begone" (334)—bored him greatly. He obviously thinks he can do better, only to discover that his literary gifts are not suited for the theater. In any case, Siggi's rejection of Mackenroth's writing is not because of its psychological orientation any more than his annoyance with *Götz* necessarily constitutes a critique of theater as a genre. Rather, in each case he objects to a language and an implicit worldview that fail to clarify his own experience. With specific regard to dramatic form, his abandonment of it merely reflects his ever-growing sense of where his artistic talents lie.

Siegfried Lenz is using Siggi's transition from essayist to novelist to raise the question of literature's role in attempting to clarify the wartime experience. Lenz entertains the seemingly paradoxical notion that the very weakness of the fictional enterprise—namely that what is recounted need not always be factually accurate (at one point Siggi's sister Hilke criticizes his narrative for distorting somewhat the characters of their mother and father)—might ultimately bring one closer to the truth. When Siggi was in high school, he realized that history left him cold (393), because the facts were just not enough. What hindered him in his schoolboy efforts at objective evaluation are the very qualities and/or faults that aid him as a novelist. Siggi cannot offer the instantaneous judgments his teacher demands because he is troubled by generalizations about complex matters. Behind his imaginings and occasional distortions is a fidelity to his own particular experience:

For I don't want my plain to be mistaken for any other plain. I am not speaking of *some* **landscape, just any landscape, but of my own landscape, and I am not trying to rediscover some unspecified misfortune, but my own particular misfortune—in short, I am not telling just** *somebody's* **story, some story that doesn't commit me personally. (203–4, emphasis in text)**

It is Siggi's fixation with the concrete, his rejection of theoretical explanations, facile or otherwise, and his ability to invent what might have happened that open to him, the incipient novelist, means of examining the *Hitlerzeit* that are forbidden to the historian, psychologist, or sociologist, whose investigations are guided, and perhaps limited, by the need for putatively objective analysis.

Through his depiction of both Mackenroth's research endeavors and the terminology and generally misguided judgments of the graduate student's more established colleagues—"'Wartenburg perceptual defect,' 'angular vision,' or even 'cognitive block,' which struck me as particularly repulsive," (17)—Lenz is underscoring the subjective elements implicit in psychological inquiries: a patient has an alleged problem; the doctor has a variety of theories at hand; the diagnosis is somehow making one fit the other. In an article in *Die Weltwoche* of September 17, 1965, he entertained similar doubts concerning the objective knowledge contained within historical documents:

The document is not as documentary as it appears. It only supplies clippings, profiles, extracts. Considering the necessity of this attempt, I personally expect from an author that he changes something, that he shifts

things, that he filters materials through his temperament. His personal involvement remains decisive. (25)

Lenz's preference is for a "Literatur von erklärter Parteilichkeit" (25), a
literature of declared partisanship, in which the personal, subjective contribution of the author is transparent. The novelist's undertaking is more
overtly speculative than that of the social scientist, and the results are
tentative. This, of course, places a great burden on the reader, who is, for
Lenz, "necessary, in order that a book can win commitment" (25). In *The
German Lesson* the *Verbindlichkeit* (commitment) asked of the reader is
not to any particular proffered explanations but to ongoing, unresolved
questions. Nothing in the novel illustrates this better than the treatment
of the painter, Nansen, and Siggi's father, the Rugbüll policeman, Jens
Jepsen.

Nansen's choice to continue painting precipitates the crisis in the novel.
However, the artist's decision to avoid the government's *Malerverbot* (the
order forbidding him to paint) is not quite as heroic as circumstances
make it appear. Although the paranoid fantasies of Nazi bureaucrats in
Berlin are sufficient to permit their finding subversive elements in Nansen's seascapes and vaguely erotic paintings of Siggi's sister, the artist is not
attempting to make any serious political statement with his canvases—
despite the former *Art and the People* critic's belated discovery of political
activism. He is a painter who, quite simply, has to paint. It is Jens Jepsen's
stubborn persecution of him that catapults Nansen's harmless activities
into gestures of political defiance.

Lenz is using Nansen's situation to examine, in an ironic way, the controversial issue of the *innere Emigration* (inner emigration), the decision
by prominent Germans not to leave Hitler's Reich but retreat instead into
private, apolitical worlds. Nansen really did nothing that was noticed to
oppose the Reich. (His protection of Theo Busbeck remained unrecog-
nized by either the Nazis or Jepsen.) He was like others who opted to stay
in Germany and pursue their careers as best they could while turning
their backs on the events around them. Although it may be fashionable
today to scorn such persons, Lenz is suggesting that many honorable
Germans were so angered, confused, and overwhelmed by what was happening in their country that all they could do was to seek to defend,

within the narrow realm of their professional expertise, norms of dignity and beauty in a society conspicuously lacking in both.[1]

It is a chance occurrence that spares Nansen the opprobrium usually heaped on those who chose the path of inner emigration. Shortly before the war's end he is imprisoned by the Gestapo. He emerges unharmed from this experience, but postwar Germany's need to discover resistance heroes leads to his lionization. Despite himself, despite the modest courage he did display during the war, Nansen finds himself part of contemporary Germany's fiction about German opposition to the Reich. Nansen may be a hero of sorts, but not on the scale accorded him by the *Wirtschaftswunderkinder* (the children of the industrial postwar miracle).

The irony in all this is that if Nansen is praised by some for the wrong reasons, he is attacked for equally wrong reasons by other, younger Germans, whose judgments are also distorted and self-serving. When Siggi sees Nansen at his first postwar exhibition, the painter is decked out like a "figure in the reconstructed eighteenth-century Frisian house" (432). Ill at ease with his clothing and environment, Nansen is clearly out of place, and in a larger sense his art is too. The painter nods approvingly when the art critic Hans-Dieter Hübscher praises his achievement as bearing "testimony to the fact that the sonority of color can transform an intuitively grasped meaning into pure paint" (434). Be that as it may, all the descriptions of Nansen's paintings in the novel, coupled with the implicit correlation between Nansen and Emil Nolde, suggest that he is working within the Expressionist tradition, and this exhibition, this celebration of the painter's genuine accomplishment, occurs precisely at a moment when contemporary art is moving in different directions and toward other concerns. Thus it initially seems natural that the younger artist Siggi meets, "a fat, sulky fellow" accompanied by a skinny girl with a doll who "evenly distributed her attention between the fat fellow and the rag doll" (428), expresses contempt for the "dauber . . . the greatest of cloud-cuckoo-painters" (442). Yet the fat guy is wrong—not in sensing that contemporary art has moved beyond Nansen but in criticizing him for knowing nothing about perspective. The issue here is more than painterly perspective, depth of field; rather it involves perspective as a broader, deeper understanding of things. When Siggi attempts to correct the younger painter's mistake, he is rewarded for his efforts with a smack in the mouth.

The full weight of this scene becomes apparent only when the reader recalls an earlier incident during World War II at Rugbüll, when Siggi was involved in a search for two lost children, a fat boy and a skinny girl with a doll (390). These retarded children, who are declared "worthless" by Siggi's pro-Nazi mother (392), have their contemporary avatar in the angry young painter and his girlfriend, who have become as marginal in mainstream society as were the handicapped kids during the Nazi era. The young painter and girlfriend represent postwar German youth whose values and perceptions have been so distorted by the activities of the older generation that they are incapable of achieving any coherent perspective on the recent past. The young painter scorns the older artist, but the boy's work, however different it is in form, shares one quality with Nansen's art: the depiction of fear (443). The younger artist's anger is misplaced because he has not understood the true object of his wrath. Without his realizing what he is doing, he is attacking not Nansen the painter but Nansen the adult, a member of the generation responsible for Hitler's rise to power. Lenz does not hammer away at this theme; he simply suggests the similarities and parallels between the retarded children, on one hand, and the artist with his girlfriend on the other. Both sets of young people are handicapped, albeit in different ways and for different reasons. It is left to readers to draw their own conclusions, to appreciate how the past affects and then continues to impinge upon young Germans' understanding of the present.

In *The German Lesson* the most striking example of Lenz's effort to commit the reader to an examination of the past with an eye to its implications for the present concerns the depiction of the Rugbüll policeman, Jens Jepsen. In a novel replete with significant choices (*Auswahlen*)—Siggi chooses how to write; Nansen chooses to defy the Nazi interdiction—the most perplexing is the apparent nonchoice of Jens Jepsen, who does what he does because "anyone who does his duty has no call to worry—not even if the times should change sooner or later" (107). Unlike the art critic who served the Nazis and then after the war proclaimed his secret opposition, Jepsen is no hypocrite. He is something more difficult to fathom and, perhaps for that reason, more frightening as well. At the war's end he places his Nazi badge in a drawer, whence he can presumably reclaim it should ever the need arise. He acts this way without displaying any secret sympathy for the Nazis; were he to have any, his conduct would perhaps be less disturbing, since it would imply a belief in some set of values, however twisted. But the policeman appears to believe in nothing except the rote performance of his assigned task. Thus he can serve the Federal Republic as dutifully, and in his own mind as honestly, as he did the Reich. Jens Jepsen represents those Germans who survived the war morally unaffected by it because, on some unconscious level, they were neither for nor against it. They simply did their duty, which they interpreted to mean doing exactly what they were told. The only choice they made was to permit others to choose for them.

To some extent the foregoing sketch of Jens Jepsen provides nothing more than a standard description of the *Mitläufer,* the passive collaborator, who has become something of a fixture in postwar German literature. Yet what makes Jepsen such an arresting figure is not his character per se but Lenz's refusal to supply stock explanations for the policeman's behavior. The originality of Lenz's treatment of the policeman lies in the author's efforts to demonstrate that the by now traditional analyses of the Mitläufer's mentality are insufficient.

It would be tempting, for example, to borrow the approach used in discussing *The Tin Drum* and argue that Jens acts as he does because he is a typical *Kleinbürger:* a person of limited social and educational background who behaves as he does out of a combination of boredom and slavish devotion to authority. To support such a viewpoint there is Siggi's observation concerning his father: "He sets himself in motion, as so often, only—it seemed—because he was now properly dressed and equipped" (23). When the Kleinbürger dresses like a policeman, he must act like one. Nevertheless, Lenz makes clear that so convenient an explanation is impossible. If Jens is a Kleinbürger, then so too is the postman Okko Broderson, who quietly tries to dissuade the policeman from harassing Nansen. For that matter, Nansen is himself a Kleinbürger, but his sense of duty has little in common with Jens Jepsen's. And then there is the redoubtable schoolmaster, Tetjus Prugel, whose mad insistence upon continuing a biology lesson about the survival of superior organisms as the invading British soldiers enter his classroom makes Jens's adherence to his duty seem pale in comparison. The Rugbüll policeman's astonishment at how Nansen, with a background so similar to his own, could behave so differently (173) would seem to be a superficial version of Lenz's puzzlement at the differing comportment of Germans from the same social caste.

Another possible explanation for Jens's conduct involves a question of sexual or emotional frustration. Certain hints of this occur throughout the novel, but the fact that Siggi *chooses* not to pursue this line of inquiry because it is not apposite to his story indicates that for Lenz, such an approach is best left to pulp novelists and makers of pornographic movies.

A more intelligent attempt to understand the Mitläufer mentality comes from an application of Hannah Arendt's thesis adumbrated in *Eichmann in Jerusalem: A Report on the Banality of Evil.* Hamida Bosmajian relates Arendt's findings directly to Jens Jepsen:

Jepsen has been analyzed as an example of the little man as a cog in the machine of authoritarianism. He is the Eichmann self in all its banality of evil, for whom Kant's categorical imperative has come to mean duty and obedience to the state to which the individual surrenders his selfhood and always acts in a way that the Führer would approve (75).

Such a perception initially makes a great deal of sense. It was perhaps an implied analogy with Eichmann that prompted another critic to remark: "Why he does his duty so narrow-mindedly . . . why exactly he is so stubborn, when there are others in the village, scarcely more educated or intelligent than he is, yet nevertheless not such inhuman pedants—that remains an open question" (Drews, "Siegfried Lenz," 363).

Yet the comparison does not really hold. If both Eichmann and Jepsen were "merely following orders," Eichmann knew where they led and Jepsen did not. Also, while Eichmann's loyalty to Hitler was conscious and genuine, Jepsen displays no clear attachment to the Führer, who is scarcely mentioned in the novel. Eichmann was a high Nazi official who profited in many ways from his fidelity to the Reich and who actively participated in the fantasy of National Socialism. Eichmann was a boring little man the way Himmler was a boring little man, but the banality of these "leaders" was quite different from that of low-level bureaucrats who, like Jepsen, were party members in name only. These comments are not intended to excuse the likes of Jens Jepsen but rather to suggest that the very brilliance of Arendt's analysis tends to obscure the fact that the motivations of the lowest echelons in Nazi Germany were not the same as those for people in leadership positions.

One of the most recent attempts to resolve this conundrum owes much to Arendt. In his *Modernity and the Holocaust* (1989), Zygmunt Bauman argues that the moral opacity of the bureaucratic Mitläufer is merely one reflection of the triumph of the modern, highly technological state, where the language of efficiency and professionalism replaces whatever moral impetus the individual may possess. Bauman's description of this phenomenon practically amounts to a portrait of the "dutiful" Jens Jepsen:

Inside the bureaucratic system of authority, language of morality acquires a new vocabulary. It is filled with concepts like loyalty, duty, discipline—all pointing to superiors as the supreme object of moral concern and, simultaneously, the top moral authority. (160)

Bauman also maintains that *"modern, rational, bureaucratically organized power"* can induce individuals to act in ways that serve the state even though the particular actions may be contrary to *"the vital interests of the actors"* (122, emphasis in text). This too speaks to Jepsen's situation, since his persecution of the painter puts him at odds with the majority of the Rugbüll community. Nevertheless, as valuable as is the analysis of Bauman, Arendt, and others, by the very nature of their generalizing approaches to the Mitläufer mentality, they cannot do full justice to an individual's complexity. Jens Jepsen is almost always a "company man," but "almost always" is not always. Toward the end of *The German Lesson* there is a scene in which the policeman would have been well within his rights to yield to his anger and frustration with Nansen. As the British forces move toward Rugbüll, the painter is conscripted, along with several others, into a Home Guard defensive unit. After a day of trench digging in expectation of the British arrival, Nansen becomes so overwhelmed with the futility and sheer silliness of what he and his friends are doing that he just walks away. In any legal terms this is desertion in wartime, and Jensen would have the law, the law of any nation at war, on his side if he were to shoot the painter. He threatens to do so; the painter keeps walking and the policeman does nothing. However slavish his devotion to authority and duty, a moment occurs in the novel when even Jens Jepsen says no.

Let us recall for a moment the earlier cited assessment of Jens Jepsen, where Jörg Drews expressed annoyance at Lenz's refusal to clarify the policeman's motives (Drews, "Siegfried Lenz/*Deutschstunde*," 363). It is certainly true that Lenz raises a question in this novel that he does not answer. In terms of the information that *Deutschstunde* provides, there is little effort to explain away the motivations of a Jens Jepsen, and this refusal to claim to solve a problem, categorize it, and then forget it constitutes the strength of the novel.

Whatever the reasons for Jepsen or others acting as they did, these reasons remain far from understood. This is why at the novel's end Siggi remarks: "My cable . . . would never extend beyond Rugbüll. Anyway, if ever I put through the connection, a bellowing voice will be certain to answer: 'Rugbüll Police Station speaking.' . . . Nothing that can ever happen, no tidal wave, no earthquake, will break this connection; I am linked to this place forever" (474). Despite Siggi's initially modest aim of merely remaining true to his limited experiences, Rugbüll eventually becomes Germany in miniature during the war, and the reason it will haunt Siggi (and Lenz) is that the deeply disturbing questions about human behavior that surfaced at that time continue to defy a thoroughly satisfying analysis: "All that I had left were questions that nobody gave me an answer to, not even the painter—not even he" (476).

Siggi's attempt to respond to the questions his childhood experience raised began with a choice (*Auswahl*) concerning a way to write. However, this choice was only the final one in a group of three. Siggi's first choice was to break free of his father's influence. He does this when he violates the policeman's orders and hides Nansen's paintings in an old mill he considers his secret museum. Yet his devotion to the museum is as much a retreat from the complications of reality as is Jens Jepsen's relentless performance of his *Pflicht* (duty). Siggi creates for himself a mysterious, highly personalized universe that permits him, through an obsessive concern with certain pictures, to forget about everything else. In this respect his supposed rejection of his father's attitudes turns out to be but a parody of them.

Siggi's second choice, despite appearances, is a more positive one. His theft of Nansen's paintings marks a clear break with his father, while at the same time it becomes an initial, albeit confused, affirmation of the young man's own values. Siggi realizes, in some inchoate form, that in postwar Germany Nansen's work will be misunderstood; it will be appreciated and despised for the wrong reasons. Just as Lenz rejects current explanations of the Mitläufer, Siggi prefers that the truth contained in his friend's paintings remain unknown for a time. Better not to know than to know badly, his gesture would seem to imply. But such an essentially negative attitude cannot suffice, and it is only with his third and final choice, his decision to develop in all its complexity "Die Freuden der Pflicht," that Siggi discovers his true vocation, which is to be a writer.

Siegfried Lenz once remarked that "Writing (*schreiben*) is an excellent way to learn about people, actions and conflicts" (cited in Bassmann, *Lenz*, 16). One could quickly add that psychologists, historians, or sociologists might well say the same thing about the knowledge their professional techniques yield. What Lenz is saying is in fact wonderfully tautological: writers must write, because the act of writing is their best chance for bringing them as close as they will ever come to something resembling truth. Thus *schreiben* is not *a* choice; for a writer, be it the mature novelist Siegfried Lenz or the neophyte Siggi Jepsen, it is the *only* choice. The young beginner is not the established artist, but Lenz is using his fictional character to make a statement about the need to continue writing, especially for young artists who cannot find the sought-after answers in works of their predecessors (Thomas Mann, Stefan Zweig?). This next generation of writers and painters must seek out new perspectives about a German experience that was more than a temporary delusion, and the lessons of which remain largely unlearned.

It is at this juncture that the suggestiveness of the title, *Deutschstunde,* becomes important. *Stunde,* which means at once an "hour" and a "lesson," and which is intriguingly close to *die Sünde* (sin), is not just any hour or lesson. It is specifically *deutsch*. On the level Siggi most values, his story is about Germany, the drama of which is reflected in a little village, and while the tale might have broader ramifications, the young author has insisted that he wants primarily to talk about his region and his misfortunes (412). Since the Germany embodied in Rugbüll is part of the Third Reich, Siggi's determination to avoid generalizing is especially noteworthy. By means of Siggi's insistence upon being specific, Lenz appears to be following Hannah Arendt, who in a discussion of war guilt allowed that Nazism could perhaps have occurred anywhere, but because it did happen in Germany, the Germans must bear the responsibility.

The war was undoubtedly Germany's gravest "hour," yet how and for whom was this *Stunde* a lesson? After the war many Germans sanctimoniously branded this *Stunde* as a *Sünde*, a sin to be sure, but also a temporary aberration that some public breast-beating of the type Oskar witnessed in *The Tin Drum* and some contributions to the right charities would remedy. Those of a more cynically pragmatic bent might have sided with the late Franz Josef Strauss's thesis of exoneration through accomplishment: "The nation that this industrial achievement has orchestrated has the right to want to hear about Auschwitz no longer" (Letsch, *Auseinandersetzung*, 12).

Still other Germans, like Wolfgang Mackenroth, have chosen the sorts of intellectual, psychoanalytical approaches that explain the most while creating the fewest concrete problems and do not hinder either the business of daily living or the continued development of the Wirtschaftswunder. For these people, analyzing the war has become a veritable "Deutschstunde," an academic exercise periodically undertaken and leading to predictably tame conclusions.

The German Lesson reaches no ultimate conclusions about the war, tame or otherwise, and therein lies its great merit. With regard to the final pages, Schwarz notes: "The verb 'to question' appears on half a page no less than eight times, and he [Siggi] finds no satisfying answer" (*Erzähler*, 75). What is true of the ending holds throughout the novel: questions are raised and answers rejected. As Lenz puts it, his task as a novelist is "to supply references, to furnish arguments: that is enough" (Schwarz, *Erzähler*, 128). This may appear a thankless task for the writer and at times a frustrating experience for the reader; yet this is a job that still needs to be done. For Lenz it may be the ultimate achievement of the literary text.

Conclusion: The War, the Novel, and the Present

10

In the readings I have offered of the six novels, I have allowed what I considered to be the exigencies of each text to dictate my approach, building, for example, my discussion of *The Tin Drum* around the theme of "the black cook," placing *Patterns of Childhood* in the larger context of women writing about World War II, and using Roland Barthes' ideas about mythology to illuminate the self-deception at the heart of *The Ogre*.

A salient feature of at least five of these novels was that, although at times difficult in structure and content, they all captured a large audience.[1] I believe that this fact merits special attention. In what follows I indicate some of the qualities in these texts that contributed to their popular appeal and then offer reasons why, in a world where all sources of information remain deeply suspect, the novel continues to function as a valued repository of insight and intelligence.

What distinguishes these six texts from novels written in the immediate aftermath of World War II is that they do not try to focus on the war exclusively as a phenomenon that, however terrible, was simply yet another instance of a periodically recurring bellicose pattern in Western history. To the extent that there was any continuity between past and present, as in the works of Céline and Grass, it had to do with a continuum of fear: an existential anxiety that was altered and enhanced by the unique horror of World War II.

In the works of the authors I have discussed in detail, World War II was radically different, primarily because of the extent of the Nazi genocidal practices. As Jabès succinctly put it, "the abyss has been seen" (*Aely*, 98). Céline, Grass, Simon, Wolf, Tournier, and Lenz reflect in their fiction a sense of the war's having created in the contemporary consciousness a rift that remains far from healed. Hence their novels demonstrate that the moral and psychological shocks of World War II continue to have an impact upon the contemporary world.

Céline's widow, Lucette, in an interview with novelist Philippe Djian, remarked about her late husband: "He was writing for the young people, because he knew he could expect nothing from adults" (19). In a sense Céline's hypothetical audience was also the audience of the other authors, whose texts likewise have a special interest for those either yet unborn during the conflict or too young to have participated actively in the war. Theirs is a readership of questioners, of people who live with the aftershocks of World War II, and who, while they certainly want to understand what they can about the whys and wherefores of this bloodbath, must also make their lives in a world very different from that of their parents. One possible explanation for the widespread appeal of these novels to a postwar generation is that in each case the narrator or main character is either a young person or possesses behavioral patterns normally associated with a child, and often an unpleasant one at that. Almost all these narratives are told in part by a young man or woman whose perspective may well contain a degree of freshness, but this potential quality is constantly offset by the narrator's immaturity and simple lack of experience. The result, of course, is to place the burden of interpretation on the reader.

One might immediately object that the Célinian protagonist-narrator is hardly a child. Yet the narrative voice, exculpatory, whiny, and accusatory, has the attributes of a spoiled, insistent child who accepts no blame for the chaos orchestrated by supposedly mature and rational creatures much more powerful than himself. If the Célinian narrator is something of a child, he is certainly not an innocent one. Occasionally quite witty, this narrative voice is mostly annoying and alienating; however, despite the consistent offensiveness of the Célinian narrator, what he has to say provides a valuable perspective on the human capacity for hypocrisy (including his own) and self-delusion (that of others).

In *The Flanders Road* Georges is old enough to have participated in the war, yet his subsequent comportment is resolutely juvenile. He reviles his father even as he copies the older man's behavior by retreating to the countryside to write a book that finally is more about the past than the present. He abhors his mother's social snobbism but remains unwilling to confront any issues that might cast aspersions on his family background or class privileges. His revolt is adolescent and his behavior with Corinne at best immature.

Reflecting upon *The Ogre*'s main character in his autobiographical essay *Le Vent Paraclet* (*The Wind Spirit*), Michel Tournier maintains that "Abel is not an adult" (117). Oskar Matzerath in *The Tin Drum* is a dwarf who decided at birth never to exceed the size of an average three year old and to give the world the impression that his intelligence has remained on that level as well. Siggi Jepsen, the young narrator of *The German Lesson* who is incarcerated in a home for youthful offenders, recounts events that transpired when he was eleven years old.

By far the most fascinating manifestation of the child motif occurs in *Patterns of Childhood,* where the adolescent Nelly acts like a "young adult," while the middle-aged narrator stews over the injustices perpetrated on her when she was still quite young. As noted, it was only with the discovery of the dual narrative, by the "young adult" schoolgirl and the still angry middle-aged woman, that Christa Wolf was able to write this book.

Much like the Célinian narrator, the other protagonists are contemptuous of what they consider the "grownup" world. Abel thinks that any book or person admired by an adult must be worthless. His hero in literature as in life is Rasputin (*The Ogre* is, in fact, dedicated to his memory), and this fondness for the murdered Russian seer is for a time shared by Oskar. Both respect the Russian as an opponent of all forms of bourgeois conventionality. Oskar scorns adults so intensely that he even refuses to look like them, and he is always critical of what "big people" do. Siggi has contempt for his father along with the various purveyors of psychological wisdom who strive to turn him into a responsible citizen.

Georges might well be frustrated in his efforts to be a *nouveau romancier,* but his inability to articulate his thoughts and feelings in a truly original manner does not prevent his understanding that his forefathers' values have been deeply compromised by the war. Perhaps more clearly than in any of the other novels, the "role reversal" in *Patterns of Childhood,* where the older narrator articulates a young person's anger, illustrates that the adult generation of World War II (at least in Germany) had deeply failed its children and that this failure remains a sensitive issue for those children now become adults.

In one of Heinrich Böll's short stories, "Entfernung von der Truppe" (Distance from the troop), the narrator mentions that people denigrate his comments about World War II because in their view all he does is repeat what every child knows. The narrator seems to agree but then points out that children are not the problem. Those who appear to have difficulty grasping what he says are the adults who participated in the war (217). The narrators of the novels I have discussed are equally suspicious of the adult community. Right-thinking citizens are for them a triumph of social conditioning: people who know how to align themselves with all that is for the moment acceptable and to separate themselves from any and all acts that are currently out of favor. Grownups are adept at spotting the potentially accusing finger and then directing it toward someone else. At one point in *The German Lesson* Siggi wonders whether he and the other boys are in jail for the crimes of their fathers (459). Siggi exaggerates, of course, but the visceral distrust of alleged adults implicit in his comment is largely typical of the other narrators as well.

In at least three of these novels, those by Céline, Tournier, and Lenz, the protagonist is overtly something of a child, alienated from adult society, and indifferent to the question of whether his narration inspires much confidence on the part of the reader. While the unreliable narrator is hardly unique to novels about World War II, the particular context gives special significance to this literary device. These novels raise such serious issues as war guilt, collaboration, genocide, and the difficulty of establishing a morally coherent existence in the shadow of Auschwitz—but then deprive the reader of the trustworthy perspective that is supposed to facilitate "correct" analysis. The result is to engage and challenge readers rather than to reassure them, to leave them fascinated if ill at ease before a text and the questions it poses. Readers whose curiosity has led them to one of these novels are compelled to remain mindful that it is their own task, not the author's, to establish an interpretive approach. The reader who persists has to accept the obligation of deciding when and where, if at all, there are elements of truth or value in the narration. In *Le Vol du vampire* (The Flight of the Vampire), Tournier notes that "a novel can certainly contain a thesis, but it is important that it be the reader, not the writer, who puts it there. Because the interpretation—tendentious or otherwise—emerges from the sole competence of the reader" (14). Precisely this sort of narrative strategy suffuses the other novels as well and, I would maintain, conforms to the disabused sensibility of the contemporary reader.

All of these books evidence a deep distrust in symbolism, which, translated from the literary realm to the world of daily life, suggests a deep suspicion concerning grandiose, overarching syntheses and a profound distrust for all-encompassing explanations. More often than not, symbols are parodied throughout these texts and serve as vestiges of a literary heritage that is no longer viable. To take a single example, it really does not matter whether or not the young Jewish boy, Ephraim, whom Abel Tiffauges carries on his shoulders at the end of *The Ogre,* represents Jesus Christ or the entire Jewish population slaughtered by the Nazis; what matters is that he was a human being prevented by circumstances from living out his existence. Ephraim might well have possessed the potential to be a genius, someone capable of making great contributions to humanity, but he might just as easily have grown up to be an ordinary, rather mediocre person who would leave no mark on history. What matters, of course, is that whatever he might have made of his life is irrelevant. His needless death is tragedy enough, and no type of allusion, literary, religious, or otherwise, will lessen the apprehension of the senseless destruction of a human being.

There is one curious exception to this general distrust of symbolism in three of the novels. It concerns animals. Céline dedicated the last work in his trilogy, *Rigadoon,* "to the animals," and throughout his frenzied wanderings through war-torn Germany he is accompanied by his cat, Bébert. In the trilogy animals are constantly portrayed as innocent victims of human violence; Bébert's helplessness and vulnerability are emblematic of the situation in which the protagonist and his entourage find themselves. The character Céline is not, of course, an innocent victim, but the irrationality that surrounds him and his friends in the collapsing Reich is best symbolized at one truly insane moment in *North,* when a Nazi official asks Céline whether Bébert is a purebred—that is, an Aryan—cat.

In *The Tin Drum* there is a kindly musician named Meyn who drinks too much and keeps cats. After he becomes a Nazi and joins the mounted

S.A., his personality changes. All his hitherto repressed anger against real and imagined enemies emerges when, in a drunken rage, he bludgeons his cats to death. Another association of Nazi violence with animals occurs when Oskar visits the German bunkers that dot the Normandy coast. An officer proudly explains that each one has a puppy buried within its walls, in accordance with a tradition that dictates that putting a live animal in a foundation of a new building assures success. This scene takes place just days before the Allied invasion with its well-known consequences for the Nazis.

The animal pattern in *The Tin Drum* changes once the war ends. The proprietor of the Onion Cellar, the cabaret where Oskar plays his drum, regularly goes out and kills twelve sparrows. One day he exceeds his limit and kills a thirteenth. On his way home he is attacked and killed by hundreds of birds. Critics have suggested that the twelve sparrows represent the twelve years that Hitler's "thousand-year" Reich actually lasted. Without denying that particular significance of the number twelve, the birds in general can also symbolize the eventual revenge that the oppressed took on the oppressors. The birds, like Hitler's concentration camp inmates, suffered consistent, carefully regulated cruelty. However, there were rare instances toward the end of the war—Treblinka is a case in point—when the tortured prisoners finally struck back at the torturers, just as the sparrows eventually reaped vengeance on the cabaret owner.

Little violence occurs in *The German Lesson,* but what there is mostly centers on animals. When Siggi's sister and her boyfriend attempt to steal eggs from birds' nests, they are attacked by screaming gulls. This scene foreshadows the single raid in the novel by the British Air Force, whose pilots, incidentally, fly planes called mosquitoes. Ducks pelted by stones and a cow destroyed by an errant bomb represent the innocent victims of the conflict.

Animals play an especially complex role in *The Ogre.* Carrier pigeons are the first innocent victims of the fighting, but other animals embody evil. The artificially bred wild oxen roaming the forest preserve of Rominten in East Prussia are transparent images for the young German boys perverted in the *napola,* the school where children are trained to become future S.S. officers.

In *The Ogre* the horse is primarily associated with the Nazis, a motif introduced by Blue Beard, the animal Tiffauges rides as he pursues boys for the *napola*. The horse chases the magnificent and defenseless deer during the hunts that Göring and his cronies enjoy.

A change in the pattern of equine imagery reflects Germany's military defeat. As the regular German Army retreats before the advancing Russians, a peasant's cart overturns, and the symbol of the victimizer suddenly becomes the victim: "the pole . . . had been driven like a pike into the chest of one of the army horses. The dying animal had fallen to its knees" (338).

Tournier's use of animals to symbolize both the oppressor and the oppressed culminates in a scene where Abel Tiffauges embodies the two conflicting roles. As the Russians attack the *napola*, Abel tries to escape with Ephraim on his shoulders. During their flight the child refers alternatively to Tiffauges as "the Steed of Israel" and the "Behemoth." The former is an image of heroism and the latter of evil. Ephraim is the only one who understands what Abel has been throughout the novel: a person with heroic, even humanitarian aspirations but whose actions nevertheless have disastrous consequences for himself and many of those he encounters. Abel Tiffauges is at once a benighted victim of his own self-delusion and a cause of suffering to others.

There is ample justification for authors who otherwise show a certain disdain for symbolism nonetheless making significant use of animal imagery. On the most obvious level, animals are not normally perceived as cultural artifacts, although they have occasionally been used as such at various moments in history (the American eagle, the Egyptian hawk, the dove in the Christian religion and in the peace movement). Therefore they are relatively detached from precise social and literary significations, yet animals have traditionally served to mirror the human universe. The medieval bestiary is an obvious example.

With specific regard to animal symbolism as representing both the cruelty and suffering exhibited during World War II, there remains a broader implication. The animal, capable of both gentleness and ferocity, has a comportment that is at times obvious, yet at other moments unfathomable. At least outside scientific circles, the "character" of an animal species is to a large extent the product of anthropomorphism, human admirers or detractors arbitrarily assigning to these creatures a variety of attributes and faults. As such the animal may function as a modest but compelling metaphor for the contradictions and mysteries locked within the human psyche. The shocks that followed World War II did not simply concern mass murder. Traditional notions of human nature—its capacity for good and evil, deviant behavior, and mental stability—crumbled with the discovery that apparently decent people had been able to imagine and then carry out what had formerly been considered unthinkable acts. To discuss these issues without resorting to hysteria and clichés proved extremely difficult. Artists, or at least the ones I have discussed in detail, have not pretended to have the solutions to these riddles. They have simply exploited the mystery surrounding the nature of animals to indicate how little has been understood about people and to symbolize all the remaining unexplored complexities present in human behavior.

It seems to me that the willingness to pose difficult questions in an interesting fashion, and then to avoid simplistic responses, would have enormous appeal to an audience supersaturated with facile answers and insistent reassurances about a bright future. Serious readers of these novels, I hope, would not for a moment think that there is anything of substance behind the initially antiracist and subsequently antiwar slogan "Never again"—except wishful thinking. They might even agree with Martin Walser:

Naturally Auschwitz will never be repeated. The next triumph of the asocial personality will deck itself out differently. That is why it is so senseless yet satisfying to perceive Auschwitz in its unique factors and, so to speak, with one's nerves. It is possible that the end of this century will appear as boring to us as did the century's beginning to the fine people of that time. In the end we may start getting ideas again. And that is the beginning of the horror. (*Heimatkunde*, 22–23)

Walser's words are not cynical, if by cynicism one means a passive acceptance of the reality of inexcusable stupidity. Walser, by the very fact of publishing his essay, is expressing a much more nuanced position. For him, there is clearly little cause for confidence that the knowledge and memory of Auschwitz will effect positive changes in human comportment. Nevertheless, the fact that he writes and publishes an essay expressing these fears implies that there is a satisfaction in the act of putting onto paper one's doubts and concerns about the future. Writing is an action, and as such it is in opposition both to passivity and to a cynical acceptance of a confusing and frightening situation.

With regard to the texts I have discussed, the action consists of examining the remnants of a ruined culture as well as some of the literary and intellectual suppositions upon which that culture rested. In this respect it is crucial not only that the writing take the form of fiction but also that in four cases, the novels by Tournier, Grass, Wolf, and Lenz, the main characters all write fiction within the individual novels.

Oskar proclaims at the outset of *The Tin Drum* that he will deal with his experiences in terms of fiction. The only annoyance is choosing the right style:

> You can begin a story in the middle and create confusion by striking out boldly, backward and forward. You can be modern, put aside all mention of time and distance and, when the whole thing is done, proclaim, or let someone else proclaim, that you have finally, at the last moment, solved the space-time problem. Or you can declare at the start that it is impossible to write a novel nowadays, but then, behind your own back so to speak, give birth to a whopper, a novel to end all novels. (17)

Oskar's solution is to employ a deceptively straightforward narrative, one that brings to mind Tournier's assertion in *Le Vent Paraclet* that he himself uses traditional forms to express nontraditional ideas (207).

Siggi's efforts to write an essay on "The Joys of Duty" gradually push him into a fictional mode. He begins to make distinctions between that which is obvious and hence unnecessary and those descriptive elements that would enhance the story he is telling (55). Eventually he ponders methods of arranging a scene for its maximum aesthetic and thematic effect (67); he hesitates to introduce a particular incident because it may not be the right moment in the story (92), muses about the power of words to recreate experience (136), experiments with dramatic form (138), and ultimately notes with approval the painter Nansen's remark that the only way to "see" is to "invent" (138).

Christa Wolf was incapable of making progress with the manuscript that eventually became *Patterns of Childhood* until she hit upon the device of having the older novelist write a remembered/invented story of a young girl in Nazi Germany. Quite aside from the lapses of memory and distance from her own childhood that Wolf describes, it was only when the author resorted to a fictional mode that she was able to find a frame within which she could develop her narrative. *Patterns of Childhood* is not simply a tale told in a hybrid form I have dubbed the memoir-novel; it is precisely because of the combining of the remembered with the imagined, the discovered with the invented, that the book came into being.

Unlike the other three narrators, Abel Tiffauges never realizes that he is writing fiction, a fiction of the worst sort, since it purports to be objective truth. Yet it is apparent to any reader that in his narrative Abel is constantly structuring and altering his experiences to force conformity with a desired pattern. To achieve this end he invents means of controlling through language any occurrence that seems to deviate from the pattern he seeks to maintain.

Abel Tiffauges' *Ecrits sinistres* (sinister writings) illustrate fiction's ability to obfuscate; his is a narrative led astray by intellectual pretensions and aspirations to total truth. As novelists, Siggi, Oskar, and the middle-aged woman narrator are more successful because their goals are more modest; they describe rather than explain. Taken together, the narrative strategies in these four works demonstrate both the potential and the dangers inherent in attempting to use fiction for exploration of the complex issues surrounding World War II.

Abel's greatest error is never to have understood that he was reconstructing reality through his imagination, and therefore, because he was never aware that his narrative was in part invention, he constantly confused his version of events with truth. This is certainly a potential weakness in any fiction, yet when the instability of storytelling is exploited skillfully, as in the cases of Oskar, the woman writer, Siggi, and the Célinian narrator, the ambiguity of the fictional mode proves to be a source of strength. Abel's account demonstrates just how deceptive and dangerous fiction can be. The value of the fictions by the other four novelist-characters lies in the absence of any claims to objectivity or completeness. These narrators offer possible but limited perspectives; their fiction suggests without insisting, and as a result the conclusions drawn from the narratives must necessarily be those of the reader.

In *The World, the Text, and the Critic,* Edward Said argues that "texts are worldly, to some degree they are events, and, even when they attempt to deny it, they are nevertheless part of the social world, human life, and of course the historical moments in which they are located and interpreted" (4). To a certain extent it is an indication of the condition of contemporary literary criticism, too often, that so self-evident a statement has to be made, and by one of criticism's most sophisticated practitioners. "In giving up the world entirely for the aporias and unthinkable paradoxes of a text," Said adds, "contemporary criticism has retreated from its constituency, the citizens of the modern world" (4).

Contemporary literary criticism appears at times to rest on the assumption that "serious" discussions of literature can only take place within an academic context and among professional readers, an attitude largely excluding the possibility that a novel, for instance, can refer to anything outside itself or that it can be appreciated on some putatively profound level by anyone who has not made a career out of the study of literature. What is true in literary studies is also true in other areas of intellectual inquiry. University-trained historians write primarily if not exclusively for their peers, philosophers only talk to one another, and to the extent that psychology impacts upon a general audience, it is usually through the bromides of some newspaper or television advice-giver. Increasingly, each academic discipline seeks to maintain its legitimization through a highly specialized language, which, whatever its value for professionals, serves to keep the educated public at bay.

Given these circumstances, it is not surprising that the novel remains such a popular form or that academics look with some suspicion on fiction that attracts many readers. Good novels, such as the ones I have discussed, certainly have a great deal to say about literature, but their purview extends beyond the confines of the university (the failure of the *nouveau roman*, not as experiment but as fiction, resulted from its inability to interest nonprofessional readers). The novel is a social document that attempts to describe, analyze, and question issues of importance to people who are attempting to understand the world they inhabit. Edmond Jabès certainly understood this simple truth when he wrote in *Yaël* that "those who speak of a decadent literature or an engaged literature always make me smile" (28).

As Jabès' words imply, literature, whatever rubric one attaches to its form (Realist, Naturalist, Decadent, Symbolist, etc.), is always in some measure about life. However large or small the intended audience, the literary text is meant to be read, and reflected upon, and not simply by professional students of a particular genre. The subject matter can be as deeply personal as a question of sexual identity or as vast as the ramifications of World War II, but in either instance the literary text is examining issues of importance evident to anyone who thinks.

Milan Kundera claims that what fiction offers is the "*wisdom of uncertitude*" (*Life Is Elsewhere*, 21, emphasis in text). It is an invitation to a continuous questioning of one's self and one's society. Many of the significant questions that literature asks change as society changes and could indeed at some future date have coherent answers. Be that as it may, the obligation and achievement of great literature are to present queries in such a fashion that readers know these are at once important and their own.

The questions provoked by World War II are precisely the sort that must be kept before the public because, as Kundera notes, "today, the history of the planet finally makes a whole, but it is war, ambulant and perpetual, which realizes and assures this unity which has been dreamed of for such a long time. The unity of humanity signifies: nobody can escape anywhere" (26).

Tournier's *The Ogre* provides a highly suspect appearance of closure, and the ending of *The Flanders Road* is fraught with questions ("what do I know?"). In the other four the story simply stops. None of the four novels is really finished, partly because the nature of the subject matter does not lend itself to facile conclusions but also because "its potential range is always being extended by every additional reader" (Said, *The World*, 157). This is how it should be. To return to a comment cited in the opening pages of this study, the most important element pervading these four works is the implied conviction that, in Hans Egon Holthusen's words, the war's lessons remain "unmastered: the past . . . has not faded or become indifferent . . . but rather stronger, . . . more incomprehensible" (in Bosmajian, *Metaphors of Evil*, 17). It is as essential as it is difficult to articulate this sense of horror and disbelief without indulging in the kinds of sententious rhetoric that Shelley once stigmatized as "the intense inane." Novels that fulfill this task so eloquently recall to our attention that, appearances to the contrary, the contribution fiction makes to society can be eminently practical.

Notes

1. Introduction: The Writing of War

1. It also provoked a powerful, albeit short-lived conservative reaction in the visual arts that involved a debunking of prewar Cubism as a Germanic artform ("Kubism"), and a brief flirtation by prominent artists such as Picasso with Neoclassicism. See Kenneth Silver's *Esprit de Corps*.

2. The Present Made the Past

1. There is no lack of contemporary critiques or at least reevaluations of the Enlightenment heritage, but John Gray's *Enlightenment's Wake* (1995) may be the most detailed account of what its author takes to be the irrelevance of Enlightenment thinking for postmodern society.

2. A detailed analysis of Foucault's views concerning the Enlightenment appears in chapter 4, devoted to Claude Simon's *The Flanders Road*, and plays a crucial role in the discussion of that novel.

3. In this respect it is worth noting that critics well-disposed to *Doctor Faustus* at times unconsciously parody the novel's portentousness in the guise of praising the book. Consider Jon Tuska's evaluation of Mann's achievement: "a representation of a *Last Judgment* upon Western civilization, sharing Michelangelo's epic grandeur, mightiness of form, loftiness of vision. . . . It is at once history and more than history; it is portent and prophecy, closer to Isaiah and to John than to Paul, and for that reason, closer to us and the crisis of our culture" ("The Vision of Doktor Faustus," 278). Except perhaps for the clichés—"mightiness of form," "epic grandeur," "crisis of culture"—these sentiments could have been expressed by Zeitblom. More significant, they appear to do justice to Mann's goals. The question, however, is what do such comments really mean? In what respect, aside from the most pedestrian application of the allusion to *The Last Judgment* to the destruction of Germany, does a comparison of Michelangelo's fresco to Mann's novel clarify anything about World War II or Germany's participation in it? To argue that something is "history and more than history," that it is "portent and prophecy," is to apply language to an issue on such a grand scale as to deprive the words of any concrete meaning.

4. It is possible that Günter Grass is offering a parody of this somewhat simplistic dichotomy allegedly within the German character when in *The Tin Drum* he has pictures of Hitler and Beethoven staring at one another with mutual loathing.

3. Presenting the Present

1. With regard to the German novels I discuss, the influence of the immediate literary predecessor is obvious on Grass and Lenz, who were both involved with the

Group 47, but it clearly would be a mistake to read either *The Tin Drum* or *The German Lesson* purely in terms of that group. Christa Wolf opted to remain in East Germany, and while she had contacts with the Group 47, her literary activities were much more involved with the pressures, ambitions, and tensions on the east side of the Berlin Wall. Even less can be said about influence when the subject is the works of Céline and Tournier. Although both knew German well, it would be a useless effort to attempt to delineate aspects of the Group 47 style in their novels. While Grass has a fleeting, sarcastic reference to the new novel in *The Tin Drum* (17–18), the French authors I examine are at pains to take their distance from Parisian literary trends. Michel Tournier claims that his goal is "to express in traditional, safe and reassuring form a content that possesses none of these qualities" (*Le Vent Paraclet,* 190), while Céline, the essentials of whose style were formed before the war, had little but contempt for the band of scribblers he associated with someone named "Robe-Grillée" ("Interview with Pierre Audinet," in Dauphin and Godard, *Cahiers Céline,* 2:204).

4. Memory and the Collapse of Culture: Claude Simon's *The Flanders Road*

1. For the 1974 colloque, see *Lire Claude Simon,* edited by Jean Ricardou.

2. The effect of World War II on the creation of the *nouveau roman* has already been noted (see, e.g., Jacques Leenhardt's "Nouveau roman et société" in *NR I*), but the publication of Robbe-Grillet's autobiographical trilogy has added weight to the sense of shock the war engendered, particularly the Final Solution. See the discussion in chapter 3 of *Le Miroir qui revient* (1985) and *Derniers jours de Corinthe* (1994).

3. Here is the French original: "Peut-être qu'il aurait été plus intelligent de sa part de—" "Non: écoute . . . Intelligent! oh bon Dieu qu'est-ce que l'intell . . . " (20).

4. See Stephen Heath, *The Nouveau Roman: A Study in the Practice of Writing:* "Aiming for himself as subject, Georges undertakes a pursuit of identity; pursuit *against* language . . . which is grasped as a pursuit against the father—*normalien, agrégé,* teacher, writer, in short, representative and guardian of the word" (163, emphasis in text).

5. Dällenbach provides a different reading of this sentence: "Is it not because he heard for the first time . . . 'The dog ate the mud' that the narrator of *The Flanders Road* sees them as if he were there" (*Claude Simon,* 45)? The "them" in this context refers to the various chaotic and meaningless incidents that constitute Georges' wartime experience. Dällenbach suggests that Georges profits from understanding this sentence and thus has the potential to become a successful writer.

6. I want to reiterate the distinction I am making between Claude Simon, the artist who is famous for the variety of subtlety of his literary allusions, which function as useless remnants of a dead past (see Dällenbach, *Claude Simon,* 42), and the character, Georges, whose failure as a *nouveau romancier* is in part indicated by his tendency to employ cultural signposts to provide a putatively profound dimension to his musings.

7. In this context it is worth noting that Birn refers to Georges' mother, Sabine, as an "artiste manquée" (a failed artist, "The Route . . . ," 94). Birn also argues that

Sabine, by "imposing on her son her own interpretations of the past, . . . renders him impotent, incapable of orienting himself both in the past and in the present" (93).

8. The impression that Georges maintains of de Reixach can only be dependent upon his mother's: "haloed with a sort of supernatural prestige, of inaccessibility" (Andrès, *Profils*, 154).

9. Birn argues that "Corinne's body rescues Georges from a universe of ghosts and catalyzes his artistic development" ("The Route . . . ," 101).

10. In Claude Simon's contribution to the discussion at Cerisy, "La Fiction mot à mot" (Fiction word for word), the author cites with approval Olga Bernal's comment: "If the novel of the nineteenth century was a novel of knowledge, the modern novel is essentially one of non-knowledge" (*NR II*, 84).

5. Women Writing War: Christa Wolf's *Patterns of Childhood*

1. The standard source for information about German literature written by women is *Deutsche Literatur von Frauen* (*German Literature Written by Women*), a series of essays in two volumes edited by Gisela Brinker-Gabler. The second volume, published in Germany in 1988, contains sections dealing with World War II.

2. In 1992 Ruth Krüger published *Weiter leben: eine Jugend* (*Living On: A Youth*). This memoir, curiously translated into French as *Refus de témoigner* (Refusal to witness), might well serve as a rather disquieting pendant to Kofman's book. Krüger describes her travails as a frail young Viennese Jew (she was approximately the same age as Kofman) who survived incarceration in several concentration camps, including Auschwitz, through a combination of poetry, grit, occasional human decency, and good luck. At the end of the war she emigrated with her mother to the United States, where she eventually established a successful career as a professor of German literature. The major difference between these two memoirs is implicit in their titles. *Rue Ordener, Rue Labat* remains anchored in the past, in the time and space of the Occupation, as if to suggest that, for whatever reasons, Kofman was unable to overcome those days and those memories. Krüger, perhaps for equally unfathomable reasons, somehow managed to "weiter leben," to push on with her life without for a moment pretending that her past was behind her.

3. In her *Women Writers and Fascism* Gättens maintains that for "the modern period, women's 'unofficial' writings, which are mostly autobiographical, can serve as a source for women's historical experiences. Because of women's overwhelming exclusion from the public sphere, these writings tend to reproduce the division between the private and the public. Throughout *Three Guineas,* Woolf thus engages in the double strategy of reading 'official' 'unofficial' history" (11–12). The two story lines in *Patterns of Childhood* are to a degree Christa Wolf's version of "official" and "unofficial" history.

4. In "A Guarded Iconoclasm: The Self as Deconstructing Counterpoint to Documentation," Sandra Frieden stresses the pressure placed on the reader because of the "generic confusion" found in *Patterns of Childhood:* "In fact, the generic confusion that attends the reading of this book is an important feature: the dismantling of conventions within the discourse challenges the expectations of the reader, who

176

must penetrate to increasingly deeper levels of perception in order to integrate anticipations with reality, memory with actuality, and . . . narration with experience" (in Marilyn Fries, ed., *Responses to Christa Wolf,* 271).

5. Early in *Patterns* the reader learns that Nelly's mother "always wanted to be a doctor. . . . She repeated [that] until her dying day. Something in the line of medicine would have been just right for me. . . . Of course, your father always scolded her for building castles in the air" (19). Nelly's mother's youth precedes the Nazi period, so the frustration of her ambitions has no particular relation to an aberrant political system. To the extent that she is a victim, she is the victim of being a woman.

6. Wolf's alienation from her childhood self and by extension from Nelly cannot be overemphasized. In an interview, "A Model of Experience," portions of which are cited in this chapter, she expands on "an uncanny feeling of alienation. As if I would be deceiving both myself and the reader if I called this being 'I'. . . . And it was exactly this feeling which I wanted to express by using the third person" (in *The Author's Dimension,* 45).

7. One form of victimization that occurs in this novel concerns women's lack of information. A particularly painful and ironic example of this lack takes place in the midst of the flight from the Russians. Nelly's mother Charlotte describes the miserable surroundings where they are taking shelter as "the asshole of the world" (333). No reader can react to this line without experiencing the obvious contrast between the downtrodden but transient condition of these women and the infinitely grimmer fate of those prisoners in World War II's veritable *anus mundi,* Auschwitz.

8. A particularly vivid example of young Nelly's intense but partial grasp of what is happening around her occurs when she has to assist a Russian woman doctor who is checking local German women for venereal disease. Despite everything that Nelly has experienced—the deaths, the flight west, the conversation with the concentration camp survivor—it is only at this moment that "for the first time Nelly saw how women were made to pay for the things men do to them" (368).

8. *The Ogre:* Myth as Fiction, Fiction as Myth

1. See my *Michel Tournier,* 47–48.

9. Recapturing the "Deluded Years": Siegfried Lenz's *The German Lesson*

1. The painter Emil Nolde, a model for Nansen, is one such example of the "inner emigration" phenomenon. After a flirtation with the Nazi Party, Nolde abandoned all forms of political activity and devoted himself to his art while remaining in Germany for the duration of the war. In 1941 the Nazi authorities denounced his painting as "degenerate."

10. Conclusion: The War, the Novel, and the Present

1. Claude Simon's *The Flanders Road,* as important as it is to this study, never captured a large audience either before or after the author's Nobel Prize (1985).

Bibliography

Aas-Rouxparis. "Interview de Claude Ollier." *Lettura Francese Contemporanea* 8 (Iuglio, 1983): 155–60.

Adorno, Theodor. *Notes to Literature III.* Ed. Rolf Tiedemann, trans. Sherry Weber Nicholson. New York: Columbia University Press, 1974.

Adorno, Theodor, and Max Horkheimer. *Dialectic of the Enlightenment.* Trans. John Cumming. New York: Continuum, 1991.

Altbach, Edith, Jeanette Clausen, Dagmar Schultz, and Naomi Stephan, eds. *German Feminism: Readings in Politics and Literature.* Albany: State University of New York Press, 1984.

Altes, Liesbeth Korthals. *Le Salut par la Fiction? Sens, valeurs et narrativité dans* le Roi des aulnes *de Michel Tournier.* Amsterdam: Rodopi, 1992.

Améry, Jean. "Asthetizismus der Barbarei: Uber Tourniers Roman *Der Erlkönig.*" *Merkur* 28 (1973):73–79.

Andrès, Bernard. *Profils du personnage chez Claude Simon.* Paris: Minuit, 1992.

Arendt, Hannah. *Eichmann in Jerusalem: A Report on the Banality of Evil.* New York: Viking, 1963.

Bachmann, Ingeborg. *Thirty Years.* Trans. Michael Bullock. New York: Holmes and Meier, 1987.

Barraclough, Geoffrey. "Farewell to Hitler." *New York Review of Books* 22 (Apr. 3, 1975): 11–16.

Barthes, Roland. *Le Degré zéro de l'écriture.* Paris: Seuil, 1953.

Bassmann, Winfried. *Siegfried Lenz: sein Werk als Beispiel für Weg und Standort der Literatur in Bundesrepublik Deutschland.* Bonn: Bouvier, 1976.

Bataille, Michel. *Gilles de Rais.* Paris: Mercure de France, 1972.

Bauman, Zygmunt. *Modernity and the Holocaust.* Ithaca: Cornell University Press, 1989.

Beckett, Samuel. *L'Innommable.* Paris: Minuit, 1953.

Benjamin, Walter. *Illuminations.* Trans. Harry Zohn. New York: Harcourt, Brace and World, 1968.

Bersani, Leo, and Ulysse Dutroit. *Arts of Impoverishment: Beckett, Rothko, Resnais.* Cambridge: Harvard University Press, 1993.

Bessel, Richard. *Germany after the First World War.* Oxford: Oxford University Press, 1993.

Beutin, Wolfgang. *"Deutschstunde" von Siegfried Lenz: Eine Kritik.* Hamburg: Ludke, 1970.

Bevan, David, ed. *Literature and War.* Amsterdam: Rodopi, 1990.

Birn, Randi. "The Roads to Creativity: Eighteenth Century Parody in *The Flanders Road*." In *Orion Blinded: Essays on Claude Simon*, ed. Randi Birn and Karen Gould. Lewisburg: Bucknell University Press, 1981.

Böll, Heinrich. *Eine deutsche Erinnerung: Interview mit René Wintz*. Köln: Kiepenheuer und Witsch, 1979.

———. "Entfernung von der Truppe." *Als der Krieg Ausbrach*. München: DTV, 1965.

———. "The Man with the Knives." In *The Stories of Heinrich Böll*, trans. Leila Vennewitz. New York: Knopf, 1986.

Borwicz, Michel. *Ecrits des condamnés à mort sous l'occupation allemande (1939–1945)*. Paris: Presses Universitaires de France, 1954.

Bosmajian, Hamida. *Metaphors of Evil: Contemporary German Literature in the Shadows of Nazism*. Iowa City: University of Iowa Press, 1979.

Brinkler-Gabler, Gisela, ed., *Deutsche Literatur von Frauen*. Vol. 2. München: C. H. Beck, 1988.

Brosman, Catherine. *Simone de Beauvoir Revisited*. Twayne: Boston, 1991.

Buruma, Ian. *The Wages of Guilt: Memories of War in Germany and Japan*. New York: Farrar, Strauss, Giroux, 1994.

Camus, Albert. *La Peste*. Paris: Gallimard, 1947.

Carroll, David. *French Literary Fascism: Nationalism, Anti-Semitism, and the Ideology of Culture*. Princeton: Princeton University Press, 1995.

Cassirer, Ernst. *The Myth of the State*. New Haven, Yale University Press, 1961.

———. *The Philosophy of the Enlightenment*. Trans. Fritz Koelln and James Pettegrove. Boston: Beacon, 1955.

———. *Rousseau, Kant, Goethe: Two Essays*. Princeton: Princeton University Press, 1945.

Céline. *Entretiens avec le Professeur Y*. Paris: Gallimard, 1955.

———. *From Castle to Castle*. Trans. Ralph Manheim. New York: Carroll and Graf, 1987.

———. *North*. Trans. Ralph Manheim. New York: Delacorte, 1972.

———. *Rigadoon*. Trans. Ralph Manheim. New York: Delacorte, 1974.

———. *Romans II: D'un château l'autre, Nord, Rigodon*. Ed. Henri Godard. Paris: Gallimard (Pléiade), 1974.

———. *Semmelweis*. Paris: Gallimard, 1952.

———. *See also* Dauphin and Godard, eds.

Cloonan, William. *Michel Tournier*. Boston: Twayne, 1985.

Cone, Michèle. *Artists under Vichy: A Case of Prejudice and Persecution*. Princeton: Princeton University Press, 1992.

Cooke, Miriam. *Women and the War Story*. Berkeley: University of California Press, 1996.

Cooper, Helen, Adrienne Auslander Munich, and Susan Merrill Squier, ed. *Arms and the Woman: War, Gender and Literary Representation*. Chapel Hill: University of North Carolina Press, 1989.

179

Cunliffe, Gordon W. *Günter Grass.* Boston: Twayne, 1969.

Dällenbach, Lucien. *Claude Simon.* Paris: Seuil, 1988.

Dauphin, Jean-Pierre. *Les Critiques de notre temps et Céline.* Paris: Garnier, 1976.

Dauphin, Jean-Pierre, and Henri Godard, eds. *Cahiers Céline: Céline et l'actualité littéraire.* Vol. 1: *1932–1957.* Paris: Gallimard, 1976.

———. *Cahiers Céline: Céline et l'actualité littéraire.* Vol. 2: *1957–1961.* Paris: Gallimard, 1976.

Davis, Colin. *Michel Tournier: Philosophy and Fiction.* Oxford: Clarendon Press, 1988.

Dawidowicz, Lucy S. *The Holocaust and the Historians.* Cambridge: Harvard University Press, 1981.

de Certeau, Michel. *L'Ecriture de l'histoire.* Paris: Gallimard, 1975.

de Man, Paul. "The Rhetoric of Temporality." In *Critical Theory since 1945,* ed. Hazard Adams and Leroy Searle. Tallahassee: Florida State University Press, 1986.

Demetz, Peter. *After the Fires: Recent Writing in the Germanies, Austria and Switzerland.* San Diego: Harcourt, Brace, Jovanovich, 1986.

Derrida, Jacques. "Biodegradables: Seven Diary Fragments." *Critical Inquiry* 15 (Summer 1989): 812–73.

———. *D'un ton apocalyptique adopté naguère en philosophie.* Paris: Galilée, 1983.

Djian, Philippe. "Comment fut écrit *Rigodon.*" Entretien avec Lucette Céline. *Le Magazine Littéraire.* 25 (1969): 19.

Drews, Jörg. "Siegfried Lenz/*Deutschstunde.*" *Neue Rundschau* 80, no. 2 (1969): 383.

Dubuffet, Jean. *L'Homme du commun à l'ouvrage.* Paris: Gallimard, 1973.

Duras, Marguerite, *The War: A Memoir.* Trans. Barbara Bray. New York, Pantheon, 1986.

Eichner, Hans. "The Rise of Modern Science and the Genesis of Romanticism." *PMLA* 97, no. 1 (Jan. 1982): 8–30.

Eliot, T. S. "The Waste Land." In *The Waste Land and Other Poems.* London: Faber and Faber, 1952.

Elm, Theo. *Siegfried Lenz: Deutschstunde—Engagement und Realismus in im Gegenwartsroman.* München: Fink, 1972.

Enzensberger, Hans Magnus. *Einzelheiten.* Frankfurt am Main: Suhrkamp, 1962.

Felman, Shoshana. "Paul de Man's Silence." *Critical Inquiry* 15 (Summer 1989): 704–54.

Foucault, Michel. "What Is Enlightenment?" In *The Foucault Reader,* ed. Paul Rabinov. New York: Pantheon, 1984.

Friedländer, Saul. *Reflets du nazisme.* Paris: Seuil, 1982.

Fries, Marilyn, ed. *Responses to Christa Wolf: Critical Essays.* Detroit: Wayne State University Press, 1989.

Fussel, Paul. *The Great War and Modern Memory.* New York: Oxford University Press, 1975.

Gättens, Marie-Luise. *Women Writers and Fascism: Reconstructing History.* Gainesville: University Press of Florida, 1995.

Gay, Peter. *The Party of Humanity: Essays in the French Enlightenment.* New York: Knopf, 1963.

———. *Weimar Culture: the Outsider as Insider.* New York: Harper and Row, 1968.

Görtz, Franz Josef. *Günter Grass: Auskunft für Leser.* Darmstadt: Luchterhand, 1984.

Grass, Günter. *On Writing and Politics 1967–1983.* Trans. Ralph Manheim. New York: Harcourt, Brace, Jovanovich, 1985.

———. *The Tin Drum.* Trans. Ralph Manheim. New York: Vintage, 1964.

Gray, John. *Enlightenment's Wake: Politics and Culture at the Close of the Modern Age.* London: Routledge, 1995.

Gray, Ronald. *The German Tradition in Literature (1871–1945).* Cambridge: Cambridge University Press, 1965.

Guidry, Glenn. "Theoretical Reflections on the Ideological and Social Implications of Mythic Form in Grass' *Die Blechtrommel.*" *Monatshefte* 83 (1991): 127–44.

Habermas, J. *Le Discours philosophique de la modernité.* Trans. Christian Bouchindhomme and Rainer Rochlitz. Paris: Gallimard, 1988.

Haft, Cynthia. *The Theme of Nazi Concentration Camps in French Literature.* The Hague: Mouton, 1973.

Hamburger, Michel. *From Prophecy to Exorcism: The Premises of Modern German Literature.* London: Longmans, 1965.

Harris, Frederick J. *Encounters with Darkness: French and German Writers on World War II.* Oxford: Oxford University Press, 1983.

Heath, Stephen. *The Nouveau Roman: A Study in the Practice of Writing.* London: Elek, 1972.

Hewison, Robert. *Under Siege: Literary Life in London 1939–1945.* London: Weidenfeld and Nicolson, 1977.

Higonnet, Margaret Randolph, Jane Jenson, Sonja Michel, and Margaret Collins Weitz, eds. *Behind the Lines: Gender and the Two World Wars.* New Haven: Yale University Press, 1987.

Hindus, Milton. *The Crippled Giant: A Literary Relationship with Louis-Ferdinand Céline.* Hanover: University Press of New England, 1986.

Hirsch, David H. *The Deconstruction of Literature: Criticism after Auschwitz.* Hanover: Brown University Press, 1991.

Hollington, Michael. *Günter Grass: The Writer in a Pluralist Society.* London: Marion Boyars, 1980.

Hynes, Samuel. *A War Imagined: The First World War and English Culture.* New York: Atheneum, 1991.

Iser, Wolfgang. "When Is the End Not the End? The Idea of Fiction in Beckett." In *On Beckett: Essays and Criticism,* ed. S. E. Gontarski. New York: Grove, 1986.

Jabès, Edmond. *Aely.* Paris: Gallimard, 1972.

———. *Du Désert au livre. Entretiens avec Marcel Cohen.* Paris: Pierre Belfond, 1980.

———. *El, ou le dernier livre.* Paris: Gallimard, 1973.

———. *Le Livre des questions.* Paris: Gallimard, 1963.

————. *Le Livre de Yukel.* Paris: Gallimard, 1964.

————. *Le Retour au livre.* Paris: Gallimard, 1965.

————. *Yaël.* Paris: Gallimard, 1967.

Jensen, Peter. *"Deutschstunde." Die Frankfurter Allgemeine,* September 17, 1968.

Joyce, James. *Portrait of the Artist as a Young Man.* New York: Modern Library, 1928.

Judt, Tony. *Past Imperfect: French Intellectuals 1944–1956.* Berkeley: University of California Press, 1992.

Jünger, Ernst. *Jardins et routes: Journal 1, 1939–1940.* Trans. Maurice Betz. Paris: Christian Bourgeois, 1979.

————. *Premier Journal Parisien: Journal 2, 1941–1943.* Trans. Unlisted. Paris: Christian Bourgeois, 1980.

————. *Second Journal Parisien: Journal 3, 1943–1945.* Trans. Frédéric de Towarnicki and Henri Plard. Paris: Christian Bourgeois, 1980.

Kadish, Doris Y. *Practices of the New Novel in Claude Simon's* L'Herbe *and* La Route des Flandres. Fredericton, N.B.: York Press, 1979.

Kafka, Franz. *The Penal Colony: Stories and Short Pieces.* Trans. Willa and Edwin Muir. New York: Schocken, 1961.

Kaplan, Alice Y. *Reproductions of Banality: Fascism, Literature and French Intellectual Life.* Minneapolis: University of Minnesota Press, 1986.

Kaufmann, Dorothy. "'Le Témoin compris': Diaries of Resistance and Collaboration by Edith Thomas." *L'Esprit Créateur* 33, no, 1 (Spring 1993): 17–28.

————. "Uncovering a Woman's Life: Edith Thomas (Novelist, Historian, *Résistante*)." *French Review* 67, no. 1 (Oct. 1993): 61–67.

Kermode, Frank. *The Sense of an Ending: Studies in the Theory of Fiction.* Oxford: Oxford University Press, 1966.

Kitzman, Lawrence. "Duras' War." *L'Esprit Créateur* 33, no. 1 (1993): 63–73.

Klüger, Ruth. *Refus de témoigner: une jeunesse.* Trans. Jeanne Etoré. Paris: Editions Viviane Hamy, 1997.

Kofman, Sarah. *Rue Ordener, Rue Labat.* Paris: Galilée, 1994.

Korman, Gerd. "The Holocaust in American Historical Writing." In *Holocaust: Religious and Philosophical Implications,* ed. John Roth and Michael Berenbaum. New York: Paragon House, 1989.

Kosta, Barbara. *Recasting Autobiography: Women's Counterfictions in Contemporary German Literature and Film.* Ithaca: Cornell University Press, 1994.

Krance, Charles. *L.-F. Céline: The I of the Storm.* Lexington: French Forum, 1992.

Kristeva, Julia. *Powers of Horror: An Essay on Abjection.* Trans. Leon S. Roudiez. New York: Columbia University Press, 1982.

Krumme, Detlef. *Günter Grass: Die Blechtrommel.* München: Carl Hanser, 1986.

Kuhn, Anna. *Christa Wolf's Utopian Vision: From Marxism to Feminism.* Cambridge: Cambridge University Press, 1988.

Kundera, Milan. *Life Is Elsewhere.* Trans. Peter Kussi. New York: Penguin, 1986.

La Capra, Dominick. *Representing the Holocaust: History, Theory, Trauma.* Ithaca: Cornell University Press, 1994.

Lacoue-Labarthe, Philippe. *Heidegger, Art and Politics: The Fiction of the Political.* Trans. Chris Turner. Oxford: Basil Blackwell, 1990.

————. "Neither an Accident Nor a Mistake." Trans. Paula Wissing. *Critical Inquiry* 15 (Winter 1989): 481–84.

Langer, Lawrence. *Admitting the Holocaust: Collected Essays.* Oxford: Oxford University Press, 1995.

————. *The Holocaust and the Literary Imagination.* New Haven: Yale University Press, 1975.

Lassner, Phyllis. "The Quiet Revolution: World War II and the English Domestic Novel." *Mosaic* 23, no. 3 (Summer 1990): 87–100.

Lenz, Siegfried. *The German Lesson.* Trans. Ernest Kaiser and Eithne Wilkins. New York: Avon, 1971.

Lercher, Alain. *Les Fantômes d'Oradour.* Lagrasse: Editions Verdier, 1994.

Le Rioux, Dominique, Beaujour Michel, and Thélia Michel, eds. *Céline.* Paris: Cahier de l'Herne, 1972.

Letsch, Felicia. *Auseinandersetzung mit der Vergangenheit als Moment der Gegenwartskritik.* Köln: Pahl-Rugenstein, 1982.

Lettau, Reinhard, ed. *Die Gruppe 47: Bericht, Kritik, Polemik.* Berlin: Luchterhand, 1967.

Lipstadt, Deborah. *Denying the Holocaust: The Growing Assault on Truth and Memory.* New York: Free Press, 1993.

Longuet, Patrick. *Lire Claude Simon: la polyphonie du monde.* Paris: Minuit, 1995.

Lyotard, Jean-François. *Heidegger and "the Jews."* Trans. Andreas Michel and Mark Roberts. Minneapolis: University of Minnesota Press, 1990.

————. *Le Postmoderne expliqué aux enfants.* Paris: Galilée, 1986.

————. *Le Tombeau de l'intellectuel et autres papiers.* Paris: Galilée, 1984.

Mandel, Siegfried. *Group 47: The Reflected Intellect.* Carbondale: Southern Illinois University Press, 1973.

Mann, Thomas. *Diaries 1918–1939.* Trans. Richard and Clara Winston. New York: Harry Abrams, 1982.

————. *Doctor Faustus.* Trans. H. T. Lowe-Porter. New York: Knopf, 1948.

Marks, Elise. "The Alienation of the 'I': Christa Wolf and Militarism." *Mosaic* 23, no. 3 (Summer 1990): 73–85.

Matthews, J. H. *The Inner Dream: Céline as Novelist.* Syracuse: Syracuse University Press, 1978.

May, Herbert G., and Bruce M. Metzer, eds. *The New Oxford Annotated Bible with the Apocrypha.* Oxford: Oxford University Press, 1973.

McElroy, Bernard. "Lunatic, Child, Artist, Hero: Grass' Oskar as a Way of Seeing." *Forum for Modern Language Studies* 22 (1986): 308–22.

McGann, Jerome. *The Romantic Ideology: A Critical Investigation.* Chicago: University of Chicago Press, 1983.

McMahon, Joseph. *Human Being: The World of Jean-Paul Sartre.* Chicago: University of Chicago Press, 1971.

McPherson, Karin, ed. *The Fourth Dimension: Interviews with Christa Wolf.* London: Verso, 1988.

Merquior, J. G. *Foucault.* Berkeley: University of California Press, 1987.

Morrissette, Bruce. *Les Romans de Robbe-Grillet.* Paris: Minuit, 1963.

Muray, Philippe. *Céline.* Paris: Denoël, 1984.

Neunzig, Hans A., ed. *Lesebuch der Gruppe 47.* München: DTV, 1983.

Noble, Ian. *Language and Narration in Céline's Writings: The Challenge of Disorder.* Basingstoke, U.K.: Macmillan, 1987.

O'Brien, Conor Cruse. *Albert Camus.* Trans. Sylvie Drefus. Paris: Seghers, 1970.

O'Connell, David. *Louis-Ferdinand Céline.* Boston: Twayne, 1976.

O'Kane, Pat. "*La Route des Flanders:* The rout(e) of the reader?" In *Claude Simon: New Directions,* ed. Alastair Duncan. Edinburgh: Scottish Academic Press, 1985.

Owings, Alison. *Frauen: German Women Recall the Third Reich.* New Brunswick: Rutgers University Press, 1993.

Plard, Henri. "Une Source du chapitre *Niobe* dans *Die Blechtrommel* de Grass." *Etudes Germaniques* 39 (juillet-septembre 1984): 284–87.

Platten, David P. "The *Geist* in the Machine: Nazism in Tournier's *Le Roi des aulnes.*" *Romanic Review* 84 (March 1993): 181–94.

Ponornareff, Constantin. *The Silenced Vision: An Essay in Modern European Fiction.* Frankfurt am Main: Peter Lang, 1979.

Praz, Mario. *The Romantic Agony.* Trans. Angus Davidson. London: Collins, 1966.

Prigent, Christian. "A Descent from Clowns." Trans. Michele Sharp. *Journal of Beckett Studies* 3, no. 2 (Autumn 1993): 1–19.

Reed, Donna. *The Novel and the Nazi Past.* New York: Peter Lang, 1985.

Relinger, Jean. *Henri Barbusee: écrivain combattant.* Paris: Presse Universitaire de France, 1994.

Ricardou, Jean, ed. *Lire Claude Simon.* Colloque de Cerisy. Paris: Nouvelles Impressions, 1987.

Ricardou, Jean, ed., with Françoise van Rossum-Guyon. *Nouveau Roman: hier, aujourd'hui.* Tome 1. Colloque de Cerisy. Paris: 10/18, 1972.

———, *Nouveau Roman: hier, aujourd'hui.* Tome 2. Colloque de Cerisy. Paris: 10/18, 1972.

Richter, Hans W. *Hans Werner Richter und die Gruppe 47.* Broadcast. Published in München: Nymphenburger, 1979.

Robbe-Grillet, Alain. *Angélique ou l'enchantment.* Paris: Minuit, 1988.

———. *Les Derniers jours de Corinthe.* Paris: Minuit, 1994.

———. *Le Miroir qui revient.* Paris: Minuit, 1985.

———. *Pour un nouveau roman.* Paris: Minuit, 1963.

Roberts, Martin. *Michel Tournier: Bricolage and Cultural Mythology.* Stanford: Anma Libri, 1994.

Rousso, Henry. *The Vichy Syndrome: History and Memory in France since 1944.* Trans. Arthur Goldhammer. Cambridge: Harvard University Press, 1991.

184   Rubenstein, Richard. *The Cunning of History: Mass Death and the American Future.* New York: Harper and Row, 1975.

Rubenstein, Richard, and John Roth. *Approaches to Auschwitz: The Holocaust and Its Legacy.* Atlanta: John Knox, 1987.

Ryan, Judith. *The Uncompleted Past: Postwar German Novels and the Third Reich.* Detroit: Wayne State University Press, 1983.

Said. Edward. *The World, the Text, and the Critic.* Cambridge: Harvard University Press, 1983.

Sarraute, Nathalie. *L'Ere du soupçon.* Paris: Idées, 1956.

Sartre, Jean-Paul. *La Mort dans l'âme.* Paris: Gallimard, 1949.

———. *Qu'est-ce que la littérature?* Paris: Gallimard, 1948.

Schrader, Barbara, and Jürgen Schebera. *The "Golden" Twenties: Art and Literature in the Weimar Republic.* Trans. Katherine Vanovitch. New Haven: Yale University Press, 1988.

Schwarz, Wilhelm. *Der Erzähler Siegfried Lenz.* München: Francke, 1974.

Silver, Kenneth. *Esprit de Corps: The Art of the Parisian Avant-Garde and the First World War, 1914–1925.* Princeton: Princeton University Press, 1989.

Simon, Claude. *The Flanders Road.* Trans. Richard Howard. John Calder: London, 1985.

———. *La Route des Flandres.* Paris: Minuit, 1960.

Sollers, Philippe. *Logiques.* Paris: Seuil, 1968.

Steiner, George. *In Bluebeard's Castle: Some Notes toward the Re-definition of Culture.* London: Faber and Faber, 1971.

———. *Language and Silence: Essays in Language, Literature and the Inhuman.* Boston: Atheneum, 1970.

Suleiman, Susan. *Authoritarian Fictions: The Ideological Novel as a Literary Genre.* New York: Columbia University Press, 1983.

Sykes, Stuart. *Les Romans de Claude Simon.* Paris: Minuit, 1979.

Thiher, Allen. *Céline: The Novel as Delirium.* New Brunswick: Rutgers University Press, 1972.

Thomas, Edith. *Le Témoin compromis: Mémoires.* Ed. Dorothy Kaufman. Paris: Viviane Hamy, 1995.

———. *Pages de journal 1939–1944.* Ed. Dorothy Kaufman. Paris: Viviane Hamy, 1995.

Tournier, Michel. *Le Vent Paraclet.* Paris: Gallimard, 1977.

———. *Le Vol du vampire.* Paris: Mercure de France, 1981.

———. *The Ogre.* Trans. Barbara Bray. New York: Pantheon, 1972.

Tuska, Jon. "The Vision of Doktor Faustus." *Germanic Review* 40 (Nov. 1965): 277–309.

Ullmann, Stephen. *The Image in the Modern French Novel.* Cambridge: Cambridge University Press, 1960.

Vandromme, Pol. *Céline.* Paris: Editions Universitaires, 1963.

Wagener, Hans. *Siegfried Lenz.* München: Beck, 1979.

185   Walser, Martin. "Unser Auschwitz." In *Heimatkunde: Aufsätze und Reden*. Frankfurt am Main: Suhrkamp, 1968.

Weightman, John. *The Concept of the Avant-Garde*. LaSalle: Library Press, 1973.

White, Hayden. *Metahistory: The Historical Imagination in Nineteenth-Century Europe*. Baltimore: Johns Hopkins University Press, 1973.

Wolf, Christa. *The Author's Dimension: Selected Essays*. Ed. by Alexander Stephan, trans. Jan Van Heurck. Chicago: University of Chicago Press, 1995.

———. *Patterns of Childhood*. Trans. Ursule Molinaro and Hedwig Rappolt. New York: Farrar, Straus, Giroux, 1980.

Woodhull, Winifred. "Fascist Bonding and Euphoria in Michel Tournier's *The Ogre*." *New German Critique* 42 (1987): 79–112.

Woolf, Virginia. *Three Guineas*. New York: Harcourt, Brace, 1938.

Worton, Michael. "Myth-Reference in *Le Roi des aulnes*." *Stanford French Review* 6 (Fall-Winter 1982): 299–310.

Index